MORE PRAISE FOR *HEAVEN'S DITCH*

"The Erie Canal was the most audacious public works project of its day, a game-changer in American history, and the stage for some wild and intriguing characters and events—including daredevils, zealots and Mormons. Who knew? Jack Kelly's *Heaven's Ditch* tells a not-to-be-missed story in a reader-friendly style. This thought-provoking book will definitely spark discussion."

—Erica Freudenberger, Director, Red Hook Public Library,
Best Small Library in America Award finalist

"Kelly's study of upstate New York is a compelling history of ambition and religious fervor in early nineteenth-century America."

—Dick Hermans, owner of Oblong Books in Millbrook
and Rhinebeck and a past president of the New
England Independent Booksellers Association

"The book is a wonderful read and really captures much of the transformation that was occurring culturally, politically and religiously in the first half of the nineteenth century and around the canal."

—David Brooks, Education Coordinator,
Schoharie Crossing State Historic Site

"A well-researched work showing Kelly's deft ability to bring to life the strong and pivotal characters who, by will or grace, moved American history forward."

—Susan Fargione at Merritt Bookstore in Millbrook, NY

"Compelling . . . Kelly captures the enormous excitement of these heady days. An intriguing synthesis of American cultural and economic currents in the early 19th century."

—Kirkus Reviews

ALSO BY JACK KELLY AND
AVAILABLE FROM ST. MARTIN'S PRESS

*Band of Giants: The Amateur Soldiers
Who Won America's Independence*

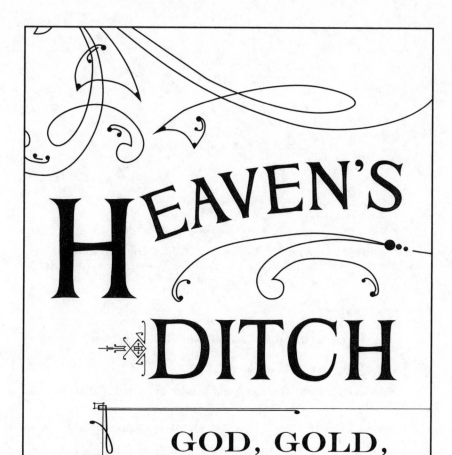

HEAVEN'S DITCH

GOD, GOLD, AND MURDER ON THE ERIE CANAL

Jack Kelly

St. Martin's Press
New York

www.stmartins.com

Library of Congress Cataloging-in-Publication Data

Names: Kelly, Jack, 1949– author.

Title: Heaven's ditch : God, gold, and murder on the Erie Canal / by Jack Kelly.

Description: First edition. | New York : St. Martin's Press, [2016]

Identifiers: LCCN 2016003174| ISBN 9781137280091 (hardback) | ISBN 9781466878990 (e-book)

Subjects: LCSH: Erie Canal (N.Y.)—History. | New York (State)—History—1775–1865. | BISAC: HISTORY / United States / 19th Century. | HISTORY / United States / State & Local / Middle Atlantic (DC, DE, MD, NJ, NY, PA). | TRANSPORTATION / Ships & Shipbuilding / History.

Classification: LCC HE396.E6 K45 2016 | DDC 386/.4809747—dc23

LC record available at http://lccn.loc.gov/2016003174

Our books may be purchased in bulk for promotional, educational, or business use. Please contact your local bookseller or the Macmillan Corporate and Premium Sales Department at 1-800-221-7945, extension 5442, or by e-mail at MacmillanSpecialMarkets@macmillan.com.

First Edition: July 2016

10 9 8 7 6 5 4 3 2 1

The Erie Canal rubbed Aladdin's lamp. America awoke, catching for the first time the wondrous vision of its own dimensions and power.

—Francis Kimball

Upon my arrival in the United States, the religious aspect of the country was the first thing that struck my attention.

—Alexis de Tocqueville

TABLE OF CONTENTS

List of Illustrations   ix
Map   x

PROLOGUE   1

1   5

Hardship * Bond of Union * A Mighty Baptism * A Perfect
Wilderness * Hair-hung * Eternity * Visionary * Navigable
* Abduction

2   39

Groundbreaking * To Feel and Shout * Damned If You Do
* Practical * All * The Spirit of God * Clouds of Heaven *
Beyond Description

3   65

Excited * On Fire * Otherwise, I Am Fine * Mania *
Magnificent * Ill-Advised Zeal * Gold Bible * Ingenious *
Whiskey * Methods * Abyss

4   111

Translation * Time * Most Imminent Danger * By the Hand
of Mormon * A Battlefield * Morgan's Ghost * Story * Awake
* Tell It to the World * Latter Days * All Rochester

5 — 157

Wedding * Big Things * Work of God * Sharp Sickle * Zion *
Fort Niagara * Salvation * Deep Prejudice * Velocity * Spirit
* Extermination

6 — 201

Packet * Unutterable Magnitude * Pagans * War * Public
Prosperity * Thunderer * The Bones of God

7 — 231

The Whole of America * O Blessed Year * As It Is * Strong
Meat * Awful Forebodings * O Lord, My God

EPILOGUE — 255

Today * Everything * Highway * Martyr * Old Mule *
Pageant

Source Notes — 265
Sources Cited — 277
Index — 283

LIST OF ILLUSTRATIONS

Elevation profile of the Erie Canal   28

Canal route   31

How a canal lock works   121

Mormon Missouri and Illinois   218

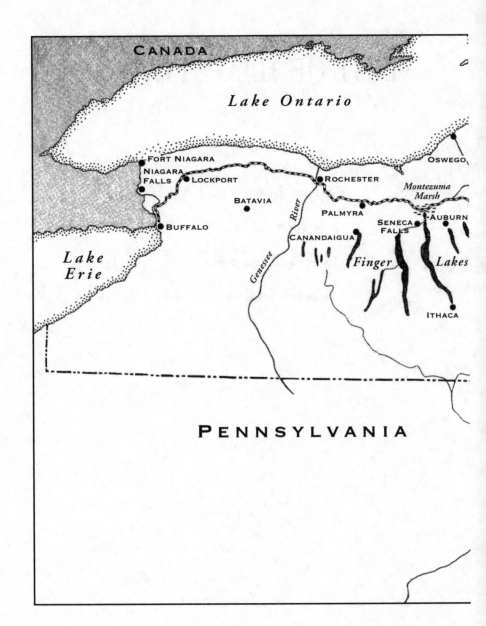

by *Joy Taylor*

PROLOGUE

Jesse Hawley paced the office of a Seneca Falls miller. The room trembled as rushing water drove the mill's cogwork. Amid the musty smell of grain, the curly-haired broker spread a map of New York State on a table and sat "ruminating over it, for—I cannot tell how long." His eyes lit on Niagara Falls. An image burst into his head. He saw the green water of the Great Lakes gushing in a mist-clad roar over that famous precipice. He imagined a great work of man diverting the flow into an artificial river, a canal running across the entire state. He saw a long parade of boats, each stacked with barrels of flour, floating down this channel toward eastern markets. To Hawley, a middleman in the western New York grain trade, it was a vision of wealth.

He had just been complaining to the mill owner about the state's miserable transportation system. Farming in the Genesee country was productive, yes, but no one could make a profit manhandling heavy barrels along mud-clogged roads or transporting them down the unreliable, rapids-filled Mohawk River to reach the nation's population centers. A canal was the answer.

Five years earlier, at the dawn of a new century, Hawley had joined the trickle of hopeful, daring Yankees who were heading west from New England, traveling beyond the wall of the Appalachian Mountains. Like most of them, Hawley was young, only twenty-seven then. Like many, he came in search of a fortune. Now, in 1805, he was facing bankruptcy.

Water was indispensable for carrying heavy loads. Teams of horses straining to pull wooden wagons could not compete with boats gliding along streams or lakes. Every major city in the nation had access to a river, a coast, or both. A horse that could move two tons along a smooth road could haul fifty tons down a canal.

Yet Hawley's idea was laughable. Three hundred sixty miles of tangled forests and dank swampland, of hills and valleys, separated

Lake Erie from the Hudson River. Hawley needed only to consider the Middlesex Canal in Massachusetts, twenty-seven miles end to end. Then the longest canal in America, it had taken nine years to build. At the same rate of construction, a canal across New York State would not be completed until the unimaginable year 1925, when everyone now living would be dead.

To Hawley, geography represented both an obstacle and an intriguing promise. The Great Lakes, all but Lake Ontario, stretched halfway across the continent at the same elevation. The Hudson crept inland entirely at sea level. Link the two and you would join the distant west with the coast. The long downhill run from Lake Erie, dropping a foot every mile across the state to Albany, could carry a placid waterway navigable in both directions.

Visions are cheap; flashes of clarity come to us all. Translating a vision into reality is always the challenge. Hawley had little formal education and no training in canal design or construction. No one in North America knew much about the subject. Even the English "expert" who designed the Middlesex Canal was often at a loss when calculating levels or constructing locks.

Soon after the canal vision came to him, Hawley watched his business go bust. He fled the state to avoid debtors' prison. Hiding out near Pittsburgh, he concluded, "All my private prospects in life were blighted." To pass the time, he wrote two essays for a local newspaper on the subject of his dreamed-of canal. Determined to avoid ridicule and to hide his status as a deadbeat, he adopted the identity "Hercules." "I will presume to suggest," he began, "the connecting of the waters of *Lake Erie* and those of the *Mohawk* and *Hudson* rivers by means of a canal."

The fugitive's conscience soon got the better of him. He returned to the Finger Lakes settlement of Canandaigua to face the music: twenty months in debtors' prison. Broken and destitute, he became convinced that "hitherto I have lived with no useful purpose." To restore his sense of self-worth, he decided to "publish to the world my favorite, fanciful project of an overland canal."

Hawley's "prison" was a Canandaigua hotel room. Confinement did not prevent his imagination from roaming freely. He managed to get hold of books and maps and to bone up on canal technology. "Hercules" wrote a series of fourteen essays published in the *Genesee*

Messenger beginning in 1807. His choice of a route for the canal and his estimate of its cost were both remarkably prescient.

While he was writing, he learned of another transportation breakthrough. In August 1807, inventor Robert Fulton sailed the first commercial steamboat up the Hudson River, covering the distance from New York City to Albany in thirty-two hours instead of the four days needed by wind-driven schooners. Fulton became an instant celebrity and would soon sign on as an important canal backer.

All eyes were on the future. Hawley said it would be "a burlesque on civilization" to continue navigating farm brooks in bark canoes. Instead, he envisioned settlers rushing along canals to populate the newly accessible interior. He foresaw barges hauling flour, lumber and other produce from the Great Lakes down to the Hudson. Of New York City, he accurately predicted that "in a century its island would be covered with the buildings and population of its city." Besotted with canals, he discussed waterways branching from his main "Genesee Canal," and similar projects in other states. He even dreamed of a "marine canal" that would slice "across the Isthmus of Darien," anticipating by a century the Panama Canal.

The reaction to the publication of his cherished idea was blunt. One critic declared that Hawley's scheme "lies in the province of fancy, and may be treated as a vision." Another described it as "the effusions of a maniac." President Thomas Jefferson judged the idea "little short of madness." The future would render a different verdict.

HARDSHIP

God and Mammon—the two words defined the age. At the dawn of the nineteenth century, Americans were waking to the possibility of salvation and to the allure of wealth. During the era of the Revolution, scarcely one American in ten had professed religious faith, and riches had been the birthright of privilege. Now the spiritual was returning to fashion and the prospect of universal prosperity bloomed. No matter how sinful, a man could find a path to heaven. No matter how poor, he could get his due if only he would dare to grab. "Go ahead!" became a catchphrase. "I'm not greedy for land," was the motto of the proverbial New England farmer, "I just want what joins mine."

When they married in 1796, Joseph Smith Sr. and his wife Lucy received a small farm from his family and a thousand-dollar dowry from hers. The couple set bright faces toward the future. Frugal Yankees, they put the cash aside and plunged into the demanding work of hardscrabble farming.

The land in east-central Vermont was rocky and unforgiving. For six years, the Smiths barely scratched out a sustenance. In 1802, now with two young sons, they took a chance. Perhaps the idea was Lucy's—she was the more enterprising of the two. They rented their homestead and set up a mercantile store in the prosperous town of Randolph, Vermont. Eager for the main chance, they soon spotted an opportunity. Ginseng's reputation as a tonic and aphrodisiac created an insatiable demand in the Orient. Ginseng grew wild in the Vermont hills. Joe amassed a large quantity of the acrid-tasting root in the course of his trade. He and Lucy boiled it in sugar to preserve it, transported a shipment to New York, and sent it off on consignment, convinced that their fortune was made. Months later, bad news: a venal merchant had hoodwinked the Smiths. The ginseng treasure had yielded only a cask of tea in return. The chance of sudden wealth had changed to a life-altering calamity.

The Smiths lived in a rat's nest of credits and debts. They owed urban merchants for the goods they had sold, but were unable to collect the money customers owed them. The ginseng loss caused their store to fail. Determined as a point of honor to fulfill their obligations and avoid debtors' prison, they drew on Lucy's dowry. Still short, they sold their farm for eight hundred dollars.

Self-sufficiency required ownership of land. The Smiths, having stepped from the "embarrassment of debt" to the "embarrassment of poverty," as Lucy put it, slipped into the precarious life of the landless. They would not soon recover. During the next fourteen years they moved seven times from one rented New England farm to another.

Joe, who was thirty-one at the time of the ginseng disaster, taught school in winter and farmed in summer. In 1805, Lucy gave birth to Joseph Jr., their fourth child. Six years later, still tenant farmers, they moved to Lebanon, New Hampshire. Lucy, ever an optimist, declared, "There is nothing which we have not a sufficiency of to make us and our children perfectly comfortable." The three older children were able to attend school, while little Joe Jr. learned his ABCs at home.

The Smiths' overriding concern with making ends meet did not mean that they neglected the spiritual. Like many on the New England frontier, they were seekers rather than members of an established church. Lucy's older brother was a lay preacher and faith healer. The supernatural was palpable to her—her sister Lovisa's miraculous recovery from illness had deeply impressed her. Her husband had a restless mind and found significance in his dreams. The family regularly prayed and read the Bible together. Like many country people, they made do with a homespun religion heavy on portents and miracles. Their faith would soon be put to the test.

In 1812, typhoid swept Vermont, killing with abandon. All the Smith children became ill. They survived, but a lingering infection invaded the bone of young Joe's leg. Twice, a physician laid open his shin from ankle to knee. When the festering returned, a group of doctors suggested drilling into the bone, then chiseling away infected sections. The boy bravely insisted that his mother leave the house so as not to be disturbed by his cries. The white-hot pain gave the six-year-old a vivid taste of hell. His father held him while the doctors removed three fetid chunks of his shin bone. The wound finally healed, but Joe spent the next three years on crutches. The doctors' bills left the family foundering in debt.

Joe Sr. hired out as a laborer, Lucy painted and sold the oil cloths that country people used to brighten drab kitchens. In 1814, most of the crops on their rented farm failed. Only day labor in town and the sale of fruits from their orchard allowed them to scrape by. They knew hunger. The next year, the weather was unfavorable and crops again withered. Discouraged and increasingly desperate, the Smiths rolled up their sleeves to try once more in 1816.

BOND OF UNION

Although many scoffed, Jesse Hawley's "Hercules" essays ignited a sudden firestorm of interest. In February 1808, only a few months after he had begun publishing his vision, the New York state legislature ordered that a survey be carried out "of the most eligible and direct route for a canal . . . between the tide waters of the Hudson river and Lake Erie." They chose James Geddes, a central New York salt merchant and self-taught surveyor, to examine the lay of the land.

Water access to Lake Erie, canal proponents argued, would make New York the portal to a western empire. From there, a boat drawing seven feet could sail all the way to "Chaquagy [Chicago] and then up a creek of that name to the Illinois River . . . and so down to the Mississippi." The link "would be an indissoluble bond of union between the Western and Atlantic states."

The idea of union was important in the early republic. "When the United States shall be bound together by canals, by cheap and easy access to markets in all directions," Robert Fulton said, it would not be possible to "split them into independent separate governments." Without a transportation network, the country might prove a fragile conglomeration of distant states.

The notion of an entirely inland canal, as suggested by Hawley, still seemed improbable. In the legislature, it "produced such expressions of surprise and ridicule as are due to a very wild foolish project." Most legislators favored the simpler option of connecting an improved Mohawk River with Lake Ontario, then digging a thirty-mile canal to bypass Niagara Falls and reach Lake Erie. To study the feasibility of such a route would be Geddes's first priority. He was to look at other alternatives only as money permitted. It would not permit much—the legislators allotted only six hundred dollars for the entire survey.

A Pennsylvania farm boy, Geddes had acquired enough book learning to teach school. Later, he traveled the country looking for opportunities. In 1794, toting two iron kettles, he moved to the Onondaga region of central New York, an area still shared with Iroquois tribes. The rich brine of local springs could be boiled down or evaporated to yield the salt so valued for preserving meat and other foods. He settled there, married, studied law, and became one of the influential men of the district. He taught himself surveying and delineated plots around the lake.

During the summer of 1808, the forty-five-year-old Geddes set out on his consequential mission. He well understood the basic problem. The rugged ridges and mountains of the Appalachian chain had hampered travel to and from the interior since Europeans had first settled the New World. The high ground stretched in an unbroken line from Maine to Georgia. Almost unbroken. The Mohawk River flowed eastward out of central New York and squeezed through a gap in the mountains a few hundred yards wide.

Geddes had a dim notion that an ice-age glacial dam had once blocked the St. Lawrence River. All the water from the Great Lakes had gushed down the path of the Mohawk, crashing through the Appalachians at this very gap—a place now called Little Falls—and on to the sea along the estuary of the Hudson. When the ice melted, the outflow resumed its natural course and the Mohawk diminished to a relative trickle. As a means of transportation, the river was unreliable. But the Little Falls gap, unique along the eastern seaboard, offered a tantalizing clue about the possibility of a water route to the West.

Focused on the Lake Ontario route, Geddes walked around Oneida Lake, which lay just past the end of the Mohawk River, and traced the streams that led west. He quickly saw a significant impediment to this route. The elevation of Lake Ontario was more than three hundred feet lower than that of Lake Erie and two hundred feet lower than the navigable headwaters of the Mohawk. Many locks would be needed to bring boats down to Ontario and back up again.

Geddes nevertheless dutifully traveled to the Niagara region to examine a route that a canal might take to circumvent the falls. Only then, with winter already coming on, did he turn his attention to the inland path. He had depleted his expenses and had to lay out seventy-three dollars of his own money to keep going.

The land through which Geddes traveled, on horseback and foot, was still largely a wilderness, into which isolated settlers had hacked primitive farmsteads. When the adventurer Estwick Evans walked the region during the same era, he found pioneers living in log huts with dirt floors and wooden chimneys. The backwoodsman was a magician with an ax, but "some of them are no less rude than the wilds which they inhabit." Their isolation and contact with raw nature left them superstitious. "In this part of the country," he noted, "many of the people entertain strange notions respecting supernatural agencies."

Geddes knew that building a canal through this landscape, much of it dominated by undulating hills, would present enormous challenges. Leaving the end of Lake Erie at Buffalo—then a collection of sixteen buildings—the waterway would have to travel north, drop down to the plain that skirted Lake Ontario, cross many miles of varied and often swampy land, and finally descend a steep drop to reach the Hudson River at Albany.

Terrain was one problem; locating sources of water was just as critical. A canal, Geddes understood, was not a stagnant ditch but a dynamic hydraulic system, with water continually flowing in and out. Volumes of water were needed to work the locks. Water was always leaking—canal engineers call it "weeping." Lake Erie could supply an abundant flow, but Geddes was already convinced that Hawley's original idea of a long, almost continuous inclined plane across the state would not work. There were too many ups and downs in between. Builders would need to channel water from reliable streams and reservoirs along the way to prevent sections of the canal from going dry.

Hills and valleys always threatened to block a canal. Streams and rivers were obstacles that had to be bridged. The demand that a canal be perfectly level required builders to fill low lands and cut through high ground. The alternative was to build expensive locks to connect sections on different levels. How could men slice through these snarling forests? How could they bring an artificial waterway across miles of mucky marshland? How could they take it over the temperamental Genesee River, so prone to flooding?

Geddes carefully threaded a path through the stern landscape. At times, the scope of the work brought Geddes close to despair. He suspected that the canal was merely a dream, a temptation that could only end in a colossal waste of money and effort. Perhaps it might be attempted by future generations, but not by this one.

A gray sky began to blanket the remote land with snow and deep silence. He pushed on. He contemplated the vast problems and imagined solutions. He was sustained by hope, drawn forward by the seductive whisper of something grand. He wrote his report: yes, an inland canal was feasible.

A MIGHTY BAPTISM

When Charles Grandison Finney was born in 1792, his parents chose to name him after a character in a popular novel. Like many Americans, they were influenced by the rationalist climate of the late eighteenth century and preferred the name over one drawn from the Bible. "My parents were neither of them professors of religion," Finney remembered. "I seldom heard a sermon." They had abandoned Connecticut to move to the New York frontier, settling near the town of Adams at the remote eastern tip of Lake Ontario.

Although barely educated himself, Finney taught school in his hometown. Six feet two, young and athletic, he was "the idol of his pupils." He joined in their games, but could bring instant order to his classroom with a glance. Finney soon gave in to a bout of wanderlust. For several years, he lived in different parts of New York and New Jersey, teaching school and trying to find a profession that better suited him. He displayed "manners plain and bordering strongly on the rough and blunt," an acquaintance said, but his "warm heart" won him friends.

In 1818, at the age of twenty-six, he returned home and took a job as a law clerk. His imposing physical presence—the prominent forehead, commanding blue eyes, erect posture—suited him to the profession. So did his orderly mind and his gift as a public speaker. He settled into the community. Displaying a "great vivacity of spirit," he was "self-reliant, but full of kind and tender feelings." The attractive bachelor spun the ladies around the floor at dances and added to the music with his bass viol.

Finney noticed that spiritual seeking had become a pressing topic of conversation in Adams. He admitted to being "as ignorant of religion as a heathen." As a boy, he had on rare occasions listened to the ludicrous sermons of traveling Methodists and to the tedious preaching of Calvinist Congregationalists. The one spoke of a divine light, which made no sense to him, the other of innate human depravity and predestination, which seemed illogical and unfair.

Now revivals, spates of enthusiastic exhortation by itinerant preachers, were netting new church members. Finney observed one in 1819 that created enough excitement in Adams to inspire more than a hundred residents to offer their lives to Jesus. He became friends with George Gale, a local pastor and choir director with whom he shared a love of music. While Finney found Gale's Calvinist sermons wearisome, he enjoyed the young man's company. He also began to court Lydia Andrews, a seventeen-year-old from a nearby town. Her devout Christian faith made him reconsider his own beliefs.

As part of his legal education, Finney studied Biblical influences on common law. He contemplated references to the Mosaic Code, then read more deeply in the sacred book. He began to formulate his own views. He did not reject the precepts of Calvinism out of hand, but he seriously questioned the notion that all of humanity could be condemned for the sin of Adam, or that free will played no role in salvation, as orthodox Protestants in the Puritan tradition believed. His ideas meshed with a widening mood in the country. As Americans pushed out into the frontier, the old dogma loosened and the sovereignty of the individual took precedence.

His growing interest in religion troubled rather than soothed Finney's mind. He searched his soul. He attended his first inquiry meeting. He tried and tried to fit notions of the divine into his broader scheme of things. Analytical by nature, he wanted to categorize manifestations of the spirit, to make sense of them. In vain. Unease preyed on him. He felt a crisis gathering around him.

The process of transformation led a sinner through recognizable steps, beginning with concern about the fate of his soul. Then came a period of inquiry, a search for a path to salvation. The realization that only God could save him ramped up the person's anxiety. The mental tension peaked with what was called "conviction," the awful certainty that without divine intercession he was condemned to eternal suffering. This unbearable trepidation would, through God's mercy, end in a glorious, life-altering change, the "conversion" that was the essence of the evangelical Christian experience.

The Bible told Finney he must become as a child in order to enter the kingdom of God, but he found that he could not shed his adult pride. He tried to pray, but he was "ashamed to have a human being see me on my knees before God."

On a mild October day in 1821, the air spiced with the aroma of fallen maple leaves, Finney finished an early breakfast and started toward his law office. The weight of the decision suddenly became too much for him. Anxiety swelled to panic. A terrifying conviction of his sinfulness came over him. He found himself walking north, out of town, into the surrounding woods. He needed seclusion. He was sweating. He resolved, then and there, "to give my heart to God."

As he plunged through brambles, the lash of a twig left his eye weeping. He lost himself among molten coins of sunlight and shadow. He wanted to understand, to understand. He reached out to take the truth in his arms and clasped nothing. "I was dumb," he remembered, "that is, I had nothing to say to God."

He made a rash vow. If God converted him, he would give up his law career and become a preacher. His agitation gradually left him. He breathed more easily. The forest smiled at him. He returned to the village through the same mild sunshine. It was past noon. His mind was "most wonderfully quiet and peaceful." An intimation of glory had touched him and now hovered around him.

The law office was empty. He sat and played a hymn on his viol. The music entered and lifted him. "I began to weep," he later remembered. "It seemed as if my heart was all liquid." He was engulfed by a "mighty baptism of the Holy Ghost." It was "like a wave of electricity," he said, "like the very breath of God." He felt he would die if the ecstatic waves continued. He saw Jesus "face to face."

A friend from the church choir found him in his office. Finney was no longer embarrassed by his gushing emotion, but the visitor was alarmed and asked if he was sick. "No," he answered, "but I am so happy that I cannot live."

The choir member sought out a church elder. On seeing Finney in the very embrace of conversion, the man gave out a "most spasmodic laugh," a holy laugh of wonder. Another friend came in as Finney was describing the extraordinary experience to the elder. This man asked for help with his own soul and Finney prayed for him, prayed for another person for the first time in his life. He made up his mind. Yes, he would fulfill his vow.

The next day, Finney encountered a church deacon who had hired him to handle a case in court. When asked about the legal matter, the young lawyer declared, "Deacon Barney, I have a retainer from the Lord Jesus Christ to plead his cause, and I cannot plead yours."

A PERFECT WILDERNESS

DeWitt Clinton almost missed the boat when he joined the 1810 expedition to consider an inland canal. He had paid a servant a month's wages in advance to accompany him. When the man did not show, Clinton went looking for him. He had to rush to jump aboard the paddle-wheel steamboat, the novel contraption that would carry him from New York City up the Hudson River to Albany. From there, most of the members of the recently appointed canal commission would ascend the Mohawk River by boat, cross Oneida Lake, and travel down the Seneca River as far as Geneva. Carriages would take them west to Lake Erie.

James Geddes's hopeful report had spurred the state to action. The idea of the canal lay at the center of the contentious national issue of internal improvements—what we would nowadays call infrastructure investment. What was needed? Who would pay? Who profit? Federalists saw in improvements a path to national prosperity. Republicans, followers of Jefferson (unrelated to today's GOP), agreed only in part—they were skeptical about big government. Federalists dreamed of national support for markets and commerce; Republicans favored states' rights and a nation of yeomen farmers.

The issue was a pressing one. The size of the republic made it difficult to control from Washington. A murky 1805 plot by former vice president Aaron Burr to carve out a new nation in the Southwest emphasized the point. The ambition of southerners to turn the middle of the continent into a slaveholding empire worried northerners. A canal to Lake Erie would provide a convenient link between the coast and the interior. It would also make it easier for antislavery New Englanders to populate the Middle West.

The New York State legislature voted to form a seven-man commission that included Clinton, a Jeffersonian Republican; Gouverneur Morris, a Federalist; and Stephen Van Rensselaer, a landed Dutch patroon from Albany. James Geddes came along to show the commissioners the details of his 1808 survey. The men were to look over the state of navigation to the west and explore the possibility of some kind of artificial waterway. The state footed the bill for the trip with a grant of $3,000. The travelers brought along wine, cigars, and a trunk full of books, including a well-thumbed edition of Jesse Hawley's "Hercules" essays.

DeWitt Clinton had learned politics at the knee of his uncle George Clinton, New York's first governor. DeWitt had been elected to the U.S. Senate at thirty-one. He had also served several terms as mayor of New York City. He was known for his stature—more than six feet tall and powerfully built—and his *hauteur* of manner." Newspapers called him "Magnus Apollo."

Now forty-one, Clinton was no shallow politician. He was rational and curious, highly educated, concerned about the poor, opposed to slavery and to imprisonment for debt. He promoted New York's schools and libraries and pushed for scientific improvements in agriculture. The canal would become both his obsession and his lasting legacy.

Gouverneur Morris had lived an event-filled life in his fifty-eight years. Like Clinton a native of New York City, he had served in the Continental Congress during the Revolution. At the Constitutional Convention, he had helped organize the founding document and had penned the famous preamble, "We the People . . ." He had served as minister to France, openly bedded a succession of French women, and witnessed the chaotic revolution there firsthand. The aging bachelor, whom enemies considered "irreligious and profane," was now starting a new life. He had recently married a thirty-five-year-old

Virginia gentlewoman who had fallen on hard times and taken a job as his housekeeper.

Morris was an enthusiastic canal booster who had dreamed of a New York waterway as far back as the 1790s. Although he had lost his left leg in an accident, he had limped on his awkward wooden replacement to northern and western New York to speculate in frontier land. A canal would benefit his purse, but he had his eye on far grander results. "As yet, my friend, we only crawl along the outer shell of our country," he had written to a friend in 1800. "The proudest empire in Europe is but a bauble, compared to what America will be."

Morris and Van Rensselaer both decided to make the entire journey by carriage, leaving it to the others to explore the existing waterways. Morris brought his bride along—they would enjoy one of the earliest Niagara Falls honeymoons—and, in a separate carriage, his French chef and a hired English painter to record the scenery. All the men wore frock coats and square-crowned beaver hats. Morris sported knee breeches, hopelessly old-fashioned now that pantaloons had become standard for men.

Clinton and his group started from Albany in early July 1810. Travel in flat-bottomed boats showed them the drawbacks of the Mohawk River, as their crew struggled to pole the vessels upstream. They found that the refinements of New York City did not prevail in the backcountry. At an inn near Canajoharie, Clinton noted that "the swarms of flies which assailed the food, were very disgusting." The guests were served custards that "exhibited the marks of that insect as a substitute for the grating of nutmeg." At Little Falls, a settlement of forty houses, gigantic rocks were heaped in piles. Clinton correctly speculated that the formation indicated "a violent rupture of the waters through this place." He also noted that "we saw on the north side large holes dug, which we were told were made by money-seekers from Stone Arabia." These rustic treasure hunters—Stone Arabia was the name of a local town—imagined that chests of gold had been buried in the earth by pirates or ancient inhabitants.

Utica displayed a bit more civilization, with three hundred residences, some of them quite elegant, and two newspapers. At Rome, the commissioners examined a three-foot-deep canal, part of a never-completed, poorly designed system intended to connect the Mohawk with Lake Ontario.

Accommodations could be primitive. At an inn east of the Salina salt works, "Our ears were invaded by a commingled noise of drunken people in an adjacent room, of crickets in the hearth, of rats in the walls, of dogs under the beds, by the whizzing of musquitoes about our heads, and the flying of bats about the room." At another hostelry, Clinton was "assailed by an army of bed-bugs, aided by a body of light infantry in the shape of fleas."

On July 25, they passed Lyons, east of the Genesee River and near the village of Palmyra. Outside town, they came upon a meeting of Methodist zealots in a clearing. "In one place," Clinton noted, "a man had a crowd around him, to listen to his psalm singing; in another, a person was vociferating his prayer." It was a sudden encounter with the religious intensity for which the region was becoming famous. One man had his arm around the neck of another, and was "looking him full in the face, and admonishing him of the necessity of repentance."

Two hundred seekers, a huge crowd on the frontier, were called together by a trumpet. Four preachers mounted a central platform. One of them "opened the service with prayer, during which groans followed every part of his orisons, decidedly emphatical." Afterward, the clergyman began "preaching up the terrors of hell." The travelers had to depart, but "we met crowds of people going to the sermon. On the margin of the road, we saw persons with cakes, beer, and other refreshments for sale."

All along the way, Clinton took delight in the unfamiliar surroundings of the west. He was an experienced ornithologist and noted "wood-ducks, gulls, sheldrakes, bob-linklins, king-birds, crows, kildares, small snipe." Forbidding forests covered most of the region, save the vast Montezuma Marshes and the scattered wheat fields. In 1810, no regular stagecoach traveled beyond Rome.

Clinton knew they were traveling through a land that had, in their lifetime, belonged to another people. His father, General James Clinton, had been one of the leaders of a 1779 Revolutionary War expedition to destroy the villages of Iroquois as punishment for the Indians' raiding of pioneer homes on behalf of the British. The excursion had alerted the white men to the bounty of western New York, where the Indians grew rows of corn ten feet high and peaches in abundance.

DeWitt Clinton knew and respected the fading culture of the Six Nations. All through his account of the trip, Indians fade in and out like ghosts. He saw a small group of them fishing with spears near Rome, others paddling canoes at Oneida Lake. Their drawings decorated rock walls. He examined the wampum and kettles recovered from burial mounds. He watched an Indian boy hit a coin with a dart from a six-foot-long blowpipe used for hunting birds.

The Quakers, Clinton wrote, were trying to teach the natives civilized behavior in order to rescue them "from the evils of savage life." Yet the morals of the Christians in the area were often "worse than those of the Pagans." Clinton speculated about how native peoples might have arrived in North America via Asia.

Clinton's account of the trip rarely mentioned the building of a canal. One exception was at Irondequoit Creek. James Geddes explained his plan to carry the waterway across the creek's deep valley, the preglacial outlet of the Genesee River. It was a keystone to the project's feasibility. "Mr. Geddes proposes a great embankment for his canal," Clinton recorded. The obstacle would prove to be one of the most daunting along the entire route.

They moved on to the nearby Genesee Falls, where the village of Rochesterville would soon explode into being. West of the Genesee, the travelers found much of the land "a perfect wilderness." They reached Buffalo on August 4, having made the 360-mile journey in a month.

On their way back, canal commissioner Thomas Eddy took a detour to visit the settlement of Jemima Wilkinson. Her religious community near Seneca Lake was known as "the second wonder of the western country" after Niagara Falls. Wilkinson was a radical visionary, her followers among the first white settlers in western New York. Now fifty-seven, Wilkinson had undergone a mystical conversion as a young woman. After a serious illness, her doctor reported, "she Conceived the Idea, that she had been Dead and was raised Up for Extraordinary Purposes." She felt that "the heavens were open'd." Having been visited by angels, she said that she was no longer Jemima, that her body had been taken over by the "Public Universal Friend." She put on a man's clothes and preached her own version of the Quaker doctrine she had grown up with.

Her message appealed particularly to women. "I was sincerely a Seeker," said Ruth Prichard, a school teacher from Wallingford, Connecticut. She heard the Friend preach in a nearby house. "It was the Voice that spake as never Man Spake." The Friend beckoned her to "that peace that the world can neither give nor take away." She became a follower and never looked back. The Friend amassed a substantial congregation in New England. In 1790, she set up her settlement thirty miles south of the site of Palmyra, which would sit astride the canal route.

She was already a legend in 1810, notorious for her radical ideas about gender and spirituality. A tale was told of her that she had responded to a challenge to prove her divine power by walking on water. She came to the pond's edge, the story went, and demanded of the crowd, "Do you have faith?" When they answered in the affirmative, she declared, "If ye have faith, ye need no other evidence." In another version, the viewers were doubters and the Friend pronounced that "without thy faith I cannot do it." An almost identical story would later be told about another divinely inspired prophet named Joseph Smith Jr.

Commissioner Eddy reported that "her dress, countenance, and demeanor are masculine in a great degree." She opposed war and did not favor marriage. "She veils herself in mystery," he said, and "represents herself as a spirit from heaven."

After the commissioners returned from their expedition, they enthusiastically backed the idea of an inland canal across the state. Boats traveling such a waterway would proceed more safely than those on the lake. Propelled by reliable animal power, untroubled by storms, they could gather and distribute merchandise at towns along the route. Only a long, excavated channel, the members thought, would fit the bill.

The commission recommended that the great project be funded, built, and operated by the government. "Too great a national interest is at stake," they said, to entrust the undertaking to a private company, which, in seeking a profit, "would defeat the contemplated cheapness of transportation." They asserted that "large expenditures can be made more economically under public authority." They left open the question of whether the state or federal government should bear the cost.

Gouverneur Morris, their senior member, wrote up the report they submitted in March 1811. A month later the state legislators passed the first canal act, allotting $15,000 to pay for the preliminary steps, the most important of which was to pin down a source of financing.

The great project immediately stumbled. Years of conflict with Great Britain came to a head. War broke out. By the end of 1812, western New York was on the front line of the fighting. All thoughts of building a canal there were put on hold.

HAIR-HUNG

The outdoor meeting that the canal commissioners had seen near Lyons was a sign of a tectonic spiritual change in America. The Great Awakening of the 1730s had encouraged the semi-mystical, born-again experience that became central to evangelical faith. It had fueled the spread of Methodist ideas, which emphasized zealous evangelizing of God's Word. But during the latter half of the eighteenth century, religion had faded from national attention. The Enlightenment-influenced founders leaned toward secularism.

Spiritual faith came roaring back during the first decades of the nineteenth century, a period that would be known as the Second Great Awakening. It was a prolonged spasm of enthusiasm and devotion far more intense than the First, and it would leave a permanent stamp on American Christianity.

"Outbreaks occur," Alexis de Tocqueville wrote of Americans after his 1831–32 tour, "when their souls seem suddenly to burst the bonds of matter by which they are restrained and to soar impetuously towards heaven." He found this enthusiasm most often west of the Appalachians, where "there is nothing of tradition, family feeling, or example to restrain them."

Tireless Methodist preachers, who roamed the backlands spreading their message one household at a time, were prominent in this transformation. On the frontier, neither clergyman nor listener had time for contemplation or deep study. The message had to be simple, short, vivid, and heartfelt. Better for the clergyman to portray the torments of the damned, than to waste time with what was known as "velvet-mouth preaching."

Sometimes, a group of preachers joined forces and drew religious seekers to a single location. Because some participants traveled long distances, they had no choice but to camp near the revival. These "camp meetings" typically lasted through several days of sermonizing, emotional intensity, and exaltation.

Pioneers' lives were a relentless routine of hard work, isolation and anxiety. When they took time off, they wanted a peak experience, not the nuanced theology of sophisticated clergymen. They wanted lurid imagery and clear options. They judged ministers by their enthusiasm, their lung power, and their ability to stir the soul. If they were going to be saved, they wanted to crash through to the divine quickly before they had to journey home and return to their chores.

The archetype of the camp meeting had taken place at Cane Ridge, Kentucky, in August 1801. Barton W. Stone, a twenty-nine-year-old Presbyterian minister, led a week-long meeting that created a sensation in the backcountry. At least ten thousand seekers attended, maybe as many as twenty-five thousand. They camped in the forest and slept under tents or in wagons. Dozens of preachers proclaimed the Word simultaneously, sermonizing for hours in different parts of the camp, each competing to attract listeners. Participants were dazed by a crowd larger than any they had ever seen. They sang hymns. They shivered to preachers' warnings, threats, and vivid depictions of eternal damnation. They were "hair-hung and breeze-shaken over the pit of hell." Some began to tremble all over. Some danced, shouted, laughed hysterically. "The noise was like the roar of Niagara," a participant reported.

Those touched by the electric fervor that shot through the crowd often dropped to the ground, "slain in the spirit." They moaned, screamed, wept, fell into trances. Egged on by cries of "Sic Satan, sic 'em!," they dropped to all fours and barked the devil up a tree. Crowds rushed to gawk at the latest outbreak, to encourage and join manifestations of divine rapture. *Amen!* was the shout. *Hallelujah!* At night, lamps and torches turned the scene into an infernal spectacle.

These hysterical conclaves were criticized and caricatured. Those who embraced Christ in a minute, said orthodox churchmen, would turn away from Him just as quickly. "Must a man draw his mouth out of all shape, and bellow like a bull, in order to become a Christian?" a critic demanded. With so many young, sex-starved men and women caught in prayerful passion, cynics hooted, there were "more souls begot than saved."

Yet the meetings represented the genuine yearning of pioneers. They did not want to be told that divine election had already decided their eternal fate. They wanted to tackle salvation barehanded, the same way they grappled with nature. They burned with the desire to feel, to be alive in the bosom of God. When Reverend Stone was successful in driving home his message, "the people appeared as just awakened from the sleep of ages."

ETERNITY

Anticipation is hell in war. For days the thud of distant artillery worried the dreams of the American troops at Plattsburgh, New York. It was 1814 and the British army was invading America. The red-coated soldiers had marched from Canada down the western shore of Lake Champlain. They outnumbered the defenders, almost all of whom were new to the terror of armed conflict.

The War of 1812 had not gone well for the Americans. Their efforts to invade Canada and perhaps add that territory to the union had failed. The British had crossed New York's western frontier and captured Fort Niagara. They had marched into the nation's capital in August and burned government buildings, including the president's mansion; First Lady Dolley Madison had barely managed to save a full-length portrait of George Washington. In a few days, the bursting of bombs and the rockets' red glare would challenge Fort McHenry in Baltimore Harbor.

William Miller, waiting at Plattsburgh, was unsure of how he would perform when the crisis came. He had volunteered for the army when the war broke out, but he was by profession a farmer. At thirty-two, he was married and raising a crop of children. Unlike some of the men around him, Captain Miller did not murmur prayers as the British approached. He was a deist and doubted that God interfered in human affairs.

Miller straddled two worlds. He had grown up when the humanist Enlightenment, with its high regard for knowledge and rationality, was in fashion. He had watched the country enter the romantic age marked by sentiment and visionary speculation. Born in 1782 in the rural New

York village of Low Hampton on the Vermont border, he was the son of a devout mother and a skeptical father. Although taught to fear the Lord, young Bill also read Thomas Paine's 1794 essay *The Age of Reason*, an attack on romanticism and the "priestcraft" of organized religion. Paine said the Bible was "a history of wickedness." Miller sided with the skeptics. "While I was a Deist," he would later remember, "I could not, as I thought, believe the *Bible* was the *word of God*."

Like Joseph Smith Jr., William Miller grew up on a rented farm. He longed for an education "with an intensity of feeling that approached to agony." He borrowed books from a subscription library in his hometown. A passionate reader, he soaked up pirate tales, *Robinson Crusoe*, and Captain James Cook's account of his voyage to the South Seas.

At fifteen, he finally began to attend the new school that had opened near his home. Having outpaced the other students in reading, he wrote letters for them and composed poetry. He learned arithmetic, a discipline that he would put to a unique use later in his life.

In 1803, at the age of twenty-one, Miller married and settled near the home of his wife, Lucy, in Poultney, Vermont. He distanced himself from his pious mother and preacher grandfather. He continued to farm, but he had higher ambitions. He joined the enlightened Freemasons and dabbled in politics, winning a position as constable, then county sheriff.

Deists—President Jefferson was one—believed that God was the prime cause of reality. But after the creation, they reasoned, the Almighty stepped back and allowed the world to operate according to natural laws. They viewed the world as a rational place. Miller agreed with them that the Bible was filled with "many contradictions and inconsistencies." He thought that clerics used its complexity to monopolize religion.

Miller joined the Vermont militia in 1810 and transferred to the regular army when war broke out two years later. In the late summer of 1814, his company hurried to Plattsburgh. They joined three thousand American troops to face the eight thousand British soldiers bearing down on them. A small fleet of American ships and gunboats stood guard over the town's harbor.

On September 11, 1814, the attack came. "What a scene!" Miller wrote in a letter home. British rockets and cannon fire slammed into the town. Sulfur stained the air. A shell burst within two feet of him, lacerating three men. He listened to "the shrieks of the dying, the groans of the wounded." The din of guns, the bursting of bombs and the deadly whizzing of musket and cannon balls dazzled him.

The American naval gunners bested their British counterparts and forced the enemy fleet to withdraw. Unable to hold the town without naval support, enemy commanders pulled their land forces back. The seemingly miraculous victory, along with the stubborn resistance at Fort McHenry and the Americans' triumph at the Battle of New Orleans in January 1815, provided a balm for national pride in the wake of a pointless war and the desecration of their capital.

The experience left Miller troubled. He had seen his fill of death. In addition to the slaughter of war, he had lately endured the passing of a brother and sister, then of his father and another sister. In the best of times, he was a moody man. Now he grew "moross and ill natured," plagued by melancholy—what we would call depression.

Deism, which reserved judgment on an afterlife, offered no solace. "To go out like an extinguished taper," Miller wrote, "is unsupportable." He summed up his desolation by paraphrasing Deuteronomy: "The heavens were as brass over my head and the earth as iron under my feet."

A spiritual change came over him. He purchased the farm his father had rented, built the house that he would occupy for the rest of his life, and encouraged his mother to give his five children religious guidance. At thirty-three, he became a patron of the local Baptist church.

He continued to suffer the dread of death. He wanted to "cling to that hope which warrants a never ending existence." Annihilation was a chilling thought. "Eternity, what was it? And death, why was it?"

One Sunday in 1816, when the local pastor was absent, elders asked Miller to preach the sermon. He began to speak on "the importance of Parental Duties." Suddenly he was overcome with emotion. The Holy Spirit entered his heart. It was not the earthshaking, heaven-opening shock experienced by Charles Finney and so many others, but his experience that day transformed Bill Miller.

"God by his Holy Spirit opened my eyes," he later recorded. Jesus became "my friend, and my only help," the Bible "the lamp to my feet and light to my path." His mind "became settled and satisfied."

Because he had been a notorious deist, Miller's conversion made local news and influenced others to reconsider their unbelief. He urged his friends to save their souls by accepting Christ.

Having become an "ornament and pillar in the church," Miller found the religious world he reentered more chaotic than the one he remembered. Believers now felt they could and must take responsibility for their own spiritual lives. They were looking for a new God, an approachable, merciful deity, a God of the heart.

To Miller, these yearnings were too modern. He believed in the stern, judging God of his boyhood. He believed in a God of reason. A Christian should not approach Jesus with blind faith. "To believe in such a Saviour without evidence," he asserted, "would be visionary in the extreme."

Miller was no visionary. He needed proof for his beliefs. His solution was to return to the Bible. "There never was a book written," he asserted, "that has a better connection and harmony than the Bible." Losing taste for all other reading, he studied Scripture endlessly. "I wondered why I had not seen its beauty and glory before," he wrote. He put aside all suppositions, commentaries, and interpretations. The Bible was "its own interpreter." Armed with a concordance, he studied the context of each word wherever it occurred. He was determined to "harmonize all these apparent contradictions."

For two years, he spent "whole nights as well as days" turning pages and mulling over the verses. The more the Scriptures came into focus, the more he was able to see through the symbolic surface into the certainties at the book's core. What he discovered astounded him. He read and reread, calculated, pondered. There was no avoiding it. The holy Word of Almighty God was pointing toward a truth of terrifying importance.

VISIONARY

Snow! Surveyors tracing the route of the hoped-for canal through the western New York Finger Lakes looked up amazed. It was June 7, 1816, and snow was falling from the summer sky. William Miller, poring over his Bible in Low Hampton, felt the unseasonable cold and wondered if it was a sign. To members of the Joseph Smith family, struggling to grow enough to eat in Vermont, the chill was the last straw. Everyone in northeastern America would remember the "year without a summer" for the rest of their lives. Temperatures varied wildly, crops failed, ice grinned from the shores of lakes.

Half a world away and a year earlier, a British naval officer assigned to the Dutch East Indies had heard the sound of distant artillery. Suspecting pirates, he sent a ship to investigate. After a few days of sailing, the captain of that ship encountered darkening skies. Soon, noonday turned to midnight.

Mount Tambora, on the island of Sumbawa, had exploded in April 1815 with a roar heard more than nine hundred miles away, the distance from Philadelphia to St. Louis. The explosion, ten times as violent as the later one at Mount Krakatoa, set off "one of the most frightful eruptions recorded in history." Of the twelve thousand inhabitants of the island, only twenty-six survived. In all, the disaster took the lives of fifty thousand humans.

The cataclysm blew a staggering quantity of ash and sulfurous gas into the stratosphere. The following year, residents of New York City noticed a dry haze in the air. The reduction in sunlight cooled the earth and disrupted weather patterns around the globe. New England was particularly hard-hit. Sixteen inches of snow fell in Vermont in June. During July, farmers lifted ice "thick as window glass" from troughs in Maine. Killing frosts swept the region in August. "Our teeth chattered in our heads," a woman wrote in her diary that summer. A minister reported that because of the widespread anxiety "almost all the newspapers now publish religious intelligence." Lucy Smith stoically described the cold as an "untimely frost." But having lost most of their crop during the two previous years, "eighteen-hundred-and-froze-to-death" was a grievous blow to her hungry family.

That summer, Joe Smith Sr. joined the caravan of discouraged farmers headed west, leaving Lucy to settle their affairs. The trek to the hinterlands was not for the fainthearted. A traveler would describe the area around Syracuse as "so desolate it would make an owl weep to fly over it." Joe kept going, stopping at Palmyra, a larger and more prosperous village than the one he had left. At age forty-five, he prepared to start again from scratch.

Fertile land and an influx of savvy Yankees were building the area's prosperity. Wheat thrived there. The plan for the canal from Lake Erie to the Hudson, if it materialized, would bring the ditch right through Palmyra. Land prices were already soaring in anticipation of canal prosperity. Smith hoped to catch hold of the galloping opportunity. But the Smith family was, as one historian put it, "the visionary rather than . . . the acquisitive Yankee type." They would spend the next fifteen years in Palmyra watching the lucky and the canny prosper around them.

That winter, Lucy extracted herself from the grip of creditors and started from Vermont with hardly enough cash to buy food along the way. Ten-year-old Joe Jr. was forced to walk much of the way through the snow in spite of his throbbing leg. His mother was nursing an infant of eight months named Don Carlos and herding seven other children. At one point on the month-long trip, a hired driver tried to throw the family out of their own wagon. Lucy wrenched the reins from his hands, denounced him loudly and declared she would drive the wagon herself. She arrived in Palmyra with nine cents, having traded her daughter Sophronia's eardrops to cover their bill at the last inn. With joy and tears, she threw herself into the arms of her husband.

NAVIGABLE

In 1815, DeWitt Clinton's fortunes had reached a low ebb. He had audaciously challenged incumbent James Madison for the presidency in the 1812 election and lost. During the war that broke out that year, Clinton's canal commission had been stripped of its spending authority. Many thought the idea itself had run out of steam.

With peace restored, commissioner Thomas Eddy tried to breathe new life into the project. He helped organize a public meeting to demand that state lawmakers reconsider an inland canal. Clinton threw his influence behind the effort. An assembly of influential New Yorkers met at the plush City Hotel on Broadway in New York City just before the end of 1815. Clinton was the author and lead proponent of a petition to the legislature. He pointed out that a canal would forge a permanent link through New York between the Atlantic and the west.

Clinton let his rhetoric soar. The project was "without parallel in the history of mankind." The legislature must act now—"delays are the refuge of weak minds." Tens of thousands of citizens across the

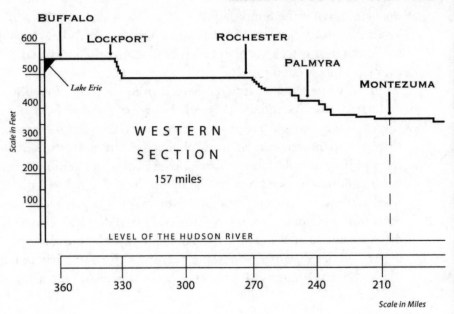

ELEVATION PROFILE

state agreed and rushed to sign the petition. This quasi-referendum revived the canal concept and turned Clinton into its champion. Enthusiasm began to percolate from Albany to Buffalo.

The renewed call brought a vocal response from critics. Folks in the Hudson Valley, Long Island, and the southern tier of the state saw nothing in the project but cost, risk, and increased competition for their own farm produce. The project was just too big. The technical challenges were beyond the abilities of inexperienced engineers. As for Clinton, an opponent said, he was "determined to seize on the canal project as a ladder to climb into power." The accusation was true.

The representatives in Albany could not, however, ignore the tidal wave of support for the project. The issue of the canal had to be addressed. Lobbyists from around the state descended on the legislature for its 1816 session.

Clinton "had a delicate and difficult game to play" as he tried to navigate the opposition. He focused on creating a detailed study of the route, one that would win over legislators by making the project seem less fanciful. He supported a compromise bill to appoint a new

OF THE ERIE CANAL

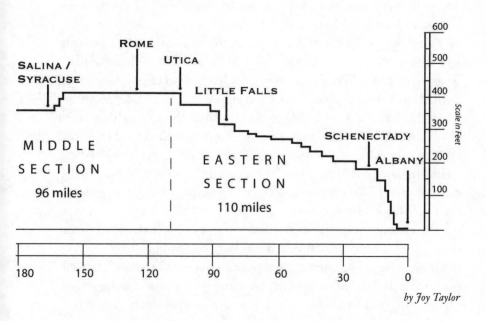

by *Joy Taylor*

commission, with himself as president, and to authorize money for a thorough survey of the proposed route.

The bill passed on the last day of the legislative session in April 1816. The next step was to lay out an exact, not an approximate, plan for the canal's path. This was a grueling task that foreshadowed the enormous challenges of the actual construction. James Geddes led the team that plotted the route through the most remote section of the waterway, from east of Palmyra to Lake Erie. The commissioners assigned the middle section to Benjamin Wright, a plump, round-faced judge from Rome, New York, who knew the local terrain well. Charles Broadhead, another surveyor, would cover most of the upper Mohawk Valley, from Utica eastward.

The forty-six-year-old Wright had more experience with canals than most Americans, but he was no expert. Having settled on the western frontier, he had helped the English canal planner William Weston with the largely unsuccessful improvements to navigation along the Mohawk River. Wright was now taking on a far more daunting challenge. Heading west from Rome, the canal would pass through deep forest, scrubland, and swamp. Unlike the Mohawk Valley, little of this territory had been cleared or settled. With a covered wagon to carry their gear and supplies, Wright's team of a dozen men plunged into the wilderness.

The goal was to find a path west that was as level as possible and as straight as could be managed. Hills and valleys were both to be avoided. Once Wright determined a likely direction, his surveyor sighted on a distant object, took a compass reading, and walked toward the landmark. An axman accompanied him, notching trees along the trail. Two additional woodcutters hacked down brush and trees to clear a four-foot-wide path. Men carrying sixty-six-foot-long chains measured a section almost the length of a football field. They marked each end with two stakes, one extending above the ground, the other flush with the soil.

An assistant engineer next set a level on a tripod halfway between these points. Two rodmen rested graduated poles upright on each of the flush stakes. The engineer put the crosshairs of his device on each pole. He noted the difference in elevation, if any, between the stakes. His reading had to be precise to the fraction of an inch. Any errors would accumulate, throwing off the final calculation.

Meanwhile, Wright would be examining the terrain: streams, property lines, rocks, knolls, drainage. The survey and investigation would eventually be translated into a detailed map of the route. Cost was always on the engineer's mind. Aqueducts to cross streams, locks to navigate elevation changes, embankments to carry the canal over low stretches, all would be expensive. Periodically, Wright directed his men to dig ten-foot-deep holes in order to examine the nature of the soil. He was always on the lookout for sources of water. Would the local streams, lakes, and ponds provide enough water to keep the ditch filled?

The men pushed into increasingly dismal terrain. At first, they negotiated forests and hacked through underbrush and "woods of hemlock, cedar, alder bushes and weeds." Here and there they encountered the Oneida Indians who still lived in the area. The crews traded with them for game to supplement their regular diet of smoked pork and stale bread.

Later they moved into "swamp and swale," areas that Indians avoided. Here thick brush and brambles had to be cleared, along with

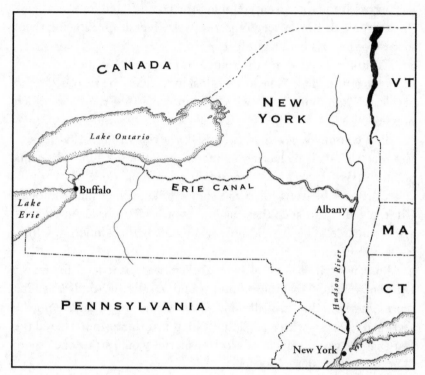

Canal route   *by Joy Taylor*

cattails and reeds nine feet high. They dodged the occasional hiss of a rattlesnake, swatted mosquitoes day and night. Conducting the survey at the height of summer, they sweated in the thick air and drank stagnant swamp water to slake their thirst.

The men were learning as they went. Except for West Point, which taught military engineers, no school in America offered courses in engineering. A young farmer named John Jervis was hired by Benjamin Wright as an axman to clear brush and trees. "The mystery of the level," he said, "the taking of sights, its adjustment, and the computations of these observations were all dark to me." Little by little Jervis learned by doing. In time, he would become a supervisor on the canal, then one of the premier civil engineers in American history.

While the survey teams did their work, Clinton and the commissioners were drawing up a plan for building the canal. They arrived at a design: the profile of the ditch would be an inverted trapezoid forty feet across at the top, twenty-eight at the bottom, and four feet deep. Locks would be ninety feet long and twelve feet deep, allowing them to raise or lower a boat eight feet.

Clinton ranged along the route, examining the work of the surveyors as it unfolded. "The mind is lost in wonder," he recorded, "and perplexed and confounded with the immensity of the ideas which press upon it."

The commissioners had proposed a series of taxes and fees to pay for the canal, including an increase in the duty on salt, a tax on steamboat tickets, and imposts on sales at auction. They would collect reasonable tolls for cargo shipped along the canal, although Clinton wanted to keep these as low as possible in order to encourage commerce. They would borrow money, perhaps finding willing lenders in Europe.

But the highest hope of New Yorkers was for federal financing. Clinton went to Washington and found an ally in South Carolina representative John C. Calhoun. Although he would later embrace sectional interests with a passion, Calhoun, at thirty-four, shared the fear that the vast distances of North America would strain the union. "Let us conquer space," he declared.

In February 1817, Congress passed the Bonus Bill, which allotted the charter fee and royalties from the Second Bank of the United States to internal improvements, with the Erie Canal the main beneficiary. On March 1, three days before he was to hand over his office to James Monroe, President Madison vetoed the measure. Neither he nor Congress, he declared, had the constitutional authority to allot public money for such purposes. So said the "Father of the Constitution."

Madison, a New York newspaper wrote, had "suddenly become wonderfully delicate and squeamish upon the provisions of the constitution." DeWitt Clinton called his action reprehensible and "totally indefensible." Like many, he suspected that Madison's devotion to the interests of Virginia, his home state, played as big a role in his decision as his concern for the fine points of the Constitution. But the decision was final. Federal financing was out. New Yorkers would have to go it alone, or not at all.

The canal commissioners had estimated the cost of the project at six million dollars, not far from the figure Jesse Hawley had suggested in his "Hercules" essays. This amounted to more than a quarter of the budget of the entire federal government and a huge chunk of all the capital in the state. It would be a desperate gamble. Critics were sure that in the "big ditch would be buried the treasure of the State, to be watered by the tears of posterity."

New York City representatives generally opposed the canal. The city would sink under canal debt, they said. The cost was "too great for the state," the magnitude of the project was "beyond what has ever been accomplished by any nation." Peter Livingston, whose family owned tracts of land in the Hudson Valley, had become a fierce Clinton antagonist. "The man who will enter into this project," he declared, "must be a *madman, a fool, or a knave*." The levels of taxation would be oppressive. "It will make paupers of the state."

"Who is this James Geddes, and who is this Benjamin Wright?" another assemblyman asked. "What canals have they ever constructed?" The engineers sent a message to reassure the legislators, expressing "their confidence in their ability to locate and construct the canal."

Popular support made the difference. On April 10, 1817, the state assembly took the plunge. The representatives passed *An Act respecting Navigable Communications, between the great western and northern lakes, and the Atlantic ocean.* In May, DeWitt Clinton capped his political rebound by winning the governorship of New York. Construction on the greatest engineering project in the nation's history was set to begin July 4.

ABDUCTION

The master stonemason Hiram Abiff supervised the construction of the temple of King Solomon in Jerusalem ten centuries before the birth of Christ. Accounts of the sacred geometry of Solomon's fabulous house of worship would be sung down the ages, fascinating thinkers like Isaac Newton. The precisely proportioned temple was lined with cedar overlaid with gold.

During its construction, a group of journeyman masons approached Hiram. They knew that if they completed their tasks well, they might, at the end of the project, be given the Master's Word. This was the sign by which an unknown workman could signify his ability when seeking a job on a distant project; it was the key that would unlock a master's wages. The three dissidents wanted the word now.

When Hiram refused to divulge the secret, one of the disgruntled workers struck him with a 24-inch ruler. Hiram survived and stumbled away. A second journeyman demanded the word. Again a refusal, a blow with a mason's square. When the master would not reveal the arcane knowledge to the third worker, the man hit him with a setting maul, this time killing him. A search party found Hiram's hastily buried body. Solomon himself raised the corpse from the makeshift grave for proper burial.

Any nineteenth-century candidate for entry into the third degree of Freemasonry was required to learn and act out Hiram Abiff's story. The drama drove home the tradition of faithfulness to the brotherhood, even unto death. It suggested that the modern order of Free and Accepted Masons drew sustenance from ancient roots.

William Morgan knew the story well. During the early 1820s, he had joined the Freemasons in Le Roy, New York, thirty miles southwest of Rochester. Like Joseph and Lucy Smith, William and his young wife, Lucinda, had tried for the main chance and failed. Like the Smiths, they had migrated to western New York, where the canal shouted opportunity.

A native of Culpeper County, Virginia, William had spent his early life as a vagabond. Rather than sticking to his trade as a bricklayer, he had traveled the world. He had tried the pirate's life, a rumor had it, crewing with the celebrated Jean Lafitte. Captured, Morgan had been dragooned into the U.S. Army. He claimed that during the War of 1812 he had fought under General Andrew Jackson at the Battle of New Orleans, rising to the rank of captain.

In 1819, at forty-five, he was ready to settle down and start a family. He returned to his home turf, set up as a merchant in Richmond, and courted a comely young lady named Lucinda Pendleton. She was only eighteen and her father, a planter and Methodist minister, opposed the match. Lucinda, strong-willed and perhaps moved by Morgan's war stories, married him anyway. After two years of settled life in Virginia, William's restlessness returned. He and Lucinda moved to Canada.

The Morgans invested their capital in a brewery in the town of York (now Toronto). A fire soon ruined their plans and left the couple destitute. By 1823, they had relocated to New York State, settling near the town on the Genesee River that had just changed its name from Rochesterville to Rochester. William worked as a clerk and may have returned to his original trade. It's likely that the construction of the canal offered him the promise of work as a stonemason. Lucinda gave birth to their first child, named Lucinda Wesley, the next year.

Like many of their generation, the Morgans strove to climb the slippery slope of economic opportunity. For William, joining the Freemasons seemed a smart move. In the brotherhood, he would rub elbows with a better sort—the lawyers, merchants, judges and politicians who might provide an entrée into some lucrative business. He was initiated soon after arriving in Le Roy and ascended through the first three degrees of the order.

The origins of Freemasonry are obscure, but the brotherhood probably began in the Middle Ages, when itinerant masons roamed Europe building cathedrals. A master mason combined the professions of architect, engineer, and builder. Masons developed guilds to set wages and regulate the trade. Skilled "free masons" worked on "free stones," completing fine ornamental carving. "Rough masons" shaped ordinary building blocks. As in the legend of Hiram Abiff, masters on a particular site needed a convenient way to distinguish the expertise of unknown applicants. Signs and passwords, kept secret from the general public, served as credentials.

The guilds maintained hostelries and clubhouses, offering aid and conviviality to traveling members. Townspeople who had never hefted a trowel or a chisel petitioned for inclusion as well. The guild officers allowed respectable gentlemen to become honorary or "accepted" masons. Some of the new members were clients or benefactors of the lodges. A distinction developed in the seventeenth century between "operative" masons with calloused hands and "speculative" Masons, drawn by the guilds' rituals and bonhomie. The society appealed to traveling merchants, who could be assured of congenial companions in a distant city.

Over time, speculative Masons took over the guilds entirely. Working with stone and mortar became largely a symbolic aspect of the brotherhood. The lodges became clubs. Freemasonry attracted forward-thinking individuals imbued with the ideals of the Enlightenment. In America, many of the founding statesmen, including George Washington and Benjamin Franklin, were Freemasons. Besides offering social connections, the fraternity constituted a kind of secular religion. It satisfied a hunger for ritual, mystery, and dress-up.

Secrecy, which had once had a practical purpose, appealed to speculative Masons fascinated by mystery and arcane knowledge. The special handshakes and cryptic rituals added to a sense of exclusiveness and fun. Elaborate oaths were part of Masonic rites. Initiates like William Morgan were required to swear not to reveal the brotherhood's esoterica "under no less Penalty than to have my Throat cut, my Tongue taken from the Roof of my Mouth, my Heart pluck'd from under my Left Breast, then to be buried in the Sands of the Sea at the low-water mark."

A sophisticate like Ben Franklin would have dismissed this rigmarole as part of the Masons' boyish histrionics. A worldly striver like William Morgan probably thought nothing of it. But to the naive and literal rustics of western New York, such an oath was serious business.

At twenty-five, Lucinda Morgan was strikingly pretty, light of hair, small of stature, and possessed of an iron will. She had been drawn to a man who did not wallow in the humdrum, who dared. She did not regret her marriage, even though it had made her intimate with the anxiety of poverty and the uncertainty of a rootless existence.

Captain Morgan, she knew, was determined to prosper. Wage labor had barely earned him enough to keep ahead of his creditors. In 1825, they had moved to Batavia, a village sixteen miles from the canal. A Masonic brother had hired William to help construct a building there.

Morgan had added his signature to a petition to start a new Masonic lodge in Batavia. For some reason, his brothers had dropped his name from the list. Was he, at fifty-two, out of sync with the younger members? Did he possess a cantankerous personality? Was he, even in an age of heavy drinking, an annoying lush? An obvious social climber? A bombastic braggart among the more sedate locals? The rejection rankled. Bad blood flowed. He stopped attending lodge meetings altogether.

Having fallen out of favor with the brotherhood, Morgan hit on a new idea. If money was not to be had by cozying up to respectable gentlemen, perhaps he could find it by indulging the public's curiosity about the Masons. Some outsiders suspected them of depravity. Why else would they shroud their doings in secrecy? Some imagined that they were plotting to subvert republican values.

What were the brotherhood's precious secrets? That, Morgan understood, was what everyone wanted to know. The man who dared break the oath, scribble down the mysteries, and publish them in a book would have the world rushing to pay him for his efforts. So Morgan thought. He was sure he had finally hit on a lucrative venture. Living hand to mouth, chased by creditors, he came to see it as an indispensable venture. As his salvation.

Eager to "create a stir among the masons," he teamed up with David Miller, a printer and newspaper publisher in Batavia. Together, they would produce a book. The project would require a substantial investment in time and materials. Several backers chipped in. The members of this little consortium had high hopes. Who would not want to read the groundbreaking volume?

On the morning of September 11, 1826, Lucinda nervously watched her husband as he prepared to leave their small Batavia apartment over a silversmith's workshop. William's book was the center of a storm of wrath, and Lucinda knew that the closer the project came to completion, the greater the danger.

The Morgans' daughter, two years old, still lay sleeping in her cradle. Lucinda was nursing their two-month-old son. The baby's birth that year on the Fourth of July, exactly fifty years after the signing of the Declaration of Independence, had seemed auspicious. They named him Thomas Jefferson Morgan. They might have been struck by an eerie coincidence—on that same day, the former president and author of the Declaration had died.

Lucinda's hopes were wrapped in fear. She lived in a precarious world where fortune could make sudden turns and citizens could be thrown into prison for debt. She worried about what would happen to her and her children if the venture misfired.

All that summer, Morgan had worked on the manuscript. He recorded the rituals, the interrogations, the initiation rites, the sacred symbols. He wrote down the Grand Royal Arch word. He included descriptions to clarify the signs, known as due-guards, and the hand grips by which one Mason could recognize another. He explained the five points of fellowship, an initiatory embrace that replicated the manner in which Solomon had drawn Hiram Abiff from his tomb. Morgan added his own knowledge to information he lifted from earlier exposés of Freemasonry that had been printed in Europe. David Miller, the printer, later said that Morgan had "compiled" the book rather than written it.

To the young, enthusiastic Freemasons of western New York, Morgan's plan was an outrage not to be countenanced. When they found out about it, they harassed him. Several times he was arrested for small debts. For a time, he moved back to Rochester to avoid their attention. Now that the book was written and Miller was pulling the damp page proofs from the press, the Masons were desperate to stop the publication.

The night before, Morgan's enemies had set fire to Miller's print shop. Some teamsters headed for the canal had been sleeping in their wagons along a Batavia street that night. They noticed the fire and extinguished it before it engulfed the building.

Morgan and Miller felt that such harassment played into their hands. Why would the Masonic brothers be so determined to stop the book's publication? It must contain juicy secrets, crucial warnings, eye-widening revelations. Readers everywhere would have to have a copy. The book would sell. Let the foolish Masons drum up publicity for the volume: the more, the better.

After William Morgan walked out the door early that September morning in 1826, Lucinda never saw the father of her children again. His fate, soon to be labeled an "outrage" by newspapers, became the most publicized crime of the century. It engendered a mystery that would outlast the secrets of the Masons. The reaction to it would influence the nation's politics for years to come. "No subject has ever spread with such rapidity over the continent, and harrowed up so much ill-feeling in the minds of the people," a newspaper would later report, "as the abduction of Morgan."

GROUNDBREAKING

O n July 4, 1817, a boisterous throng of citizens paraded out of their small village in central New York before sunrise. They were armed, but not for war. Many had been up all night celebrating the holiday and the impending grand event. They proceeded to a flat, marshy meadow studded with hemlock and birch a mile south of town. Each carried a shovel.

The stockade known as Fort Stanwix, built by the British, had occupied the site of their town during the Revolution. The place was now called Rome. Applying the name of the Eternal City to a frontier outpost surrounded by wilderness did not strike the residents as incongruous. Rome had been the capital of a storied empire, and citizens here were embarking on an imperial project. Jesse Hawley had proven more prophet than madman. A dozen years after the idea took shape in his head, it had engendered a project that New Yorkers hoped would catapult them to greatness.

DeWitt Clinton, who had taken office as governor three days earlier, understood that the state was gambling its future. The canal commissioners had decided to rely on American amateurs to oversee the construction. Benjamin Wright, the chief engineer, had never built a canal. James Geddes had proven himself as a surveyor but was also a novice regarding hydraulic science. The other engineers recruited for the project had even less experience.

Delineating land parcels, the traditional work of surveyors, was largely a two-dimensional task. A surveyor laying the course of a canal had to think in three dimensions. The level of the ground was as important as direction and distance. Determining levels on undulating ground required subtle calculations. A canal demanded precision in ways that building a road or a log cabin did not. Running test levels for the middle section of the canal, Geddes and Wright had made calculations that differed by more than a foot. The water that would fill the canal would put the levels to a mercilessly exacting test. Any canal off by a foot would fail.

Canal commissioners suspected that "Geddes will be found to be right and Wright wrong." They were losing confidence in Wright, who at times put his own business ahead of his canal duties. But given the shortage of men with any knowledge of canals at all, they could not do without him.

Geddes, in an impressive demonstration of his expertise, surveyed a hundred-mile circle around Oneida Lake. Measuring up and down hills and across valleys, he found that on completing the circuit, his calculations were off by less than an inch and a half. In an age of rough-and-ready approximations, it was a remarkable feat.

Now, as the ruddy July sun flamed over the horizon, a cannon fired from the arsenal in town: time for the ceremonies to begin. Village president Joshua Hathaway declared that they were about to undertake "one of the grandest objects that ever has and perhaps ever will grace our nation." Men impatiently gripped their shovels as state canal commissioner Samuel Young spoke of the "unborn millions" who would have access to the markets of the world. His sentiment was an expression of high optimism. The odds favored the skeptics.

The citizens of Rome gathered around a butternut-wood stake labeled "No. 1, True Canal Line," which marked the beginning of the massive digging project. A second resounding cannon boom marked the end of the speechmaking. Magistrate John Richardson had won the bid to dig the first section of the canal and would enjoy the privilege of scooping the initial shovelful of earth.

The canal had been a vision, a concept, a dream, and a cause. It had set off contentious debates in the legislature and heated conversations in taverns. It had been a subject of derision, of oratory, and of hope. Now, the speculating and imagining were over. Americans were about to turn the fantastic idea into a physical reality.

Commissioner Young handed a spade to Richardson. The contractor plunged it into the soil. The gesture touched off a frenzy of flying dirt. Everyone in attendance began to dig, "each vieing with the other," said the Utica *Gazette*, in the pure joy of participating in history.

TO FEEL AND SHOUT

Palmyra was buzzing when the Joseph Smith Sr. family arrived in 1816. Its population of three thousand souls was twice that of Rochesterville, the settlement around the falls of the Genesee River. In November 1817, the town gained its first newspaper, the *Palmyra Register*. It already had four churches. The Erie Canal was on its way and would pass straight through the village.

At first, the Smiths and their children lived in a rented house in town. Joseph Sr. and the older boys—Alvin was almost nineteen, Hyrum seventeen—sought day labor from local farmers. They helped weed gardens, dig wells, plow fields, clear ditches. Lucy continued to paint canvas oil cloth rugs. She and the girls also sold refreshments from their home: boiled eggs, ginger cakes, birch beer. On public occasions, they loaded a cart with sweetmeats and peddled them to the crowds.

By 1818, the family was able to contract for a farm: a hundred-acre plot two miles south of the village in the township of Manchester. It was the first time Joseph and Lucy had lived on their own land since the ginseng disaster fifteen years earlier. Not entirely their own—the contract required payments each autumn to the agent of the New York City land speculator from whom they were buying the property. They would be in debt until the purchase price of seven hundred dollars was paid off.

Before the deal was finalized, they constructed a log cabin on a small adjacent plot, which they also planned to purchase. Two rooms, a bedroom in a shed at the rear, and two sleeping lofts for six boys, two girls, and their parents. Lucy, always upbeat, called it a "snug log house, neatly furnished." Three years later, at the age of forty-six, she would give birth to another baby, a girl named for herself.

Next came the work of clearing the land. Tocqueville wrote that upstate New York's virgin forests consisted of "trees of all ages, foliage of all colours, plants, fruits and flowers of a thousand species, entangled and intertwined." From this, pioneer families like the Smiths had to produce sustenance. They chopped the trees, removed the branches, amassed logs into giant pyres, set them ablaze. They sold the ashes to potash dealers, who turned them into the alkali used to make soap, gunpowder, and glass.

A good axman could clear ten acres in a year. The Smiths, working together, cleared thirty. At the same time, they gathered maple sap and boiled it down to sugar. They set up hives for honey. Lucy and the girls made brooms and baskets for sale in town.

That first year, the tangle of roots allowed only a crop of Indian corn and squash. The second year, they planted wheat, their cash crop. The land was far from picturesque. Like most raw farms, it was blighted with charred trees and stumps. Crops had to be grown in the midst of the debris left from clearing.

In 1819, just as the Smiths were harvesting their first wheat and preparing to make their land payment, a financial panic collapsed grain prices. The family was not able to accumulate enough cash, even with Alvin's paid labor, to meet their obligation. The debt piled up.

The work was dirty, monotonous, wearying, and endless. It began at dawn and continued until dark. Respites were few, the mental stress intense. Yet Lucy was proud of what they accomplished. Having arrived in Palmyra "destitute of friends, house, or employment," they had carved out a life by their own industry. When a group of Lucy's women friends gathered in her cramped log house, a merchant's wife commented that Lucy deserved better. "I am the wealthiest woman that sits at this table," Lucy told her. "I have never prayed for riches of the world, as perhaps you have." Pride amid poverty was a principle Lucy conveyed to her children.

The world had its delights. Sunshine. Air scented with juniper and honeysuckle. A meal eaten with capacious appetite. An abundance of wildlife. The deep quiet that left room for the voices of nature. One upstate pioneer remembered these sounds: the whisper of rustling leaves, the notes of the whip-poor-will, a wolf's distant howl. They formed a delightful chorus that left the careful listener with a sense of pleasure and awe.

Soon after arriving in Palmyra, Lucy attended a revival, accepted Jesus, and cast her lot with the Presbyterians, a Calvinist sect in which local congregations were guided by bodies of elders. God's sovereignty and his plan to grant salvation to only an elect few were fundamental tenets. Her sons Hyrum and Samuel and her daughter Sophronia were baptized with her. The other family members stayed home, but discussion of religion dominated evenings by the fire.

Unlike his brother Alvin, whom observers described as "the soberest of men," young Joseph had a lively personality given to whimsy and play. He could be "joyously funny." A great talker, he entertained his family with "amusing recitals" about the Indians who had populated this region. He described their dress and houses, their beliefs and wars, his mother reported, "with as much ease, seemingly, as if he had spent his whole life among them."

Always restless of mind, Joe Jr. had been searching for a "liveing faith" that he could embrace. He was partial to the Methodists, enthusiasts who declared heaven open to all, but he remained unconvinced. The competition for souls that accompanied the revivals seemed to him contrary to Christian sentiment. He commented, "All their good feelings for one another (if they ever had any) were entirely lost in a strife of words and a contest about opinions."

By 1819, when he turned fourteen, Joseph's yearning, charged with the bewildering energy of adolescence, had ratcheted the tension inside him. His "mind at times was greatly excited," he later wrote. He wanted "to get Religion too wanted to feel & shout like the Rest but could feel nothing."

To feel and shout was a common desire in those days of religious excitement. When you saw your neighbors fall into an ecstasy of belief, it was easy to sense you were being left out. The following year, Joseph came across the Bible verse, "If any of you lack wisdom, let him ask of God . . . and it shall be given." His eyes were opened. "Never did any passage of scripture," he would declare, "come with more power to the heart of man." He would ask God, would turn to prayer. Privacy was impossible in the crowded log cabin. On a mild spring morning in 1820, Joseph walked off into a nearby grove of trees. "I made a fruitless attempt to pray," he later recorded; "my toung seemed to be swolen in my mouth, so that I could not utter."

Suddenly the sweet air, laced with birdsong, came alive with grandeur. Joseph felt his heart leap. "A pillar of light above the brightness of the sun at noon day come down from above and rested upon me and I was filled with the spirit of god." Charles Finney would undergo a similar glory in a grove of trees the following year. So would many others during that enchanted time.

"The Lord opened the heavens upon me," Smith marveled, "and I saw the Lord and he spake unto me." He saw "two personages (whose brightness and glory defy all description) standing above me in the air." He was told his sins were forgiven. His soul was "filled with love and for many days I could rejoice with great Joy." It was now clear which religion he was to join: none of them. One of the personages told him that "all their Creeds were an abomination in his sight."

Still tingling from his soul-shaking experience, Joseph sought out a Methodist minister and described the vision. This was standard procedure. A learned man of God could distinguish a genuine conversion from a childish fantasy, or, worse, a notion planted by Satan. The clergyman was not impressed. He had heard similar tales before. Frontier eccentrics had long been encouraging religious seekers to turn away from the corrupt churches. All creeds an abomination? No, no. The young man had been deceived.

The clergyman's pat dismissal turned Joseph even more strongly against the established sects. He had seen heavenly beings in the forest, and "they did in reality speak to me."

DAMNED IF YOU DO

In the early nineteenth century, itinerant Methodist preachers traveled the American frontier, setting fires of religious enthusiasm. The most incendiary of them was Lorenzo Dow. A Connecticut native, he was "thin and weather-beaten, and appeared haggard and ill-favored, partly on account of his reddish, dusty beard." Asthmatic and sickly as a child, he had found himself, at fourteen, "taken up by a whirlwind and carried above the skies." Like Jemima Wilkinson, he had rubbed shoulders with angels and had looked into the face of God. He had returned to earth reluctantly, clutching a promise of salvation.

In 1799, at the age of twenty-two, Dow headed to the hinterlands to preach. He had a phenomenal gift for oratory. He could spin yarns, tell jokes, mock, exaggerate, and enthrall. He understood life in all its squalid richness, and he used earthy parables to thrust home his points.

Dow understood country people, their canniness and limitations. He knew that ordinary folks loved sarcasm and humor, gripping stories and vivid imagery. He catered to their taste for histrionics. He shaped his appearance to resemble the popular image of John the

Baptist. He could act out the role of the devil, bringing his congregation "messages from hell."

Few persons in the age before railroads traveled as far as Dow. He routinely covered six thousand miles in a year, either on horseback along bad roads and forest paths, or bushwhacking through uncharted backlands.

In 1802, two decades before the Erie Canal transformed the region, he made his first visit to what would become the epicenter of religious enthusiasm on the New York frontier. He converted a hundred sinners in three hours at the town of Western, near Rome, whose inhabitants would later quake to the preaching of Charles Finney. Dow returned to the area three times and showed the profound influence a revival could have in the hands of a master preacher. His spiritual bonfires would burn across the backcountry for decades to come.

Most Methodist preachers roamed the frontier with simple hearts, their way lit by the glow of their own conversions. Lorenzo Dow called himself "the Cosmopolite." Cosmopolitan thinkers had enjoyed a vogue during the Enlightenment—the archetype was Ben Franklin, a man of the world, free of prejudice and parochialism. Dow's wide travels justified the label. So did his open-minded stance—he shunned all religious denominations and urged universal repentance. So did his uncommon lack of race prejudice—he routinely preached in the churches of African Americans and mingled socially with blacks. He spoke out against slavery as a "Moral Evil."

Dow rejected the pretension of the established clergy. "In a religious point of view," he declared, "all men are on a level." A devotee of Thomas Jefferson, he took the term "born equal" literally. Yet around him he saw men treated like animals and forced to bow and scrape. "One hath thousands," he said, "gained by the labour of others." There was no reason why a man should not think for himself in every field, including religion. He opposed "purse proud" elites, "men of self importance." He sneered at religious denominations.

The tottering ideas of Calvinism often came into Dow's crosshairs. Calvinist orthodoxy held that man was a depraved sinner, salvation a gift from a merciful God, bestowed on only a few regardless of merit. Jesus died only for these elect. Based on the thinking of French theologian John Calvin in the sixteenth century, these notions had been taken to heart by the Puritan dissenters who first journeyed to New England. Clergymen urged believers to pray and wait for God to act.

Dow attacked this passivity and raged against the complex, elitist doctrine of Calvinist theologians. He dismissed their insistence that the prize of salvation had been awarded or denied a person before birth. He mocked the paradox that a condemned man still had free will. He often repeated the sneering chant:

> *You can and you can't*
> *You will and you won't;*
> *You'll be damned if you do,*
> *And you'll be damned if you don't.*

The common people cheered. They wanted a spectacle and Dow gave them one. He became the darling of the camp meetings. He understood the power of celebrity—his very presence launched his followers into a kind of intoxication. He induced a spiritual agitation so powerful that it set his audience twitching and writhing, a phenomenon known as "the jerks." He encouraged the "holy laugh," a burst of hysteria that overtook those flooded with grace. Enthusiasts at his meetings got down on their hands and knees and barked like dogs in their ecstasy.

The gentry dismissed "Crazy" Dow as an ignorant barbarian. One critic said: "His manners have been clownish in the extreme; his habits and appearance more filthy than a savage Indian." But while they found him uncouth, they had to admit that "he understood common life, and especially vulgar life."

He understood life. Dow was no anchorite. Like many in those days of heady expansion, he took advantage of his travels to make money speculating in land. He published numerous collections of his rambling writings, earning royalties as he spread his notoriety. He sold patent medicine of dubious efficacy. He admitted he could outsmart swindlers and "run the rig" as well as any of them. Detractors labeled him "imposter" and "horse thief." Dow was indeed a confidence man, but he won listeners' trust not to fleece them but to hand them over to the Lord.

Dow had a tremendous influence on frontier settlers. Thousands of children were named *Lorenzo* to honor him. The name was passed down through generations, so that well into the twentieth century the ghost of the bearded wild man haunted America. But the emotionalism he encouraged and the easy path to heaven he promised scared and infuriated the orthodox clergymen of the East. In their eyes, he was turning religion into unrestrained fanaticism.

Charles Finney was to be the man who would distill Dow's frontier spirit and inject it into orthodox Christianity. He too rejected the idea that the human constitution was morally depraved, and that God had condemned men for their sinful nature. Like Dow, Finney knew the importance of putting on a show. Religious leaders, he said, should emulate politicians. They should get up meetings, circulate handbills and pamphlets, and blaze away in the newspapers.

"The object of our measures," Finney wrote, "is to gain attention and you *must* have something new." It would be his mission to bring something new to the age-old truths of Protestant faith in America. His efforts to do so would shake the churches to their foundations.

PRACTICAL

There is no poetry in cement. Of all the products of man, it is the most prosaic. Canal locks were stone basins. Aqueducts were made of stone. So were bridges, culverts, dams, and waste weirs for draining excess water. All had to be held together with durable cement. Yet neither the canal commissioners nor the engineers they hired had thought deeply about where they would obtain this critical ingredient.

Mortar made from lime and sand had long been used for stone and brick work. But that mortar, which took months to achieve its full hardness, turned to mush when in contact with water. It would not do for a canal. The builders needed waterproof cement and there was no source of such material in America. They could not complete the canal without it.

The commissioners wisely pushed back the day of reckoning by starting the canal's construction with the middle section, almost all of it on a single level. But now they were approaching Onondaga Lake, near present-day Syracuse. They needed nine locks to step the canal down to a lower level. They did not have the material to build them.

The canal was being overseen by amateurs. A "practical nature is every thing that is necessary" to build a canal, a contemporary observer noted. Americans' innate practicality would be put to the test as the engineers grappled with the reality of construction.

The commissioners, rather than try to manage a large workforce, had decided to contract the effort to "native farmers, mechanics, merchants and professional men, residing in the vicinity of the line." These locals would dig out their section of the ditch under the direction of the engineers. The arrangement relieved New York State of responsibility for permanent employees. It set a precedent for government contracting that endures today.

The laborers were accustomed to the type of work the canal demanded. Just as Joseph Smith Sr. and his sons were sweating to clear trees and get ready to plant, the canal workers were slashing through forests and hacking brush to prepare for digging. Excavating drainage ditches and diverting streams were familiar tasks. Working out of doors in any weather was usual.

Digging a three-hundred-mile ditch by hand, however, was a Herculean task. For twelve, sometimes fifteen hours a day, a laborer dug into the soil and removed it. He sweated under a sun that hung motionless in a blistering sky. He withstood the insult of cold rain. He broke through dirt and clay undisturbed for eons, thrust his shovel into the loosened ground, lifted it out, heaped it into a barrow or cart, and repeated the movements over and over and over. Contractors, whose profits depended on accomplishing the work with dispatch, drove their men. When arms and backs began to throb with fatigue, the work went on.

Excavating dry dirt, the contractors found, was best done using a modified farm plow. A local man invented a blade for the device made from hardened steel rather than wood or cast iron. Pulled by four oxen, it could tear through roots up to two inches thick. Once the sod was broken, a nineteenth-century bulldozer, which consisted of a horse-drawn blade known as a slip scraper, removed the soil.

Inventors came up with two new devices to help clear forests. One was a winch that could pull down a tree by means of a cable attached to its upper branches. Seeing a tree so uprooted, an observer noted, was "a spectacle that must awaken feelings of gratitude to that Being, who has bestowed on his creatures so much power and wisdom."

Another new tool was the stump puller. Imagine a super winch, a thirty-foot-long axle joining wheels sixteen feet in diameter. Fixed to the center, a fourteen-foot wheel is wrapped with a rope cable. Workers attach a chain descending from the axle to a partly dug-out stump. A team of horses, their force multiplied eightfold by the machinery, pulls on the cable, turning the wheel and axle, winding up the chain, and tearing the stump from the soil. The device allowed a crew of six men to grub up forty stumps in a day.

The worst of the work came when the digging moved into marshy areas. Here the scrapers were useless: only spades and wheelbarrows would do for extracting the slimy soil from wetlands. The traditional wheelbarrow had a boxlike structure that proved inefficient for transporting and dumping mud, which clung to the corners. Rome inventor Jeremiah Brainard fashioned the bed of his new barrow from a single flexible slab of ash wood. He formed it into a semicircular shape "from which the muck slid out instantly." It was used up and down the canal.

Ingenuity and intense labor pushed the project forward. By 1818, work on the middle section was approaching completion. The construction of locks, aqueducts, and other stone work was looming. The need for waterproof cement was now dire.

The technology of cement had reached a high point around the time that Christ walked the earth. Folks in Greece and the Middle East had known how to heat limestone to 900 degrees Fahrenheit; they used the resulting lime to coat their brick buildings. Experimenting, Romans found that a mixture of lime and sand with the addition of volcanic ash made a particularly hard cement. What was more, the material was waterproof, making it ideal for harbors and aqueducts. Some cement seawalls in Italy have withstood two thousand years of battering by salt water (modern Portland cement lasts only about fifty years under similar conditions).

With the decline of Rome, knowledge of this superior cement was lost for many centuries. Ordinary mortar worked fine for laying up bricks and stone blocks in dry situations. It was used in everything from castles and cathedrals to peasant huts. Stone work in wet locations needed a more durable binder.

In the early 1700s, a lighthouse on the treacherous Eddystone Rocks at the western end of the English Channel collapsed. John Smeaton, the first man to declare himself a civil engineer, designed a replacement. Smeaton found that mixing lime with clay yielded a cement that could withstand salt water. His fifty-nine-foot tower, finished in 1759, lasted a hundred years. His discovery resuscitated interest in waterproof cement.

It made sense to American canal commissioners to look to Europe for a source of the critical material. In the winter of 1818, the canal engineer Canvass White, then twenty-eight, volunteered to travel to England at his own expense to gather information. The commissioners happily agreed to the trip. Although British soldiers had burned the White House in 1814, White, who had been wounded in the war, received a cordial reception four years later. He traveled more than two thousand miles on foot during his six-month stay, sketching and taking notes of canals, aqueducts, tunnels, and other works. He acquired new leveling instruments for use by Erie Canal engineers. Everywhere he went, he encouraged men with canal experience, whether as engineers or laborers, to emigrate to America.

During his tour, he met with John Isaac Hawkins, a prodigiously talented inventor who, in addition to devising a "polygraph" for automatically copying letters, had learned a great deal about canals and building methods. The commissioners' assumption that "common quick lime" would suffice for stonework, Hawkins told White, was sheer folly. He said he could provide just the thing they needed. He gave White some samples, hoping to sell the material to the Americans in quantity. But importing such a bulky item and transporting it to the interior would be prohibitively expensive. White was convinced that the success of the canal depended on finding a source in America.

What the canal builders needed was a type of limestone that incorporated the proper proportion of clay. Soon after Canvass White's return, Chief Engineer Benjamin Wright, accompanied by a man named Andrew Bartow, ventured out to examine rocks along the canal corridor. Forty-five at the time, Bartow had received training in medicine and other sciences and was referred to as "Doctor." He kept a large farm just north of Little Falls in the Mohawk Valley.

The two men found a quarry in Onondaga County near Oneida Lake whose stone "resembled the Welch lime." Bartow tried heating and grinding it. The results were disappointing, but he told Wright he would continue to experiment. He loaded a wagon full of the rock and took it home.

With an assistant, he burned and ground and mixed samples, adjusting the firing temperature and other variables. "Baffled at first," he recorded, "we ultimately succeeded." He arranged a demonstration in which he formed a ball of his new material and left it overnight in a bucket of water. In the morning, it was hard as rock. Suddenly, an abundant local supply of waterproof cement was available along the very path of the canal. The canal commissioners said it was "a discovery of the greatest importance."

Now in possession of the critical ingredient to complete the canal's stonework, the commissioners envisioned smooth sailing. Canal stock began to sell at a premium, loans arrived from British banks, optimism prevailed. No one seemed concerned by the fact that the engineers had finished only the easiest of all the sections of the vast project. Far more imposing obstacles would have to be surmounted before a boat would float across the state.

ALL

Joe and Lucy Smith inhabited a landscape infused with magic. Lucy recorded her husband's dreams and explained their significance. Along with their neighbors, the Smiths were drawn to a folk religion in which superstition, miraculous healing, impromptu rites, and personal visions were part of everyday experience.

Outlandish spiritual manifestations had been flaring on the fringes of New England for decades. In the 1790s, when Joseph Sr. was a young man, a prophet named Nathaniel Wood had gathered a group of believers in Middletown, Vermont, just west of the Smith home. His followers declared themselves to be New Israelites, the literal descendants of the Lost Tribes. They referred to nonmembers as "gentiles," and were said to practice polygamy. They were guided by revelations from God. Under the influence of a man named Winchell (also known as Wingate), they searched for gold with divining rods. They started building a temple. "The zeal of all increased and continued to increase until it amounted to a distraction," the town historian wrote.

Winchell predicted that the world was about to end. The Apocalypse, he said, would come on January 14, 1801. His forecast of destroying angels so alarmed authorities that they called out the local militia. Soon afterward, Winchell was exposed as a counterfeiter and the movement collapsed.

The Smiths did not leave this type of rustic religion behind when they moved to Palmyra. A German immigrant noted that western New York was a "variegated sampler of all conceivable religious chimeras and dreams." The year after they arrived, the Smiths were exposed to one of the most outlandish dreamers, a man named Isaac Bullard. He led a group of Pilgrims who scorned all denominations. They yearned to restore Christianity to the time of the Apostles. The elusive Bullard was described by some as of "diminutive stature, with a club foot," and by others as a "red-bearded giant." He declared himself a prophet guided by messages from God.

With his wife, an infant son named Christ, and six followers, he trekked southward from Canada in 1817 to the area the Smiths had left a year earlier. The appearance of the Bullardites lit a firestorm of curiosity in Vermont. Their leader, who styled himself "Elijah," outlawed bathing and hair cutting. His devotees dressed in leather girdles and bearskins, chanted endless supplications to God, and subsisted on gruel from a common trough. Filth and fasting pointed the way to heaven.

Their appearance and habits drew laughter. A local postmaster called them "insane in a degree." Like Lorenzo Dow, like William Miller with his Bible-inspired forebodings, like Joseph Smith Jr. with his visions of God, Isaac Bullard was a folk genius. He was intelligent rather than learned, intuitive rather than calculating, inspired, confident, authoritative in his naturalness. Contemporaries and succeeding generations found such characters difficult to fathom, easy to ridicule. Yet in a few weeks, Bullard convinced more than thirty Vermonters to throw over their lives, rid themselves of their possessions, and join his movement. Some elusive quality in him goaded people to accept his teaching in spite of the group's freakish eccentricity.

The lost tribes were "beginning to be gathered in," Bullard told the curious. In August 1817, the Bullardites hit the road, headed for the promised land in the west. His group picked up more adherents as they crossed Vermont. In October, they passed through the area where the digging of the canal had begun during the summer. In sharp contrast to the industrious farm boys working on that project, the Pilgrims hiked along holding short staffs, bent double and chanting, "Oh-a, Ho-a, Oh-a, Ho-a . . . My God, My God!" Their hunched backs and long beards "gave them a very ludicrous appearance" one observer noted.

Frontier settlers were hungry for excitement, and the Pilgrims attracted enormous attention. Thousands of spectators lined the roads to watch the motley procession pass through Ohio in April 1818. When they reached Cincinnati, the Pilgrims traded their wagons for a flatboat and headed down the Ohio River, then the Mississippi. Disillusionment set in. By the fall of 1819, only the prophet, his wife, another woman, and two children were left, living on the bank of the Mississippi. In 1824 a merchant on his way to New Orleans encountered the two women, dressed in rags and living in a reed hut. They refused his offer of worldly aid. They were holding out for glory.

Seven years later, a Vermont newspaper would recount, "Our readers will recollect a similar delusion which raged some ten years ago in the case of the 'Pilgrims.' . . . From the resemblance between the Pilgrims and the Mormonites in manners and pretensions, we should think Old Isaac had re-appeared in the person of Joe Smith."

On their way west, the Pilgrims stopped briefly at New Lebanon in eastern New York. The town was home to a settlement of Shakers, believers who were, in their own way, as extreme as the followers of Isaac Bullard.

Today, our impression of the Shakers is colored by their craftsmanship and their celibacy. They fashioned elegant furniture; they shunned conventional eroticism. But in their own day, they were inflammatory. They recognized the equality of women, demonstrated a viable form of communal living, preached the nearness of the millennium, and deliberately turned their backs on the acquisitive society that was taking hold of America.

They offered hospitality to the Bullardites, as they did to all visitors. The two groups shared a rejection of the world's pleasures and a yearning for salvation. But while the Pilgrims were filthy, the Shakers venerated cleanliness. The Pilgrims, as one chaste Shaker recorded in her diary, "pretend to marry a woman in God & by doing sanctify the flesh." The Shakers constructed buildings with wide hallways to prevent even inadvertent contact between male and female. Repulsed by what he found, Bullard shook the dust from his feet and continued westward.

The life of Ann Lee, the founder of the Shakers, paralleled that of Jemima Wilkinson. A blacksmith's daughter from Manchester, England, Lee fell under the influence of the Shaking Quakers whose "operations of the spirit" included violent trembling and writhing. The death of four successive children convinced her that "the marriage of the flesh is a covenant with death and an agreement with hell."

Jailed for blasphemy, consumed by divine revelation, Lee saw that she was the incarnation of the Word of God. She proclaimed the feminine church. "It is not I that speak," she declared, "it is Christ who dwells in me." A vision brought her to America just before the Revolution. She and her followers gained a reputation. "They run about in the woods and elsewhere hooting and tooting like owls," one rumor had it. They made no excuses. "We are the people who turn the world upside down," the Shakers proclaimed.

In 1780, Lee, also known as Mother Ann, converted the Baptist evangelist Joseph Meacham. She told him that God had both a male and a female nature and would soon appear on earth as a woman. She undertook a preaching tour of New England, conveying an emotional brand of Christianity. "In admonition she was quick, sharp, and powerful as lightning," a follower noted. "When she rejoiced, her joy was unspeakable . . . when she wept, it seemed enough to melt a heart of stone."

But the Shakers' celibacy, refusal to bear arms, and devotion to their English-born leader rankled a population still in the midst of war against Britain. Protestant ministers railed against her and mobs harassed her followers. In Petersham, Massachusetts, they dragged her from her horse, beat her, tore her clothing to see if she was really a woman, and sent her to prison for six months.

Mother Ann died in 1784. Joseph Meacham and Lucy Wright, another early convert, took charge. They organized self-sufficient villages, beginning with one in New Lebanon. Those who committed themselves turned over all their property to the group. "They have everything in common," a visitor wrote. "How they manage with their combs and toothbrushes, I did not presume to ask."

After Joseph Meacham's death in 1796, Mother Lucy led the sect for a quarter century. The Shakers established communities in eastern New England, along the region of the Erie Canal, and farther west. Devotees were attracted to the Shakers' unique mixture of hard work, communal sharing, and spiritual ecstasy. Renunciation, a penance for some, was a liberation for others. A Shaker elder declared, "The joys of the celibate life are far greater than I can make you know. They are indescribable."

Folks from Palmyra sometimes journeyed eighteen miles on a Sunday evening to a Shaker community in Sodus, on the shore of Lake Ontario. If the Smith family did not make the journey, they certainly heard reports from those who did. Inside their meeting hall, the Shakers set aside seating for visitors. They knew some spectators would laugh, but the services gave them an opportunity to proselytize their wonderful message.

The Shaker men and women gathered in two groups. First they intoned a strange chant, "accompanied by a gentle stamping of the feet." Then they repeatedly marched toward the audience, wheeled and marched away. All this they did "with the utmost gravity," their faces blank, bodies rigid. They began "to whisk around with greatest rapidity, like so many dervishes." They skipped in concentric circles, the men and women revolving in opposite directions, never touching. They moved "with a sort of galvanized hop, hands paddling like fins and voices chanting wild airs."

They shook themselves violently from head to foot, every limb moving "in a sort of tremulous motion." Some went into "violent hystericks" that brought to mind "the wild and maddened tenants of Bedlam." A Shaker elder declared that their rituals burned up the carnality and greed natural to humankind and left behind "delightful feelings."

Some onlookers found the display "unearthly, oppressive, and bewildering." For others, the Shakers' beliefs and example opened new possibilities of salvation. "All appeared happy," a visitor noted, "and upon each face rested the light of dignified serenity." A few who came to watch stayed to join.

Joseph Smith Jr., whose mind absorbed influences from all directions, knew about the strange habits of the Shakers, about the outlandishness of Isaac Bullard's Pilgrims, and about the experimental spirituality of other groups along the frontier. Like most believers of his day, he understood that life on earth was a path to an everlasting existence. Everything else—acquisition, renown, camaraderie, requited love, financial security, political power—was dross, or worse, an occasion of sin. Those whose eyes were open understood that eternity was all. And, as Emily Dickinson, herself born into the midst of this holy turmoil, would declare: "All—is the price of All."

THE SPIRIT OF GOD

It was a marvelous time to be a Christian in America. Preachers everywhere, especially those west of the Appalachians, could feel the rising waves of spiritual enthusiasm. On the frontier, youth predominated, and the drug of choice for young adventurers was religion. In 1821, Charles Finney left behind his promising law career to do God's work.

It was a mark of his restless energy that he would, at twenty-nine, take up a profession of which he had no experience. Many years of grueling theological training were the usual requirement to become a minister. Finney's sudden ardor for religion, combined with his native intelligence, enabled him to squeeze all the preparation he felt he needed into less than two years. At the end of 1823, Presbyterian officials in northern New York gave him a provisional license as an evangelist. He would have no permanent congregation, but would minister to isolated settlements. Finney traveled the frontier area around the western edge of the Adirondack Mountains. He preached "in school houses, and barns and groves, as best I could."

The new preacher was convinced of the urgency of his mission. Finney grieved over the sinners who died unredeemed and who "have gone down to hell, while the church has been dreaming." He was willing to do whatever it took to rescue souls before their terrifying descent.

For more than two years, Finney wore himself out organizing rural revivals. He preached, counseled, exhorted folks to repent, demanded that they embrace Jesus and give themselves over to the shattering glory of Christian rebirth. In one church, he challenged congregants to rise to their feet if they accepted Jesus. Nobody moved. "You have taken your stand," Finney blustered angrily. "You have rejected Christ and his Gospel." Compromise was not his style. When a young woman said she loved God, Finney shook his fist in her face. "You lie!" he told her. "You ought to go to hell."

He preached four times a week without notes or outline. He knew what he wanted to say, and he drove home his message with devastating effect. Winter, when the demands of farming slackened, was revival season. He trekked from one remote hamlet to the next through thigh-deep snow. In the northern New York village of Antwerp, as Finney urged repentance, membership in the Presbyterian Church leaped from sixteen to fifty-six in three months.

Finney developed a double-barreled approach to his work that combined hard logic and hot feeling. He preached like a lawyer convincing a jury. His arguments left his listeners unable to defend their refusal of Christ's love. Finney demanded a response. "You admit that what I preach is the Gospel," he intoned. "Now will you receive it?"

Yet he knew that it was more important to win hearts than minds. His own emotional fervor infected his congregation. "The Spirit of God came upon me with such power, that it was like opening a battery upon them," he said of one meeting. While preaching at Antwerp, he sensed that "something flashed over the congregation." It was a "kind of shimmering." His listeners, overcome, "began to fall from their seats; and they fell in every direction, and cried for mercy. If I had a sword in each hand, I could not have cut them off their seats as fast as they fell."

In an instant, he himself began "laughing in a most spasmodic manner." He covered his face with a handkerchief, worried that the congregants might not understand that it was "irrepressible, holy joy that made me laugh."

His work in the backcountry aroused opposition as well as excitement. Conservatives saw in him a blasphemer. Some threatened to tar and feather him. A man who was "greatly enraged" by the unorthodox goings-on attended a service in a rural schoolhouse armed with a pistol and intent on killing the evangelist. But Finney's preaching got to him first. Before he could pull his gun, the man fell from his pew, groaning that he was sinking into hell.

In three months, Finney delivered seventy-seven sermons, held prayer meetings every few days, and visited four hundred sixty-nine homes to pray with those swept up in the revivals. He fell ill from the exertion and began coughing blood. In July 1824, he received his official ordination as a Presbyterian minister.

That October, he finally married Lydia Andrews. Now thirty-two, Finney was twelve years older than his new wife, but she was his senior in religion, having converted at the age of eleven. After the wedding, she stayed with her parents in Whitesboro, just outside Utica. Charles went north to find them a home near Watertown. Called to oversee another revival, he delayed fetching his new bride. Eternal souls urgently depended on him. He stayed until spring before finally reuniting with the patient Lydia.

Everywhere he went, Finney insisted that although God might choose the elect, every man and woman was a free agent. Bad choices, not innate depravity, were what made mankind corrupt. "A sinner under the influence of the Spirit of God," he said, "is just as free as a jury under the arguments of an advocate." He reminded farmers that although God was indeed sovereign, they did not wait for the Almighty to "give them a crop only when it pleases him." They worked at it.

Finney understood that the U.S. Constitution's ban on federal support of religion had brought about a revolution in America's churches. The states were also in the process of weaning congregations from their tax revenues: in 1833, Massachusetts would be the last state to end public subsidies of religion. Citizens were left to choose their own faith. The numerous denominations had to compete for members and for their contributions.

The concept of market competition, then penetrating into more and more facets of American life, now applied to religion as well.

Americans were free people, salvation a matter of choice. Finney shaped his message accordingly. "Gospel salvation seemed to me to be an offer of something to be accepted," he declared.

Finney gained experience in the hinterlands, but he soon felt the need to bring his message to the more densely settled region along the new Erie Canal, where many more souls needed saving. He visited his old mentor George Gale at the town of Western, just north of Utica. Gale invited him to preach a revival in his church.

What the Presbyterians of Western got was a bombshell. They were accustomed to erudite, yawn-inducing explications of Scripture from pastors whose minds were more attuned to the intricacies of theology than to the urgency of salvation. The effect of Finney's words, one observer noted, was "like cannonballs through a basket of eggs." His clear voice and hypnotic gaze brought home the commonsense quality of his preaching. His sermons startled listeners out of their torpor and awakened in them a desperate desire to be saved.

Soon, congregants were "falling under the power of God," sinking to the floor, fainting. Conversion followed conversion; dead churches sprang to life. In a day when religion was headline news, Charles Finney was becoming a sensation. People flocked to Western from Rome and other nearby cities to hear this dynamic new preacher.

"Oh, God, smite that wicked man, that hardened sinner," Finney begged, pointing his long finger. "God Almighty, shake him over hell!"

CLOUDS OF HEAVEN

Men and women have at times imagined that the current corrupt age is a prelude to great change. Some become convinced that what lies ahead sparkles with happiness and sunshine. Others foresee darkness, the death of the world, the end.

Early Christians were certain of Christ's promised return, which they sensed was imminent. This Second Advent would be accompanied by the great cataclysm described in the Gospels and hinted at in the prophetic books. The sun would darken, trumpets would sound, and Jesus would establish His thousand-year earthly kingdom.

Later, apocalyptic events came to be seen in a spiritual light, not as physical realities. St. Jerome, who translated the Bible into Latin in the fourth century, deemed the Book of Revelation to contain "as many mysteries as it does words." Church fathers largely ignored the ominous prophecies. During the Middle Ages, forecasting a literal Apocalypse constituted heresy.

But the undercurrent remained. Christian visionaries ventured guesses about the timing of the end. Some thought that, as Peter's epistle taught, "the heavens shall pass away with a great noise, and the elements shall melt with fervent heat, the earth also and the works that are therein shall be burned up." Christ would appear "in the clouds of heaven with power and great glory." The dead would literally rise from their graves, and those who were saved would be "caught up to meet the Lord in the air." It would happen not in a dream but in the world of flesh and blood, of pain and ecstasy.

William Miller, shaken by his war experience and by his conversion to faith, was particularly sensitive to the unease of his times. In trying to understand it, he had turned to the source of all truth. The Bible, he said, was a "feast of reason." Paradoxically, Miller also understood that prophecies "always have a figurative meaning." When the Scriptures said Jews they meant Christians; when they said days, they meant years. The verses whispered to him in chorus. Mountains suggested governments, beasts referred to kingdoms, waters to people, the papacy was the Antichrist, a leopard stood for Greece.

Yes, an interpreter needed discernment to penetrate the dreamscape, but a common man using common sense could do it. "The Bible is a system of revealed truths, so clearly and simply given, that the 'wayfaring man, though a fool, need not err therein,'" Miller wrote, paraphrasing Isaiah.

Miller immersed himself in the phantasmagoria of the Book of Revelation—the beasts full of eyes within, the angel standing in the sun, death mounted on a pale horse. "How long shall be the vision concerning the daily sacrifice and the transgression of desolation?" Daniel asked. The Lord answered: "Unto two thousand and three hundred days; then shall the sanctuary be cleansed." Miller knew what all this meant.

He understood the parable of the ten virgins in Matthew's Gospel. The five foolish virgins brought no oil for their lamps when they went to meet the bridegroom. The midnight cry rang out, "The bridegroom cometh!," and they missed their chance to attend the marriage feast. The bridegroom was Christ, the arrival his second coming. Preparation was essential.

In 1818, after two years of intense study, Miller came to a conclusion. He had looked into holy Scripture and seen that "the end of all things was clearly and emphatically predicted, both as to time and manner." His discovery left him wide-eyed with awe and trepidation. "I believe," he finally declared, "that the second coming of Jesus Christ is near, even at the door . . . on or before 1843."

If this was true, did it mean he had a responsibility to warn others, to raise the midnight cry? The unassuming farmer agonized over the question. For now, he told no one of the impending calamity. Yet the knowledge burned in his heart.

BEYOND DESCRIPTION

On September 21, 1823, Joseph Smith and his family spent the evening speculating about eternity. Amid flickering candlelight, they discussed the Bible and the claims of competing religious faiths. Joseph, almost eighteen now, kept the memory of his earlier vision locked in his heart. He had refused to join any of the churches, all of which he had been told were abominable.

Joseph was an ordinary teenager. With his striking blue eyes and aquiline nose, he had become "a great favorite with the ladies." Like almost all males of the time, he occasionally drank too much. He "fell into many foolish errors." Talk of religion sometimes left him feeling guilty over his entanglement with the "vanities of the world."

That evening, he and his siblings mounted the narrow stairs to the sleeping loft under the pitched roof. With the candle out, the room descended into darkness. The air was tangy with the smell of dirty feet and sweaty work clothes. The silence bottomed out in the whispering, whistling breath of sleepy children. Joseph's mind would give him no rest. His thoughts kept reaching into the dark, into celestial realms.

He tossed and turned. Achingly aware of his follies and sins, he prayed for forgiveness. His eyes grew sensitive to the gloom. An eerie brightness began to erase the shadows. Morning? Moonlight? No, the unearthly glow intensified, illuminating the chamber like day. The radiance etched every object, every rafter, every sleeping face. He saw a person by the door in a robe of exquisite whiteness, a figure "glorious beyond description, and his countenance truly like lightning."

The individual spoke to him, fired words into his head like shots from a pistol. He was Moroni, a resurrected being. He caused immense ideas to flood Joseph's mind. The youth saw the great judgments and desolations that would afflict the present generation. Moroni conveyed a revelation from God that commanded Joseph to perform a fabulous, urgent mission. Then he silently gathered the light into himself and ascended toward heaven. The boy stared after him, slack-jawed with amazement.

Twice more that night, Moroni appeared in the room. Each time, he reiterated his message. The next morning, Joseph's brain still reeled with the apparition, the tumble of ideas. He could barely concentrate on his work in the fields. His older brother Alvin reprimanded him for dawdling. His father, seeing Joseph's pallor, told him to go back to the house. On the way, the boy stumbled and fell unconscious. As he recovered from his daze, Moroni appeared again to admonish him.

Joseph returned to his father in the field and whispered to him the secret. Moroni had told him of a book "written upon gold plates, giving an account of the former inhabitants of this continent." Joseph was to retrieve this treasure from an underground cache on a nearby hill. The book's value was not in its precious metal: Moroni had forbade him even to think of worldly gain. The text was something far greater, a new narrative of reality. Tools, which he would find with the plates, would allow him to see beyond earthly sight and to understand.

The teenager waited for his father's reaction. Joseph Sr. was fifty-two. A loving man, he had long known the relentless anxiety of poverty. He had acquired very little that he could pass on to his children. His tented eyes expressed the disappointment of a well-intentioned failure. Yet he lived in a world of possibilities. He knew his Scripture. "Your sons and your daughters shall prophesy," the Book of Joel declared, "your old men shall dream dreams, your young men shall see visions." He believed his son. He told him to do exactly as the angel had instructed.

The familiar hundred-foot-high hill that Joseph had seen in his vision was an elongated pile of glacial till located just off the road from Palmyra to Canandaigua, three miles south of the Smith farm. Joseph went there that very day. He dug near the top and pried a rock away. Beneath it, he found a stone box. Inside that, the golden plates, bound with rings. With them, a breastplate and diamond spectacles, the aids to vision.

Although he had been warned, Joseph succumbed to the luster, the immense value of the gold. Reaching to grasp the treasure, he received a nasty shock. He looked up to see the stern celestial being. Moroni chastised him. He must approach the plates with nothing in mind but the glory of God. Nor would he be able to retrieve them now. He must come back every year on the same day. One day, perhaps, he would be allowed to possess them.

Joseph returned home in a state of wonder. He poured out the story to his family, who had anxiously awaited his return. They sat in a circle and listened with rapt attention. His utter sincerity and compelling words instantly converted them. "The whole family were melted to tears," his mother reported. "The sweetest union and happiness pervaded our house."

Joseph warned them that revelation entailed danger. When the wicked of the world knew what was happening "they would try to take our lives." No matter. Joseph Smith Jr., not yet eighteen, had begun one of the most extraordinary spiritual journeys in modern history.

EXCITED

Life along the Erie Canal was changing too quickly. The new was rushing forward. Waves of prosperity buoyed some and left others to founder. Social status was growing more slippery, class distinction sharper. Money was the new idol, land speculation a national obsession. Fortunes were made and lost with shocking suddenness. Uncertainty generated resentment. The pace of change made citizens sensitive to anything that challenged revered values. Scandal raised the specter of conspiracy. Anxiety turned to fear.

In 1826, the popular and respected Freemasons could hardly imagine that they were about to become the targets of public wrath. Their members occupied offices at all levels of government. New York governor DeWitt Clinton held the title of General Grand High Priest of the General Grand Royal Arch Chapter of the United States. Andrew Jackson, the war hero who had run for president in 1824, was a Mason. So was Henry Clay, the secretary of state. But a storm was bearing down on the brotherhood.

In May 1826, William Morgan began writing his *Illustrations of Masonry by One of the Fraternity Who has Devoted Thirty Years to the Subject*. The title was hyperbole; the book an account, without commentary, of the first three degrees of the order: Entered Apprentice, Craft Mason, and Master Mason. On hearing of the project, local Masons inserted a notice in a Canandaigua paper that publicly labeled Morgan "a swindler and a dangerous man." The Le Roy, New York, chapter appointed a vigilante committee assigned, "in case of emergency, to guard the institution from imposition."

Locals still breathed the air of the wilderness, including a tendency toward mob justice. As the project moved forward that summer, western New York Masons turned rabid. Samuel Greene, a Batavia politician, attended a Masonic meeting and reported that he "never saw men so excited in my life. . . . Committees were appointed to do this and that and everything went forward in a kind of frenzy."

Publisher David Miller, when he began the process of printing Morgan's tome, stocked his shop with firearms, including twenty rifles, half a dozen pistols, and two menacing swivel guns. Morgan demanded that his backers put up a bond in the amount of $500,000 to secure the royalties due him and his family. The amount was fanciful, but the request was indicative of Morgan's concern.

Morgan left Lucinda and the children at home early that Monday morning, September 11, 1826, and headed for the print shop. A stranger approached him and told Morgan he was wanted at Danold's Tavern, a well-known Batavia institution. Three men, all Masons, awaited him. They had with them a constable from Canandaigua.

The men ate breakfast together. The conversation was tense but civil. The constable explained that they had traveled fifty miles from the east to arrest Morgan. The charge was the theft of a shirt and cravat that Morgan had borrowed from a Canandaigua bartender several months earlier. As a man of the world, Morgan might have been amused by the effrontery of these young hicks and their ludicrous charge. He offered no resistance. Miller showed up at the tavern and offered to put up Morgan's bail. The men refused; they wanted Morgan.

Allowing for stops along the way, the crowded stagecoach took ten hours to cover the distance back to Canandaigua. Arriving in early evening, the men brought Morgan before a justice, who promptly threw out the charge for lack of any evidence. At this point, Nicholas G. Chesebro, master of the Canandaigua Masonic Lodge, showed up with documents proving that he had purchased a promissory note, signed by Morgan, requiring him to pay $2.69. Morgan could not produce the cash; the judge ordered him locked up in the town jail.

The author spent that night and the next day, September 12, behind bars. About seven that evening, a Mason named Loton Lawson appeared at the jail. Jailer Israel Hall was absent, so Lawson asked Hall's wife Mary to release Morgan. He himself would pay the debt Morgan owed. Mrs. Hall had heard a rumor that Morgan was a dangerous man, and she would not take responsibility for setting him free. Lawson fetched Chesebro to assure her that the transaction was strictly legal. Finally persuaded, she released Morgan about nine that night. As he walked out of the jail, Lawson and another man fell in on either side of him, gripping his arms.

The encounter quickly turned violent. Mrs. Hall heard Morgan cry out, "Murder!" He continued to scream for his life. In the light of a bright moon, she saw Morgan struggling vainly to free himself from the two men. A signal from Chesebro brought a carriage. The men together forced Morgan into the closed vehicle. With the pounding of horses' hooves, they all disappeared into the night.

ON FIRE

In January 1826, Charles Finney rode into Rome, New York, on a wave of excitement. He held his first prayer meeting in the parlor of Moses Gillet, the local minister who had invited him to the city just off the canal. Finney was startled by the townspeople's enthusiasm. "There was danger of an outburst of feeling, that would be almost uncontrollable," he later wrote. He had yet to open his mouth; his very renown stirred people's emotions. Stout men writhed in their seats "as if a sword had been thrust into their hearts." Finney realized that his mere presence could "create a distress that seemed unendurable." He spoke for a few minutes, but "the agitation deepened every moment; and as I could hear their sobs, and sighs, I closed my prayer and rose suddenly from my knees."

Reverend Gillet nearly panicked at these manifestations in his flock, which seemed so like madness. Finney calmed him, but felt the peril of inducing people to approach too suddenly the emotional volcano of conversion. Stunned by his own power—the power of the Holy Ghost working through him—he told the agitated believers to go home in silence. Before they could leave, one young man nearly fainted. His friends began to swoon. Finney hurried to calm them. Go home, he told them. Be quiet. Pray. They went into the street sobbing. The revival had begun.

The Rome revival teetered between celebrity worship and mass hysteria. When Finney and Reverend Gillet stepped into the street, residents rushed to them, begging them to visit their homes. When they entered a house, neighbors crowded in to hear them speak. Finney called an impromptu gathering in a hotel dining room and watched people sprint toward the meeting place. When he spoke in homes, schools, and churches, "men of the strongest nerves" were so moved by his remarks that "they were unable to help themselves, and had to be taken home by their friends." As prayer sessions approached frenzy, he had to call off meetings "to prevent an undesirable outburst of overwhelming feeling."

"Ministers came in from neighboring towns," he wrote, "and expressed great astonishment at what they saw and heard, as well they might." Conversions came so fast that churchmen had difficulty recording them all. "Religion," a resident wrote, "was the principal subject of conversation in our streets, stores, and even taverns."

Resistance crumbled. A doctor whose daughter began to suffer under a conviction—the prelude to a full-blown conversion—said it was impossible that she should give herself to Jesus. "It is fanaticism," he declared, "it is madness." But then, while he was riding several miles out of town to see a patient, the truth suddenly dawned on him. "The whole plan of salvation by Christ was so clear to him," Finney said, "that he saw that a child could understand it. He wondered that it had ever seemed so mysterious to him."

A wealthy banker, a skeptical Unitarian, heard Finney speak and declared, "That man is mad, and I should not be surprised if he set the town on fire." Yet when he went to Utica for a bank directors' meeting, he found himself telling his colleagues, "There is something very remarkable in the state of things in Rome."

Finney worked feverishly. "I was obliged to preach altogether without premeditation; for I had not an hour in a week, which I could take to arrange my thoughts beforehand." Visitors to the town could feel the spirit of God. A sheriff from Utica, a gruff man of fifty, felt as if God pervaded the whole atmosphere in Rome. While there "he had to rise from the table abruptly, and go to the window and look out, and try to divert his attention, to keep from weeping." He noticed others around him, overcome in the same way.

The town was full of prayer. "Go where you would," Finney remembered, "you heard the voice of prayer." Townspeople began to observe the Sabbath without fail. They became self-conscious about profanity, about quarreling, fighting, and gossiping. As the revival grew, merchants closed their shops in the evening to attend services. Even those who had lived through many revivals "were now made to tremble and bow."

It was not only the poor or uneducated who were affected, but members of the affluent middle class that was rising along the canal. "My meetings soon became thronged with that class," Finney noted. "The lawyers, physicians, merchants, and indeed all the most intelligent people, became more and more interested, and more and more easily influenced." They in turn swayed others: religious piety became the fashion.

The personal, direct style of preaching that Finney introduced outraged some and excited others. "I said 'you,'" he admitted. "I said 'hell' and with such an emphasis as often to shock the people." That is, he spoke to his listeners directly and described their possible fate in no uncertain terms.

Only four years after becoming a Christian, only a year and a half after his ordination, the young minister was becoming one of the most famous men in America. A man from a village near Utica pleaded with him to visit. The regular preacher there, he said, "is not plain-telling sinners to repent and *that immediately*. His feelings are too tender." As Finney's notoriety spread, requests came from as far away as Cleveland and New York City.

He was not yet ready to venture so far. His next stop was Utica, a city whose population and prosperity were being pumped up by its location directly on the canal. He arrived in February 1826 and stayed until May. He continued to develop what were called his "new methods." He broke precedence by allowing women to pray in "promiscuous" or mixed-gender assemblies. He couched his sermons in colloquial language. He prayed for sinners by name, making them squirm in their pews.

All this was contrary to the decorum of orthodox churches. Finney's methods were associated with the shenanigans of frontier exhorters, who thought they were doing God's work when they got a Christian to howl and moan. His enemies labeled him "the madman of Oneida." He frightened congregants, one critic said, with his "descriptions of hell, and his imagery of the infernal regions," with which "he seems to be very familiar."

Finney was speaking to the young, who were enduring the shift from subsistence agriculture to an unsettled, market-oriented economy. Cast loose from the spiritual certainties of their parents and grandparents, they were quick to label an orthodox clergyman an "old hypocrite." Traditionalists accused Finney of a "levelling of all distinctions of society." He readily admitted to using the "language of the common people." There were souls to save. "The results justify my methods."

Conservative clergymen in New England were particularly outraged by his methods. All their churches were closed to him. Finney was not fazed. His conversion had left him with a connection to God that gave him a deep confidence in his actions. Once, while engaged in prayer, the Lord drew so near him "that my flesh literally trembled on my bones. I shook from head to foot, under a full sense of the presence of God." The experience left him calm, full of trust and with "the most perfectly kind feelings toward all the brethren that were misled, and were arraying themselves against me."

God seemed to sweep away opposition. Finney told the story of an older clergyman who was attending a Presbyterian convention in Utica. He had never seen a revival and did not approve. He made a speech condemning Finney and his irreverent methods. That night, Finney led congregants in asking God to keep the clergyman's speech from dampening the revival. "The next morning, this man was found dead in his bed."

An atmosphere of salvation swamped Utica just as it had Rome. Even visitors to the town were instantly caught up in the enthusiasm. "I heard of several cases of persons that just stopped for a meal, or to spend a night, being powerfully convicted and converted before they left the town," Finney noted.

Finney went to visit a nearby textile factory. The workers were mostly girls and young women. As the clergyman walked through the building examining the machinery, he noticed one girl whose hands trembled. He cast a solemn look at her and she "sunk down, and burst into tears." It did not end with her. "The impression caught almost like powder," Finney observed, "and in a few moments nearly all in the room were in tears." The pious owner ordered the mill temporarily shut down, proclaiming, "It is more important that our souls should be saved than that this factory run." Within a few days, all the workers were converted.

Conversions were always on Finney's mind. When a fire drew a crowd to a gristmill, Finney showed up and said to one of the gawkers, "Good evening, we've had quite a fire, haven't we? Are you a Christian?"

His wife Lydia led prayer meetings specifically for women. She organized teams of two or three women to visit home after home and encourage families to join the revival. The Finneys were taking advantage of the fact that women were much more likely to be church members than men. The ladies were gratified to be given a chance to exert their power for good.

The couple's efforts paid off. Hundreds were converted at Utica, more than three thousand in Oneida County as a whole. In addition to these immediate conversions, congregants continued to accept Christ for months after Finney left, influenced by his teaching and by friends and family members who had already converted.

It was during the Utica revival that Finney gained his most influential convert. Theodore Dwight Weld was an erratic, energetic young man, zealous to the point of fanaticism. The son of a Congregational pastor, he had, like Finney, grown up in the hinterlands of New York State; Weld's home was south of the salt springs that had become Syracuse. He attended Phillips Andover Academy, a citadel of orthodoxy outside Boston, with thoughts of following his father into the ministry. He was so avid for learning that he ruined his eyes by devoting too many candlelit evenings to intense study. After two years, he had to drop out. He toured the country teaching a memory-improvement system. The job polished his gift for oratory and provided him with a store of self-reliance and promotional savvy.

By 1826, the twenty-three-year-old had taken up his studies again, this time at Hamilton College near Utica. More mature and experienced than his classmates, the zealous Weld developed great influence among the students there.

While Finney was working his Utica revival, Weld visited his Aunt Sophia in the city. She had fallen under the spell of the famous evangelist and was anxious for her nephew to hear him preach. Weld sneered at Finney, his frontier emotionalism, and his criticism of established clergymen. "My father was a real minister of the Gospel," he told his friends, "grave and courteous, and an honor to the profession. This man is not a minister, and I will never acknowledge him as such."

Although the student declared he would have nothing to do with the clergyman, Weld's aunt tricked him into attending a morning service at which Finney would preach. She made sure Weld sat in the middle of a crowded pew.

The evangelist turned to the young man with what Weld called "those great staring eyes of his (never was a man whose soul looked out through his face as his did)." He spoke warnings of damnation directed at Weld, who grew increasingly uncomfortable during the hour-long harangue. "He just held me up on his toasting-fork before that audience," Weld remembered.

The next day, Weld encountered Finney at a store in town. He unleashed a retaliatory tirade against the minister. As the tongue-lashing went on, a crowd gathered. Finney took the abuse, then reminded Weld that he was the son of a minister of Christ. "Is this the way you behave?" Weld spat a final insult and fled.

But Finney's mild retort dissolved Weld's youthful pretensions. "I was so ashamed I could not live," he later remembered. He went to the house where Finney was staying. The evangelist thought the young man intended to continue his abuse. "I have come for a very different purpose," Weld said, choking with emotion. Finney threw his arms around Weld's neck, dragged him into the parlor and both men fell to their knees, "sobbing and praying and sobbing and praying."

It was a spasm of salvation, but the headstrong Weld was not about to fall so easily. Back at his aunt's home, he continued to berate Finney. He paced in his room through the night. His mind was a cauldron where anger, guilt, fear, remorse, and yearning all bubbled in an agonizing stew. He blamed Finney, he blamed himself. This was the goal of a revival, to shake up the sinner, to make him or her as uncomfortable as possible. His aunt found him in the morning lying on the floor, "his heart all broken to pieces."

Drained, unable to resist, Weld attended a revival meeting the next evening, confessed himself a sinner, let go of his selfish vanity, and embraced Jesus. His mother was delighted when she heard the news. His father may have regretted that it was Finney, not himself, who brought Theodore into the fold.

With his usual excess of zeal, Weld did not just make a decision for Christ, he signed up with Finney to carry the urgent message to others. The decision "put an end to my studying," Weld remembered. "I was with him in his meetings, speaking and laboring all that summer."

That June, Weld accompanied Finney to Auburn, New York, eighty miles west along the canal corridor. As dynamic and single-minded as Finney himself, he helped with the hard work of the revival. Finney had encouraged women to pray in company with men. Weld went further, allowing women to speak in meetings, something that was unheard of in orthodox Protestant churches.

Unitarians, who included the rational, liberal citizens of the town, criticized Finney as a fanatic, yet townspeople packed his revivals. During one sermon, a man stood and held up silver dollars clutched in both hands. He shouted at Finney, "These are my gods!" Silence fell on the church. Finney slowly swiveled his head and fixed his censorious gaze on the man. That one look silenced the scoffer and demolished his glib facade. He soon joined the five hundred souls from Auburn who converted.

OTHERWISE, I AM FINE

"It seemed to me like building castles in the air," Webb Harwood remembered, "and I did not dream of the practicability of such a thing." Harwood, the first permanent settler in what would become the village of Palmyra, was referring to the notion of constructing a canal through the wilderness. Yet by 1821, to his great astonishment, "I have had the pleasure of seeing a boat pass my door with 300 souls aboard, drawn by 2 horses."

The canal was being completed and opened in sections. This strategy drew attention to problems that could be avoided in construction farther down the line. It also brought the benefits of water transportation to the finished areas and began to generate a trickle of revenues from tolls. The section from Utica to Rome (about fifteen miles) opened in the fall of 1819. A year later, the canal reached Montezuma, thirty miles west of Syracuse.

Tiny Montezuma, briefly situated at the end of navigation, experienced a sudden boom. An entrepreneur there built a sixty-seven-foot-long boat equipped with an elegant dining room. He began to provide the first passenger service along the canal. Daily packet boats began to arrive at Montezuma carrying dozens of passengers. If the travelers wished to proceed west from the terminus, they switched to stagecoaches.

When the line reached Palmyra, Webb Harwood's wife would note that seeing a boat on the ocean was no paradox but to see vessels floating "where large timber was growing and swamps almost impassable for either man or beast, that was worthy of all our attention and very entertaining."

Having gained experience on the easy level near Rome, the engineers and contractors now had to make the canal descend, climb, descend again, then proceed through a long wallow of swamp and marsh before beginning a steady uphill journey toward Rochester.

The economic slump that followed the Panic of 1819 worked in the commissioners' favor. They paid less for both labor and materials, and they were able to borrow money at more favorable rates. British bankers and American investors, encouraged by early successes, snapped up canal bonds.

Thomas Eddy, a longtime advocate of the project, thought of a novel idea for funding it. Why not let poor people invest in an enterprise that was designed to bring prosperity to their state? Even before work on the canal began, Eddy had been mulling a "plan to *prevent* their poverty and misery by means of employment and establishing saving Banks." In 1819, the Bank for Savings in the City of New York opened in the basement of an almshouse. It took in small deposits from porters, laborers, cooks, dustmen, and other workers, promising them a 5 percent return. Within two years it had amassed half a million dollars' worth of canal bonds. The Bank for Savings would last, through several name changes, until 1991.

As the great construction project moved away from the Mohawk Valley into more sparsely settled regions, keeping it supplied with laborers became a problem. Farmers were eager to earn cash by working temporarily near their homes, but they were not about to become permanent wage laborers. Contractors had to import workers, often immigrants shipped up from New York City. Many of the first workers were Welsh; later, almost all came from Ireland.

Harwood described these workers as "some of the roughest creatures." The conditions would have roughened anyone. The swamps west of Montezuma were the worst. Workers braved snakes to hack away thick stands of rushes. Hours of digging the black mud could be wiped out when a spongy side bank slumped into the ditch. The men had to wade back in, sometimes up to their waists in muck, and start over. In places, the ground was so wet that contractors had to erect planks along the edge of the excavation, anchored by stakes driven into the clay below, in order to keep the soft earth in place.

"No person without experience can be fully aware of the disadvantages of laboring in wet earth," the canal commissioners reported. Quicksand and muck would hold on to a shovel every time it was thrust in. The workmen too "would often sink in and stick fast, so as to render it rather difficult to extract themselves." Leeches feasted on their legs.

Swarms of mosquitoes competed with deer flies and black flies to worry and sting the workers. The men resorted to hanging tin pots filled with smoldering leaves around their necks. The smoke from these "Montezuma necklaces" was hardly enough fend off all the pests. The sun baked men's backs. The mud sucked the shoes from their feet. Dehydration brought headache, muscle cramps, chills, and vomiting.

Disease began to take its toll. Malaria was common. Aided by dysentery and typhoid fever, it killed perhaps a thousand men just in the thirty-mile stretch west of Montezuma. Accidents were a constant threat as men swung pickaxes in close quarters. Any wound was vulnerable to tetanus.

A physician near Syracuse observed scenes of suffering and distress "beyond conception." Illness slowed the entire project. "Although great exertions were made to supply the place of such laborers as became diseased," the commissioners reported, work had to be suspended for weeks. "All the principal contractors, with many of the subcontractors, became diseased."

In 1818, a Welsh laborer wrote home that the "wages on the canal are one dollar a day and thirteen to fourteen dollars a month with food and washing and half a pint of whisky a day." The rate varied from $10 to $23 a month, depending on the number of workers available. To many it was not worth it. One immigrant wrote back to Wales, "I beg all my old neighbors not to think of coming here."

A laborer named Timothy Geohagan wrote to his sister in Ireland during the worst of it: "I don't know . . . if any of us will survive, but God willing, we will live to see a better day." He slept in a tent, which was stifling in the summer and drafty when the weather turned cold. "Six of me tentmates died this very day," he continued, "and were stacked like cordwood until they could be taken away. Otherwise, I am fine."

MANIA

The canal project set off digging such as never had been seen in North America. The horse-drawn plows and scrapers gouged sod, loam, gravel, and clay. Men sweated with picks and shovels to disturb, expose, and remove the soil. At one point, a Palmyra newspaper reported, workmen on the canal discovered buried under the earth the blade of a large knife, a stout nail, and "several plates of brass." The find, the paper declared, furnished "materials for speculation."

Country people in New England had long speculated about what they might find below the earth's surface. The practice of what was called money-digging spanned generations. As early as 1729, Benjamin Franklin had commented on the many pits dug by those "fed with a Vain Hope of growing suddenly rich." In Maine, wild-eyed money-diggers seeking elusive riches had excavated a pit eighty feet deep.

Most often, they sought pirate treasure. Even far inland, locals imagined that Captain Kidd or some other buccaneer might have hidden a chest of gold doubloons. Others dreamed of Spanish silver mines or payroll chests secreted by Revolutionary War soldiers. A newspaper editor in Windsor, Vermont, claimed he could name five hundred men "who do in the simplicity and sincerity of their hearts believe that immense treasures lie concealed" in the Green Mountains.

Diggers sometimes uncovered the burial caches of ancient inhabitants. Native American peoples known as the Mound Builders had occupied the Great Lakes region as early as 3500 B.C., centuries before the tribes that made up the Iroquois Confederacy.

In Rome, money-diggers had torn apart Fort Stanwix, which had withstood a British siege during the Revolution. Near Cairo, in the Hudson River Valley, a ten-year-old boy named Thurlow Weed observed the digging frenzy during his boyhood. His family, like the Smiths, were "poor but credulous people." Of his father, a farmer and cartman, Weed remembered, "Everything went wrong with him. Constant and hard labor failed to better his condition." On the treasure hunts young Weed attended, the leader would cut the throat of a black cat and "the precise spot was indicated by the direction the blood spurted."

A new outbreak of treasure hunting was usually sparked by the arrival of a charismatic seer known as a scryer. The expeditions might be directed by imaginative adolescents or teenage girls. African Americans were thought to have special insight into buried riches. Following the Smith family's arrival in Palmyra, "the MANIA of money-digging soon began rapidly to diffuse itself through many parts of the country," a newspaper editor observed.

The Smiths had high hopes during their first years in Palmyra. The conscientious son Alvin began to build a proper frame house on their land, a handsome two-story dwelling, which would accommodate the family and serve as a refuge for his parents in their old age. The family unwisely diverted some of the mortgage payment on the farm to finance the new house. Their need for cash increased.

Dreams often showed the way to wealth. A dream repeated three times was especially meaningful. The night Joseph Jr. had learned the location of the golden plates, the angel Moroni had visited him thrice.

Finding treasure usually required a tool to guide the search. A forked branch from a witch hazel or peach tree was the traditional divining rod. The seer would whisper "work to the money," and the device would point the direction, its dipping and quivering communicating details about the cache. Another popular tool was the seer stone or peep stone. To use one, the "glass-looker" would place the stone in a hat, bury his or her face below the brim to exclude light, and stare, sometimes for hours, seeking a vision. When Joseph was fourteen, around the time of his epiphany in the forest grove, he tried to use a seer stone owned by a local girl named Sally Chase. "It proved not to be the right stone for him," Joseph Sr. said, "but he could see some things."

Each seer had to find his or her personal stone. One story had Joseph traveling 150 miles, almost to the shores of Lake Erie, and digging his stone out from under a tree root. In another version, he found it twenty feet below the earth while excavating a well for a neighbor. This stone was about the size of a hen's egg, dark brown with tan stripes. It was a device, his mother wrote, "by which he could discern things invisible to the eye." Local folks from time to time hired Joseph to find lost objects or to lead treasure expeditions.

Summer was a good time for searching. "The heat of the sun caused the chests of money to rise near the top of the ground," Joseph Sr. said. Blood from a sheep or dog could indicate its precise location. Absolute silence while digging was a necessity. Any man who cried out, especially when he uncovered the treasure chest, would break the spell and ruin the project.

Locating the treasure was only the first step in a complicated process. Obtaining the cache required serious and chancy exertions. The gold would inevitably be guarded, Joseph Smith Jr. noted, "by some clever spirit." This spirit sentry might create loud noises or visions to scare diggers. One group of seekers spotted a man nine feet tall sitting on the ridge of a nearby barn. Another was startled by a band of ghostly horsemen clattering by.

One of Smith's digging partners said that after they came on a chest of money, "on account of enchantment, the trunk kept settling away from under them while digging; that notwithstanding they continued to constantly remove the dirt, yet the trunk kept about the same distance from them." Sometimes a treasure took off and burrowed through the ground like a mole, the hunters watching the earth rise and fall in its wake.

Part of the motivation for money-digging was the pure fun of it. To country people, treasure hunts were a chance for midnight rambles and arcane rituals. Sudden frights and imagined riches appealed to them, even if they returned empty-handed. The tension, the luscious hope, and the luminary effect of raw whiskey combined to make the expeditions intense and memorable.

The important thing was to keep hope alive. If the money-digging failed to yield a treasure, a Palmyra editor noted, the "deluded beings would on a succeeding night return to their toil, not the least doubting that success would eventually attend their labors."

The growing middle class of lawyers, physicians, and merchants rejected hoary folk beliefs and superstitions. Money-digging was childish, a sign of the laziness and gullibility of shiftless people. Respectable citizens complained that money-diggers "become insolent and saucy, neglect economy and industry." One observer noted that reasonable men believed that divining rods could indeed detect underground water, but "if the diviner hunts for metals, he becomes distrusted by the better sort of men."

In 1824, a Palmyra farmer named Martin Harris hired Joseph Sr. and his sons to build a fence on his farm. The father told him that "Joseph can see any thing he wishes by looking at a stone. Joseph often sees Spirits here with great kettles of money." Soon afterward, Harris dreamed about supernatural beings, who let him count their money. He awoke with a dollar in his hand. He mentioned the dream to Joe Jr., who let him know that the spirits were grieved. Harris threw the money away. Enchantment meant more to him than gain.

Money-diggers understood that looking was more important than finding. The idea of gold was more potent than the inert metal. Divining and the other facets of folk belief were spiritual exercises. Believers wanted assurance that they were in contact with the supernatural. Scryers like Joseph felt that God was sharing some of His power, was guiding the earthly seer.

Charlatans naturally rushed to take advantage of the credulity of the rubes. The Erie Canal provided an ideal corridor for urban sharpers to penetrate the interior and gull the locals. Where did the line fall between the mountebank, whose interest did not rise above the material, and the true believer seeking spiritual riches? Sometimes the boundary was far from clear.

Joseph's discovery of the gold plates in the autumn of 1823 was a bright moment for a family struggling with relentless ill luck. That November, two months after the visit from Moroni, Joseph's older brother Alvin, who had replaced his ineffectual father as the head of the family, suddenly fell ill. Doctors treated him with calomel, a mercury compound more poisonous than therapeutic. He died a few days later at the age of twenty-five. Suddenly, the family was bereft of its main breadwinner and teetered on the brink of insolvency.

The Smiths' finances did not improve over the next two years as they struggled to keep afloat. Then a prospect of cash appeared. Josiah Stowell was, like Martin Harris, a mature, established farmer and small businessman. His home in the Susquehanna Valley lay a hundred and twenty miles southeast of Palmyra. He had heard accounts of Joseph's reputation from his son, who lived near the Smiths. On a business trip to the area in October 1825, he called on the family and was mightily impressed that the young man could describe his house and outbuildings in South Bainbridge without having been near the place.

He offered to pay Joseph to travel there. The young man would guide a party intent on finding a Spanish silver mine that the fifty-five-year-old Stowell had searched for in vain on his property. Joseph enlisted on the condition that his father be included in the expedition. Formal articles of agreement were drawn up, declaring that the hunt was for "a valuable mine of either Gold or Silver." It allotted to the Smiths two-elevenths of all the property obtained.

The site of the purported mine was near the town of Harmony, twenty-five miles down the river from Stowell's farm and just over the border into Pennsylvania. The Smiths spent a month directing the search. They uncovered no precious metals, but Joseph found a treasure in Harmony that he valued more highly than any amount of wealth. He had fallen in love.

MAGNIFICENT

David Stanhope Bates had studied for the ministry and had planned to spend his life praising God's great work. Now in 1820, trudging through the soggy soil along Irondequoit Creek, he was contemplating what would be man's greatest work on the continent. The deep gorge lay ten miles east of the settlement on the Genesee still known as Rochesterville. What Bates saw disturbed him. The ground was sandy and unstable, an accumulation of sediment.

Seventy feet above him, like a chimera floating in thin air, was the path where the canal would have to pass.

"At the center of all engineering," wrote the historian of technology Elting Morison, "lies the problem of converting knowledge to practice." This problem is both obvious and profound. Knowing is one thing, doing another. Converting the abstract to the concrete is the enormous test of ingenuity.

While studying celestial truths in the seminary, Bates had become intrigued by mathematics. The interest did not conflict with his religion. As far back as Newton, men had seen numbers as a means for understanding the mind of God. For the young seminarian, science did not exclude the Lord; rather, it offered a clearer vision of His creation.

Nevertheless, Bates had abandoned his clerical studies, married, and become a merchant. In 1810, a landowner in Oneida County, still the remote frontier, hired Bates to survey his property. The young man moved his family to Constantia, an isolated settlement on the northwest shore of Oneida Lake. His three sons loved the frontier wildness and spent their youth playing with the children of the remaining Oneida Indians. The very summer they arrived, DeWitt Clinton and his delegation passed by on their tour to judge the feasibility of a canal. To pioneers like Bates, the notion seemed laughable.

But in 1817, the canal was about to become a reality and would pass just south of Oneida Lake. Bates, now forty, already knew Benjamin Wright, the lead engineer on the project. Bates parlayed his surveying experience and general ingenuity into a position as section engineer. He would plan and manage the path of the canal as it moved from Syracuse westward to Rochester.

After the execrable mire of the Montezuma Marshes, the gash created by Irondequoit Creek was the principal challenge along this part of the route. When James Geddes had surveyed the area in 1808, he came close to pronouncing the valley an absolute bar to an inland canal. He managed to trace a path from the Genesee River to the Irondequoit, avoiding all high ground. The canal could march down the western side of the valley, with plentiful water to work the locks. But there was no source of water to bring it back up the eastern slope. The only solution was to run the canal at a level straight across the wide gap. But how?

Geddes had discovered three large mounds of soil left by glaciers in the valley. Filling the gaps between these piles would create an enormous embankment on which the canal could ride. The task was Herculean but, he thought, achievable. When Geddes imagined boats that "would one day pass along on the tops of these fantastic ridges," he felt disposed "to exclaim *Eureka*."

Geddes's survey had supplied the knowledge; now it was up to David Bates to convert the plan to practice. As the canal trudged westward, the time came when the Irondequoit Valley had to be bridged. The commissioners, who were always nervous about costs, saw a cheaper alternative to Geddes's farfetched earth-moving project. A seventy-foot-high wooden trestle could be built quickly and at much less public expense. Along its top, a sealed trough would carry the canal. "Economy induced us to make the substitute," they admitted.

The commissioners were encouraged by a bridge recently constructed nearby. The town of Carthage lay between Rochester and Lake Ontario at a point where the Genesee River had gouged a deep, seven-hundred-foot-wide gorge. Bolting timbers together, workmen had built a huge wooden arch anchored on the opposing banks to carry a road two hundred feet above the water. It was the largest wooden bridge in the world, a symbol of American know-how. A master carpenter on the job was asked how he had determined what size timbers to use. "I take the average judgement," he said, "then guess and allow."

Workers finished the bridge in 1818. Fifteen months after it opened, the span failed and crashed into the river below. The canal commissioners noted the calamity and thought better of their economical approach at the Irondequoit Valley.

The decision to build an embankment, Bates saw, raised another issue. Besides its lower cost, a wooden trestle would have been far lighter than the thousands of tons of fill needed to connect the valley ridges. The embankment would have to be thirty feet wide at the top, more than two hundred at the bottom. It would tower seventy feet over the valley. Bates had no basis on which to make precise calculations, but he sensed that the ground along the creek would not support such weight. If the soil shifted, or slid, or subsided, it would disturb the trough, spill the canal water, perhaps cause the entire earthwork to avalanche down.

Guided by common sense, Bates decided to sink nine hundred log pilings, each a foot thick and up to twenty feet long, through the soil to bedrock. On top of them, workmen constructed a heavy timber mat to support the tons of dirt above. Bates informed Benjamin Wright of his plan, which was based largely on guesswork. The idea, Wright wrote back, "appears to be correct. I pray you to see that the piles are well and faithfully driven. It is all important to the safety of the whole work that there should be no settling nor any precariousness, as you know that would destroy all instantly."

Once the pilings and wooden floor were in place, stonemasons used them to support a 26-foot-high, 245-foot-long arched culvert that would allow the creek to flow under the embankment. This impressive structure was finished in 1821. The next year, workmen began to unload and pack in place wagonload after wagonload of dirt. Inspectors examined each to make sure it was not too sandy or too pebble-strewn to prevent cohesion.

Local farmers welcomed the work. They shoveled the dirt into wagons from mounds and banks around the area, hauled it to the site, and dumped it. All during the 1822 season, they amassed soil, the weight of their wagons and horses helping to pack it down as it accumulated. They piled a mound above the creek as high as a seven-story building. Incorporating the existing ridges, the whole embankment stretched nearly a mile.

Bates was quick to correct any shortcomings. He was an urbane, good-natured man, very discreet. If he saw a contractor cutting corners, he might comment to an assistant engineer within the man's hearing that he must have given unclear instructions about how the job was to be done.

At the top of the embankment, the laborers pounded in additional pilings to firm the soil. They gouged a trench and constructed a timber trough. This they lined with three inches of clay. Along the length of the ditch, workmen performed this crucial "puddling," applying layer after layer of clay to keep the water in. The work proceeded quickly. In October 1822, Bates ordered the safety dams opened. The water flowed in. Hundreds of onlookers held their breath. If the weight of the water cracked the trough or a significant leak developed, all could be lost. Bates at first restricted the section to only a foot of water. The channel held. Each night, the water was drained. After two days of this, he raised the water level to two feet. Again, the channel proved impermeable, the structure solid.

The anxiety did not abate. Bates had never designed such a work, and no one could forget the fate of the Carthage Bridge. At first, this portion of the canal carried only shallow-draft boats. Heavy shipments from Rochester's flour mills had to be moved by wagon around the embankment before being sent down the canal farther east. During the 1823 season, the trough was lined with another thick layer of clay and filled with three feet of water. Leaks were repaired over the winter, and by 1824 it was ready to be brought up to the standard four feet. The project was a success.

Crossing the embankment became an experience no traveler could forget. Passengers craned their necks from packet boats. As they glided above the tops of trees they could look down and see people gazing at them from below. The sensation seemed to presage a new era. Boosters at Rochester toasted the Erie Canal as "Stupendous! Magnificent!"

ILL-ADVISED ZEAL

Lucinda Morgan waited anxiously in Batavia for her husband to come home. His breakfast went cold. Lucinda paced. She fed her daughter and infant son. She finally left the apartment, children in tow, to make inquiries. Word had gotten around. She was told that William had been bundled off to Canandaigua by six men.

She spent a sleepless night, then went to see Sheriff William Thompson in Batavia. She knew the game. Freemasons had cooked up the spurious charges against William in order to apprehend him. They held power in western New York, and they were determined to stop Morgan from publishing his book.

She wanted her husband home, and she was ready to make a deal. If she handed over some of her husband's papers, would it secure his release? Thompson said it was "very likely." Masons probably suspected that the papers contained descriptions of rituals beyond the three degrees of the brotherhood that Morgan had already detailed in the book. The sheriff asked if Lucinda had anyone to accompany her to Canandaigua. She mentioned a friend, Horace Gibbs. Gibbs would not do, Thompson said. He was not a Mason. It had to be a Mason. He asked her if she knew a Mr. Follett. No, she did not. He was a gentleman, the sheriff said. A gentleman and a Mason. He would take her.

She found someone to care for little Lucy, but she could not leave behind the nursing two-month-old Thomas Jefferson Morgan. Before she left, she had to show her husband's papers to Mr. Follett and another man, a Mr. Ketchum. They "did not want to go on a tom fool's errand," they told her. They looked at the documents and, seemingly satisfied, set out with her in a dusty carriage.

Along the way, they stopped at the hamlet of Stafford a few miles east of Batavia, where they conferred with more Masons. These men suggested that Morgan possessed additional documents that Lucinda was holding back. Now Follett told her he would not waste his time trying to help her. Mr. Ketchum was headed for Rochester. If she wished, he would drop her at Canandaigua on the way. She agreed and they continued, stopping at an inn for the night.

In the morning, Lucinda rode in silence as they joggled and creaked past fields of late-summer goldenrod. She was scared and angry. Like many women, she hated the Masons. They made it difficult to maintain a decent home life. They encouraged heavy drinking, one of William's weaknesses. Their all-male, lodge-centered activities left women sitting home alone.

Mr. Ketchum delivered her to Canandaigua about noon on Wednesday, two days after her husband had gone missing. An outpost on the main road through western New York, the handsome city boasted five schools, several libraries, and three churches. The sidewalks were paved.

Mr. Ketchum left Lucinda and little Tommy at a tavern while he went to inquire. He returned after dinner and said that a man from Pennsylvania had appeared in the city with a warrant for William's arrest. He had taken Morgan away. No one knew where. It was the end of the road. Ketchum said he was sorry.

A frantic Lucinda demanded more information. The petite woman's powerful personality gave Ketchum qualms. He went away again. Near dark, he returned and confessed that the Masons were holding her husband. Morgan would not be killed, but the brothers needed more of his papers. They also wanted the printed book pages from Miller's shop. The project had to be stopped, the idea of the book abandoned.

Ketchum said he would keep the papers she had brought with her. He would give her two dollars traveling money and pay her stagecoach fare back to Batavia. If she turned over the required documents, he could assure her that she would receive twenty-five dollars and maybe as much as a hundred. Outraged, she rejected what was, for her, a serious sum. She wanted her husband back.

Infant in arms, she boarded the stagecoach on Thursday night for the return trip to Batavia. Back home, she received a visit from Thomas McCully, Master of the Batavia Masonic Lodge. William was still technically a member of the order, he told her. She and her children would be provided for from the Masonic Charity Fund.

Destitute as she was, she insisted that she would never take help from her husband's enemies. She had few friends in town, but she would make do. She turned to George Harris, the silversmith who ran a shop downstairs from her apartment. Harris, repelled by the Masons' actions, offered to help her through the crisis.

She learned that printer David Miller had also been abducted by the brotherhood. A mob of about fifty men, "most of whom were furnished with large clubs," had apprehended him and transported him to Stafford. He was "guarded as a criminal," before being taken on to Le Roy. A magistrate in that town could find no reason to hold him. Unlike William Morgan, he was set free.

Lucinda was at a loss. Law and order were in the hands of local sheriffs and magistrates, almost all of whom were allied with the Freemasons. None were willing to investigate William's disappearance.

But as the news spread, the people of western New York began to stir. The Masons' flagrant actions offended their sense of civic virtue. Their grandfathers had fought to establish a nation of laws, freedom, and equality. The republic was being mocked by a secretive association of quasi-aristocrats.

Citizens in surrounding towns called public meetings to discuss the matter. One, in Victor, near Canandaigua, passed resolutions that a newspaper reported "are of a very strong character, calculated to produce effect. This affair is becoming very serious." A judicious editor warned that the ancient and benevolent institution of

Freemasonry "will be brought into disrepute from the hasty and ill-advised zeal of some of its members."

The Masons, so recently considered among the most upstanding and respectable of citizens, began to appear shady. Rumors held that their secrecy stemmed from conspiratorial, even criminal motives. The common people were taking a fresh look at their betters. They saw arrogant and calculating elitists.

Sensing a crisis, Governor Clinton issued a proclamation to state officers and ministers of justice. He declared that "outrages and oppressions have been committed on the rights of persons residing in the village of Batavia." He insisted that every official make an effort aimed at "the apprehension of the offenders, and the prevention of future outrages." Grand juries were empaneled to dissect the mystery.

Publisher David Miller was eager to take advantage of the interest in the case suddenly crackling through the region. In November, two months after Morgan's disappearance, he hurriedly issued the first ninety pages of the book. Meanwhile, he continued to set type for the rest of the volume. Peddlers hawked the first portion of *Illustrations of Masonry* around the countryside. They even staged events at which citizens could pay a fee to hear a portion of the text read aloud.

By December, the entire book was available. That same month, the first grand jury to investigate Morgan's disappearance completed its work in Rochester. The members found that "the said Morgan was carried through this village on the morning of the 13th of September last, before daylight." But with numerous witnesses refusing to testify, the grand jury declared that it was "impossible to establish, by competent testimony, the unlawful agency of any citizen of this county." Before Christmas, the *Rochester Telegraph* reported that "several persons have been for some days engaged with spears and rakes, in fishing for the body of Morgan, along the Genesee River."

Soon afterward, at a public meeting in Bloomfield, on the Canandaigua-Batavia road, citizens passed resolutions condemning "unparalleled outrages upon private property and personal liberty, by an organized mob." The conclave noted the "studied silence" of journalists. "We condole with Mrs. Lucinda Morgan, in her afflictions," they stated. For Lucinda, the affair was neither a matter of public outrage nor an intriguing mystery. It was a sharp and unrelenting ache in her heart.

The political tempest along the canal continued to mount. Citizens resolved to discover Morgan's fate, "that if living, he may be restored to his friends, and if dead his murderers may be brought to justice."

And still the question remained: Where was William Morgan?

GOLD BIBLE

In December 1825, the Joseph Smith family faced acute financial pressure. They needed to get their hands on enough cash to satisfy several payments they had missed on their farm mortgage. They also had to meet the demands of Calvin Stoddard, the carpenter they had hired to finish the frame house after Alvin died two years earlier. The situation escalated to crisis when Stoddard showed up with two other men and told Hyrum, "We have bought the place."

Lucy rushed to the office of the land agent in Canandaigua. He told her that Stoddard had accused Hyrum of cutting down sugar maples, hauling off fence rails, and doing "all manner of mischief to the farm." That was why he had agreed to sell. Now he felt he had been duped. At a meeting, the land agent asked Stoddard and his friends not to crush the Smith family's prospects. But rumors of what Joseph had found on the hilltop had become common knowledge. "Oh, no matter about Smith," the carpenter scoffed, "he has gold plates, gold Bibles, he is rich." He relented slightly. If the Smiths could produce a thousand dollars in two days, he would hand over the deed.

Lucy sent a message to her husband and son, who were returning from their treasure hunt in Pennsylvania, urging them to make haste. In her memoir published years later, Lucy wrote, "The anxiety of mind that I suffered that day can more easily be imagined than described." Joseph Sr. rushed home, bringing money he had borrowed from Josiah Stowell, using next year's wheat harvest as collateral. It was not enough.

A local man, Lemuel Durfee, agreed to pay the money, take possession of the farm, and allow the Smith family to live there as tenants. On December 20, 1825, title to the farm, which the Smiths had toiled and sweated over for eight years, passed permanently out of their hands.

Back in 1803, a similar calamity had crashed down on them after the ginseng debacle. Then, Lucy was twenty-eight, Joe thirty-two. Now both were in their fifties. They knew what a life of poverty meant. The loss of the first farm, Lucy remembered, "I did not feel so keenly, for I then realized we were young and by making some exertion we could better our circumstances." Now they were old and the future glowered.

As tenants, the Smith family had to come up with a yearly rent payment. Joseph Jr. returned to Josiah Stowell's home in the southern tier, where he could earn wages of fourteen dollars a month as a farm laborer and mill worker. The money was welcome, but another attraction drew him south. While hunting for Spanish silver the previous autumn, he had boarded in Harmony, Pennsylvania, at a tavern owned by Isaac Hale, the first white settler along that stretch of the Susquehanna. At sixty-two, Hale was a hunter of local renown. He had a daughter.

Emma Hale was a year and a half older than Joseph. She was tall and dark-haired; a visitor described her as "fine looking, smart, a good singer." She was an excellent horseback rider, with arms hardened by canoeing up and down the river. Her people were frontier Methodists, and it was said of Emma that "she often got the power."

When Joseph returned, he began to court her. During that winter of 1826, he even found some time to attend school. With a curious mind and a shaky grasp of spelling and grammar, Joseph welcomed the chance for some learning. During his stay, the naturally voluble young man told Josiah Stowell, his friend Joseph Knight, Knight's sons, and probably Emma herself, about the breathtaking visit from Moroni, and the "gold book of ancient date" that he had found. He formed a small cadre of believers among the country people there. The Knights lived in Colesville, New York, thirty miles north of Harmony.

Joseph had told his mother that Emma "would be my choice in preference to any other woman I have ever seen." But Emma's father would not hear of a match. Smith had a bad reputation. He was, Hale said, "a stranger, and followed a business that I could not approve." Hale knew about the money-digging, having been an investor in the business himself. In March 1826, his opposition was further hardened when Joseph was arrested and hauled into court. A nephew of

Josiah Stowell had brought charges against the young man as a "disorderly person and an imposter." He may have thought that Joseph was hoodwinking his gullible uncle.

Joseph admitted in court that he had "a certain stone, which he had occasionally looked at to determine where hidden treasures in the bowels of the earth were." He had given up such activity of late, he said, because looking at the stone made his eyes sore. His father traveled down from Palmyra to testify for Joseph, saying that he had been mortified that his son's "wonderful power which God had so miraculously given him should be used only in search of filthy lucre." Josiah Stowell, far from feeling duped, stated he had "faith in the prisoner's skill." Joseph later told Emma's brother Alva that seeing with a stone was "a gift from God" but that "'peeping' was all damned nonsense." It was a strange double notion typical of Joseph's homespun metaphysics.

During the trial, Joseph swore that when he looked at his stone he "discovered that time, place and distance were annihilated; that all the intervening obstacles were removed, and that he possessed one of the attributes of the Deity, an All-Seeing Eye." It was an astounding claim.

The court found him guilty in the ambiguous case; his sentence, if any, was not recorded. He went back to work, and back to his pursuit of Emma Hale.

In January 1827, Emma visited the Stowells' home. "I had no intention of marrying when I left home," she later remembered. But Joseph proposed, Josiah Stowell urged her to say yes, and "preferring to marry him to any other man I knew, I consented." Joseph was twenty-one, Emma twenty-two. Emma's mother thought Joseph had "bewitched her."

Having married in South Bainbridge, they traveled to Palmyra and moved in with the Smith family. A neighbor remembered, "Joseph's wife was a pretty woman, just as pretty a woman as I ever saw."

During the summer, Emma wrote her father. She had left everything behind and wanted to collect some clothing, furniture, and cows that belonged to her. Joseph hired his neighbor Peter Ingersoll to drive them the 150 miles to Harmony and bring the goods back. Isaac Hale was still seething over Joseph's theft of his daughter, but the deed was done and he was unable to resist Joseph's charm. Smith promised to steer clear of money-digging; Hale agreed to allow the couple to live on his property. He would help his new son-in-law establish himself.

First, Joseph and Emma had to return north, ostensibly to fetch their belongings, but also to keep an important date. During the journey, Smith remarked to Ingersoll that it would be hard to keep his promise to Emma's father because of his connections to the Palmyra treasure hunters. "They want me to look in the stone for them to dig money."

In September 1827, Josiah Stowell and Joseph Knight made what had become a regular seasonal trip to the Rochester area to buy wheat. They scheduled their visit to the Smith family to coincide with the day when the angel had instructed Joseph to make his annual pilgrimage to the hill. They were not the only ones who knew of the routine. Joseph was afraid of being waylaid by locals greedy for the "gold Bible." Instead of waiting until the evening of September 22, he decided to make the visit on the twenty-first. Staying past midnight would fulfill his vow.

After Stowell and Knight had retired, Joseph asked his mother if she had a wooden chest with a lock. The request made her nervous. Would this be the year that the angel's promise was fulfilled? Would her son bring back the gold plates? She had no chest, but Joseph told her not to worry. He went out, followed by Emma in her riding clothes and bonnet. They borrowed a wagon and horse belonging to Joseph Knight. They disappeared into the late-summer darkness.

We can only imagine the excitement of the young couple as they traveled the three miles to the spot so familiar to Joseph. The height that would be named Hill Cumorah overlooked the Palmyra-Canandaigua road. Emma waited in the wagon. Joseph climbed the mound. Time passed. History was about to pivot.

In the morning, Knight reported that his horse was missing. Lucy made an excuse: the animal had probably wandered to a far corner of the pasture. Joseph Sr. sat down to breakfast and asked where his son was. Give him and Emma their privacy, Lucy said.

Why was it taking so long? Lucy was well aware of how many treasure-hunting ventures had come to ruin at the last moment. If instructions were not followed to the letter, an offended spirit could snatch away the cache forever. The angel had suggested that Joseph would have the plates only "if he would Do right."

Suddenly, Joseph walked in. He was glowing. He took his mother aside and whispered, "I have got a key!" He showed her "three-cornered diamonds set in glass" with frames that resembled old-fashioned spectacles. After breakfast, Joseph told Knight what had happened. It was "ten times Better than I expected."

He was not sure of the significance of the plates, which were "writen in Caracters." He would have to have them translated by scholars. But the two "keys," which would be known as Urim and Thummim, divination tools mentioned in the Bible, excited him immensely. "I can see any thing," he exclaimed, "they are Marvelus."

Returning from the hill, he had hidden the gold plates in a hollowed birch log and carefully replaced the bark. He would retrieve them later. For now, he had to be careful. During his money-digging days, he had been part of a group of searchers who pooled their talents and labor. Having renounced worldly gain from the plates, Joseph found himself in a precarious situation. "The money-diggers," Martin Harris stated, "claimed that they had as much right to the plates as Joseph had, as they were in company together."

As always, the relentless drumbeat of poverty sounded at Joseph's back. The day after making his wondrous discovery, he hurried to the nearby town of Macedon to dig a farmer's well, glad for the work.

The news of the gold plates soon reached Willard Chase, one of Joseph's partners. Chase plotted with a dozen men to get their fair share. They sent for a necromancer and diviner who could direct them to any precious metal Smith might have hidden. The Smiths heard about this plot. They called Joseph back from his well-digging. Suddenly anxious, he retrieved the plates, which reportedly weighed fifty pounds, from the birch log. He wrapped them in his work frock and headed home. A man appeared in the forest and attacked him with the butt of a rifle. Joseph escaped. Another man assailed him, Joseph eluded him as well. Then came a third attack, just as in the Masonic story of Hiram Abiff. Unlike the ancient stonemason, Joseph managed to flee. He reached home battered and with a dislocated thumb.

He concealed the gold plates in a locked cherrywood chest that Hyrum had arranged to have made. Now everyone was burning with curiosity. Knight and Stowell asked questions. As gossip spread the news, neighbors stopped by and offered cash for a glimpse of the treasure. Joseph Sr. declared that because of the plates "my family will be placed on a level above the generality of mankind."

Joseph looked into his seer stone to warn him of threats. The gang organized by Chase approached the house, accompanied by their hired diviner. The Smith family helped Joseph bury the wooden chest under the hearthstone of their fireplace. Just in time.

Later, they moved the plates to the nearby workshop where Joseph Sr. carried on a coopering business. They buried the box under the floor, but removed the plates and hid them in a bundle of flax in the loft. Chase returned with his sister Sally. Looking into her green glass, she determined that the treasure was nearby. The searchers tore up the floor of the shed and smashed open the expensive box. They found nothing inside.

Martin Harris took a special interest in the affair. The forty-four-year-old Palmyra farmer was a religious seeker—a Presbyterian minister called him "a visionary fanatic." Harris stood up to Smith's local detractors. "I do not wish to make myself a fool," he declared, and only a fool would dismiss Joseph's discovery without a thorough investigation. As with many country people, Harris's credulity was combined with skepticism. To avoid being duped, he questioned members of the Smith family separately to test their stories against each other. Joseph refused to let him see the plates, but did allow him to heft their weight in the box. He told Harris to appeal to God whether they were genuine.

Harris warned Joseph that the money-diggers were planning more forceful methods for getting the plates. They might even tar and feather Smith for holding out. Joseph became alarmed. In December, he wrote to Emma's brother Alva Hale, asking him to help move the couple back to Harmony. By now they knew that Emma was pregnant with their first child. Martin Harris lent Joseph fifty dollars. Before leaving, Joseph concealed the gold plates in a barrel of beans. A mob of men appeared but did not discover the hiding place.

Joseph and Emma endured the long trip to Harmony and settled into a small house on her father's farm. The work of translating the gold plates was about to begin.

INGENIOUS

While the Irondequoit embankment was under construction, engineers were also tackling the difficult eastern section of the canal. To bypass the thundering Cahoes Falls and descend more than four hundred feet to sea level at the Hudson River required fifty-five locks. Among those working on the project was the engineering prodigy John Jervis. Hired to clear brush in 1817, the slight but sinewy twenty-one-year-old farm boy had been promoted to targetman the next year.

He was assigned to help David Bates, whom he described as "a man of very pleasant manners." Jervis had a keen head for mathematics and for envisioning the complexities of a three-dimensional design. Bates allowed him to practice with the equipment and was himself "ready to learn," Jervis said, "even from me."

Jervis spent the winter of 1818 weighing stone for the locks. The following season, he found himself replacing Bates, who was to move westward, as resident engineer for a portion of the middle section. On his way home that winter, Jervis was lucky enough to borrow a copy of the *Edinburgh Encyclopedia* from his uncle. He studied the book's state-of-the-art canal articles during the cold months. After another year as resident engineer, he took over as a principal builder on the eastern section under the direction of Canvass White, who was himself only thirty.

Jervis's section, from east of Utica to Little Falls, fell a hundred feet in thirteen miles. Guided by White but increasingly making his own decisions, Jervis pushed the work forward. When water was let in to test the section, the canal leaked so badly that it had to be drained and relined with clay. Puddling was a learned art.

The work went on, the learning continued, and the eastern section was finished. In October 1823, a month after Joseph Smith first uncovered the gold plates on Hill Cumorah, DeWitt Clinton rode the prow of the canal boat *DeWitt Clinton* in a procession through Lock No. 1, a mile and a half above Albany. Clinton, the nation's highest-ranking Freemason, watched his brothers give their solemn blessing to the stonework that completed the eastern section. Church bells rang, fireworks blazed, the West Point band hammered out a triumphant march. The canal was edging toward completion.

Barely a month earlier, more than two hundred miles inland, a similar celebration had unfolded. Life in the nation's fastest-growing city, a city for which the term "boomtown" had just been invented, offered a continual stream of excitements to the citizens of Rochester. Only a hamlet a few years earlier, the town would soon be connected to the distant Hudson River by the canal that was being constructed through the middle of its business district.

By now, everyone in town knew David Bates, who had, over the past two years, overseen the work on the Irondequoit Creek embankment. He was a likeable man, smart but not snooty. When he reprimanded workers, he often accompanied the scolding with a humorous story to soften the blow.

Nathaniel Rochester had come to the area from Virginia in 1803 to speculate in western New York land. The tremendous falls, almost a hundred feet straight down, made the location ideal for mills. At first, few pioneers wanted to settle in the remote, swampy, and rattlesnake-infested area, but the rumors of a canal had sent seven hundred residents rushing to buy plots. Mills began grinding flour and sawing wood. Forges hammered iron. The town grew up almost overnight.

Bates was now supervising the building of an eight-hundred-foot-long aqueduct of his own design to take the canal across the Genesee. It would be the greatest mass of masonry along the entire canal. His friend Benjamin Wright was advising him, but it was Bates's project. Both Wright and Bates agreed that the arches should be constructed of hard limestone shipped from quarries farther east on the canal. But the commissioners, always penny-wise, directed Bates to use the cheaper sandstone that could be had locally.

Nine stone arches, each fifty feet across at the bottom, supported the structure. Two more spanned the mill races that drew water along each bank of the river to power the factories. A feeder canal was being constructed along the bank to connect the canal to the Genesee. This channel would furnish water for the canal even as it allowed boats to navigate to and from the river.

Locals made sure that Bates understood how ornery the Genesee could be. It was the only major north-flowing waterway in the region, running a hundred fifty miles from Pennsylvania and draining an enormous swath of the country. It flooded every few years, having swamped the village in both 1817 and 1818. An aqueduct with its feet planted in the water would have to withstand the river's periodic wrath.

Managing the actual construction of the long bridge was William Brittin, an experienced carpenter. Four years earlier, Brittin had built the state prison in Auburn, a Finger Lakes settlement just off the canal's path sixty miles east of Rochester. He had served as its first warden. The commissioners considered Brittin "an ingenious and enterprising man." Knowing of the chronic labor shortages in the region, they allowed him to employ convicts from his prison to work on the aqueduct.

"Who can contemplate without horror," a newspaper editor gasped, "one hundred and fifty convicts, in the constant view of the children and youth of this populous settlement." In fact, only twenty-eight laborers accompanied Brittin, all of them Irishmen who had been imprisoned for petty crimes. They joined the four hundred workmen already hired. Seven of the jailbirds took the opportunity to hightail it—none were recaptured.

Rochesterians stood along the riverbank to watch work begin in June 1821. Coffer dams were erected to divert river water, horses strained to haul stone, steel rang against steel. By autumn, Brittin's workmen had bolted the sandstone foundation blocks solidly to bed-rock in the river. Would they hold? No one knew. Trial and error was the ruling method.

That winter, river ice piled up, the water heaved, and the piers gave way. When the level dropped, watchers could see the twisted remains of the bolts. It was reported that the canal commissioners were impressed by the "prodigious violence and power" of the river. Wright begged Bates to "see that no bad material or ill workman-ship is permitted." But neither Bates nor the chief engineer could convince the cost-conscious commissioners to upgrade the materials. The bureaucrats were determined to try again with sandstone.

Brittin had become ill and died over the winter. In the spring of 1822, a new contractor, Alfred Hovey, adopted Bates's more rigorous building plan. Great booms shook the town as workers used blasting powder to carve out squares in the river bedrock the same shape as the piers. They fit heavier foundation stones into these spaces and secured them with larger bolts than Brittin had used. They fixed iron rods and clamps inside the stonework as it rose.

Bates, as was his habit, watched the progress patiently. Maybe it was his early theological training, but somehow Bates could be thorough without fretting. "In conversation," somebody noted of him, "he was cheerful, witty, and often brilliant." The enormous arches rose slowly. Like his predecessor, Hovey found there were not enough stonemasons and laborers to keep the work going at the pace he wanted. He ordered more Irish immigrants to be recruited from New York City. Townspeople wrinkled their noses at these filthy and smelly vassals, some of whom spoke no English, only a guttural Gaelic.

The immigrants knew how to work, though. By the end of 1822, all the arches stood fourteen feet above the river. They survived the ice. The next season workers built up the canal channel and lined it with layers of clay. On October 6, 1823, residents cheered as decorated canal boats went gliding across the longest stone bridge in the world. Seventy-one-year-old Nathaniel Rochester mounted the dais and called the aqueduct "the most stupendous and strongest work in America." The town band played the Masonic hymn, "The Temple's Completed." Freemasons, always eager to enliven occasions of civic pride, conducted an opening ritual and hosted a banquet for the city's notable citizens.

One of those on hand for the aqueduct celebration was Jesse Hawley. The bankrupt visionary had climbed back from ruin to become a postmaster, then a customs collector at the port where the Genesee River joined Lake Ontario. He would later be elected to the state assembly. His identity as "Hercules," the man whose plan for the great work had inspired the canal, remained a secret known to only a few. His thick dark eyebrows bouncing, he gave a toast at the banquet, praising canals as "the modern monuments of national glory."

The aqueduct, "the grandest single feature of the Canal," was an object of pride for engineers as well as for the enthusiastic populace of the town. Rochesterians, almost all of them young, had come west seeking opportunity. Now they were watching it arrive.

But the aqueduct reflected amateurism as much as achievement. Too narrow for boats to pass each other, it became a bottleneck to canal traffic. The sharp turn at its eastern end, almost a right angle, further hampered movement and was the scene of many brawls among canal boatmen waiting to get across. As Bates and Wright had foreseen, the sandstone was too soft. Water seeped in and froze, the stone eroded, leaks developed in the canal. Barely a decade after it was completed, the bridge would have to be rebuilt.

No one at the 1823 celebration was looking that far ahead. With the canal open all the way to the Hudson, Rochester was about to become the greatest flour-milling city in the world. "Hercules" was vindicated. Opportunity beckoned.

WHISKEY

During the 1820s, thousands of folks along the Erie Canal corridor were becoming intoxicated with religion. Many more were succumbing to the mind-blasting effects of raw alcohol. America was reeling through the most phenomenal drinking binge in its history. Hordes of citizens were living their lives in the woozy, dislocated haze of permanent inebriation.

Western farmers who grew barley, corn, and rye found it more profitable to ferment and distill their crops into strong liquor than to ship the grain to market. Whiskey was plentiful and cheap. Each man older than fifteen was drinking on average fourteen gallons of hundred-proof whiskey every year. By the middle of the decade, more than a thousand distillers were operating in New York State. Whiskey was cheaper than wine or beer, more readily available than imported luxuries like tea and coffee, safer to drink than water.

Whiskey was considered "so conducive to health," a journalist wrote in 1830, "that no sex, and scarcely any age, were deemed exempt from its application." Children drank. Adults deemed it more patriotic to drink whiskey than French wine or Dutch gin. Liquor filled the role that coffee would later assume as a morning bracer. A glass of whiskey with breakfast was commonplace.

A man need not go to a tavern: he could stop for a glass of whiskey at a grocery or candy store. He could down a shot at a barber shop. Theaters served strong drink. Millers provided the refreshment to waiting farmers. Militia musters always ended with heroic drinking. Casual sellers of grog set up bars in their basements.

Men during this period habitually drank at work. Before the spread of factories, artisans typically operated workshops that employed a dozen or so journeymen and apprentices. The master was expected to provide ale or whiskey for his employees' dinner and breaks. He often drank with them. He tolerated a degree of absenteeism on what was known as Saint Monday, as workers recovered from Sunday binges.

Drinking on the job peaked among canal workers. With whiskey cheap and cash in short supply, contractors favored pay in kind—bed, board, and ample drink. The typical canal worker drank at least a pint, often a quart, of whiskey daily. Whiskey "was provided bountifully and in true western style." Thirsty from a salty diet and abundant sweating, the men drank and drank.

"Along the line of the canal," one observer noted, "at convenient distances, was to be found a barrel of whiskey, pure old rye, with part of the head cut out and a tin dipper laying by and all were expected to help themselves."

Some contractors assigned boys, known as "jigger bosses," to portion out the rations along the line. All this in spite of the fact that alcohol accelerated dehydration in warm weather and increased the danger that tipsy workers would maim their fellows while swinging picks and operating cranes.

Irish workmen were increasingly filling the canal workforce as the project moved westward into sparsely settled regions. Scorned as aliens and Catholics, they found solace in *uisce beatha*, the Gaelic "water of life."

But workers of any nationality, exposed to the harsh conditions of canal labor and the easy availability of alcohol, would have done the same. As one former worker said, "You wouldn't expect them to work on the canal if they were sober, would you?"

When drunk, laborers sometimes passed out and lay exposed for hours to the sun or chill night dew. "Fever, and death," a physician noted, "were but too often the melancholy results."

A traveler from England observed that Americans "quarrel in their drink, and they make up with drink. They drink because it is hot; they drink because it is cold. . . . They drink early in the morning, they leave off at night; they commence it early in life, and they continue it until they soon drop into the grave." Although dangerous and debilitating, booze could be a shortcut to heaven, a way to bring one's mind, however briefly, into tune with the mind of God.

Drinking frequently initiated violence. Drunks fought each other with tedious regularity. They went home and assaulted their wives and children. They squandered their money, committed petty crimes, and shamed themselves in innumerable ways. The intense drinking of the 1820s was corrosive to both individuals and society.

The pattern was about to change. The casual, paternalistic approach to drinking at work was doomed. There would be no room for a midmorning glass of whiskey as the factory became the workplace for more and more wage earners. Bosses ceased to tolerate tipsy employees. When the machines chugged into operation on Monday morning, workers had to be in their places or lose their jobs.

An even stronger reaction to heavy drinking was looming. It would burst on the American scene in the 1830s and become one of the nation's most enduring social movements. The country that English visitor Frances Trollope called the "alcoholic republic" would undergo a dramatic transformation. The building of the Erie Canal marked the peak of American intoxication. The idea of temperance hardly existed in 1825. Five years later it was a middle-class obsession. Those whom one newspaper editor called the "cold-water, pale-faced, money-making men" soon pledged a "war of extermination" on whiskey, America's first drug war.

METHODS

Even in our time, religion has retained its power to generate deep controversy. In the 1820s, belief was a far more potent source of dispute, the central concern of a significant portion of the population. The more Charles Finney's wildly successful revivals spread, the more the established men of the cloth grumbled. They talked of the "animal feelings" that Finney was letting loose in his congregants.

The most prominent of the conventional clergymen was the New England Presbyterian minister Lyman Beecher. He had been trying to steer a gradual, limited course away from the more severe dictates of Calvinism. Presiding at churches first in western Connecticut and then in Boston, Beecher toned down the doctrines of human depravity and predestination. But he loathed the unrestrained enthusiasm that had erupted at Cane Ridge, the exhibitionism that made Christians seem like lunatics. The success of Finney's unorthodox "methods" threatened to infect New England, the bastion of Puritan piety, with a similar mania.

Photographs show Beecher with the vinegary face of a farmer swallowing medicine, but the preacher was no mossback. In 1818, when Connecticut stopped supporting religion with state tax funds, he thought the damage was "irreparable." Soon he admitted that disestablishing the churches was the "best thing that ever happened," that the change had injected a new spiritual vitality into religion.

Beecher pushed for religious unity and was on guard against any idea that might set Christians at war with each other. He prized social order. "The importance of truth in religion," he stated, "is perhaps more frequently admitted than *the importance of order*." A loose cannon like Finney, who allegedly advocated falling, groaning, and dancing in church, could "throw us back in civilization, science and religion, at least a whole century."

Beecher had sired several accomplished daughters, including Harriet Beecher Stowe, who would become the most famous novelist of her day; Catherine Beecher, a prominent education reformer; and the early suffragist Isabella Beecher Hooker. Yet the prominent roles that women played in Finney's revivals disturbed their father. Beecher saw in females "a softness and delicacy of feelings which shrinks from the notoriety of a public performance." He resented Finney's attempts "to disrobe the female mind" and dress it in coarse masculine garments.

Repelled by men like Lorenzo Dow, Beecher insisted on the importance of an educated clergy. "Illiterate men," he declared, "have never been the chosen instruments of God to build up his case." Another orthodox churchman pointed out the foolishness of those who demanded a seven-year apprenticeship for a shoemaker but assumed that the skill of saving souls could be "comprehended without learning, labour, or time."

In the autumn of 1826, Charles Finney was feeling the wrath of Beecher's New England colleagues. They circulated a caustic booklet taking him to task for "his shocking blasphemies, his novel and

repulsive sentiments, and his theatrical and frantic gesticulations."
The controversy came to a head in July 1827. Beecher, hoping to calm
the waters, invited Finney and some of his supporters to a meeting
with leading clerics. He was willing to cross the Berkshire Mountains
and hold the conclave at New Lebanon, in eastern New York. Finney
agreed.

At fifty-two, Beecher arrived brimming with energy and authority. He brought with him prominent ministers from Andover,
Hartford, and Amherst, the cream of New England's religious establishment. Finney's entourage included pastors from Troy, Utica, and
Auburn. It was to be a contest of West versus East, innovation versus
tradition, youth versus age. Finney was not technically on trial, but
his methods were to be judged.

The men met in the parlor of a local doctor's home. The suf-
focating summer heat chafed their already testy nerves. The first
point of contention was the question: Should a man of God permit a
woman to participate in mixed prayer services and to speak publicly?
The two groups were immediately at loggerheads. "Let your women
keep silence in the churches," St. Paul had commanded. For traditionalists, it was also a matter of good taste. Surely Finney and his
colleagues could see that simple decency would dictate the exclusion
of females.

Finney, the lawyer, demanded proof that he had ever allowed
women to speak in his assemblies. Beecher was insulted. What need
was there for documentation of something everyone knew to be true?
"Our spiritual dignity forbids us to answer any such questions," he
blustered. Finney kept his cool, requiring his opponents to reveal the
source of the accusation.

As antediluvian as the arguments sound today, Finney's refusal
to back down at the New Lebanon meeting opened a crack in the
long tradition of patriarchy in mainline American religion. The
trend Finney started would have important consequences down the
decades.

After much sweating and debate, the churchmen could not reach
a clear agreement about the issue of women in the church. For an oppressive week, they continued to discuss a laundry list of complaints
about the methods propagated by Finney and his followers. The New
England clerics lambasted the westerners for their colloquial language

and their praying for sinners by name. Finney's alleged practice of invading a town without an invitation from a local clergyman incensed them. The revivalists, they said, blackmailed pastors into accepting their presence "only by 'crushing' or 'breaking them down.'"

The New Englanders could not countenance Finney's excessive familiarity with the Almighty in public prayers, "talking to God as a man talks to his neighbor." They said that pressuring congregants by inducing them to come to the front of the church was inappropriate. Hours of discussion were devoted to a motion declaring that "audible groaning in prayer is, in all ordinary cases, to be discouraged."

In spite of his relative newness to the ministry, Finney counterpunched effectively. He argued that the supporters of orthodoxy were themselves in the wrong when they published diatribes critical of him and his followers. Late in the meeting, he proposed a resolution condemning "lukewarmness in religion." Beecher was flabbergasted at the implied criticism. He threatened Finney that if the younger man tried to bring his methods to New England he would "meet you at the State line, and call out the artillery-men, and fight every inch of the way to Boston, and I'll fight you there."

When the meeting ended, Finney stood unscathed; Beecher went home rattled. He reportedly told a follower, "We crossed the mountains expecting to meet a company of boys, but we found them to be full-grown men."

ABYSS

On November 13, 1829, ten thousand pairs of eyes stared at a man dressed completely in white standing on a platform above the High Falls of the Genesee River in the middle of Rochester. Like Joe Smith, the man bore a prosaic name. Like Smith, he was no stranger to poverty. And he was, in his own right, a visionary.

Much of the population of Rochester had turned out to watch. Folks had traveled for days over bad roads. They had come in from the country, down from Canada. They had journeyed the canal on packet boats. This was Sam Patch, the famous daredevil. They had to see him.

Like the Smiths, the Patch family had dwelt on the margins of society. Sam was born in 1799 to a father who had worked as a tenant farmer and a sometime shoemaker around their home just north of Boston. In 1807, the family moved to Pawtucket, Rhode Island. The elder Patch put his children to work in the nation's first textile factory.

Samuel Slater, an English cotton worker, had brought the secrets of mechanized spinning to America in the 1790s. His water-powered mill cracked the British monopoly and speeded the process of making cloth. Slater had an idea of integrating his mill into the existing agricultural economy of America. Men would farm the fields around Pawtucket, their wives and children would earn cash working in the mill. But industry trumped agriculture; Slater hired whole families at low wages. Sam Patch, eight years old, became one of the nation's first factory hands. His father took to drink, abandoned his family, and later went to prison for counterfeiting.

Spinning thread on cog-driven machinery was an intricate task. Skilled "mule spinners" operated the complicated machines in the Slater Mill, while children climbed through the contraptions to tie broken threads and perform other routine tasks. Head-pounding noise filled the buildings, heat baked the workers in summer, cold made fingers numb in winter, and lint clogged the air year round. Painful accidents were common: hands were crushed, limbs broken. The work day typically lasted twelve hours, sometimes more. Children who lagged were slapped by impatient foremen.

Sam's mother joined a church when they moved to Pawtucket. Calvinist doctrine, which dripped with resignation, gave solace to the downtrodden. All was God's will. Mill owners encouraged churchgoing. In the Puritan way of thinking, depraved humans had no control of their spiritual destiny. Dependency and degradation were God-given.

Sam lost his childhood to the mills. Work limited his time for playing ball or chasing cows or romping in the wildflower fields of imagination. Farm children worked hard, too, but in the country the pace was not set by the relentless pulse of machinery. In later life, friends described Sam as melancholic. Like his father, he drank.

On rare breaks, young factory workers found fun in jumping from bridges into Pawtucket's Seekonk River near the falls. The drop was fifty feet, and they had to leap out over rocks. The most daring—Sam Patch was among them—jumped from the six-story stone mill that Slater erected in 1813. This dizzying, hundred-foot plunge gave Sam an electric thrill and the pride of showmanship. Watchers marveled at his audacity. Every jump was a small four-act drama: the tense anticipation, the thrilling leap, the heart-stopping disappearance, and the joyful restoration. He stayed under for as long as he could to prolong the suspense.

But life, for Sam, was work. He became a mule spinner himself. He heaved and guided the biggest machines in the plant, careful not to thrust too hard and snap the threads as they formed. The job required strength and delicate skill.

Americans did not take easily to the servile conditions of factory work. In 1824, workers in Pawtucket walked off the job, protesting a decision by mill owners to cut wages by a quarter and extend the work day by an hour. Women and girls instigated the nation's first industrial strike. Men, probably including Sam Patch, joined in. They blocked the doors of mills and marched to owners' houses. In a spasm of anger, they threw stones and curses. The chaotic "turn-out," as it was called, lasted only a week and ended in compromise. It was the harbinger of an endless struggle.

Having acquired a skill, Patch traveled to Paterson, a prosperous mill town in New Jersey. On a whim, he interrupted the opening of a pleasure garden by leaping from the top of the Passaic River Falls. Maybe he was drunk. Maybe it was pure bravado—he would later call leaping "an art which I have knowledge of and courage to perform." On the Fourth of July 1828, Sam again defied death at the Passaic Falls. When he completed the harrowing leap, he proclaimed the terse phrase that would become his motto: "Some things can be done as well as others." It was the working man's sneer at the pretensions of the elite.

Two weeks later, Paterson mill workers, led by children, walked off the job to protest a change in their dinner time and to demand that the workday be cut from thirteen and a half hours to ten. The carpenters, masons, and mechanics of Paterson laid down their tools in sympathy. Sam scheduled a leap over the falls to encourage his fellow mill hands. Labor turmoil engulfed the city for three weeks. During August, the workers returned, with little to show for their defiance. The owners kept the grindingly long workday and fired the strike's ringleaders. Sam Patch may have been one who lost his job.

Now Sam traveled the country, jumping. In October 1829, he became the first of the Niagara daredevils, leaping from a platform into the seething cauldron at the bottom of the falls. He did a half turn in the air and created a mighty splash when he hit the water. "He's dead!" came murmurs from the spectators. His appearance at the surface released a "flood of joy." He waved off the boat sent to fetch him and swam to shore. With this feat, he "immortalized himself," a newspaper said. He became "The True Sam Patch." The Buffalo *Republican* declared, "He may now challenge the universe for a competitor."

A month later, Sam traveled down the canal to Rochester. He announced that he would leap from the terrifying precipice of the Genesee cascade on November 6. Word went out, handbills circulated. The sporting young men of the town band served as Patch's unofficial sponsors. They put him up in the Recess, a downtown tavern and inn, and made sure he had no cause to complain of thirst.

While in Rochester, Patch brushed against the Anti-Masonic agitation, which had spread like a fever across western New York ever since William Morgan had gone missing three years earlier. Supporters and detractors of the brotherhood had turned the mystery into a political fistfight. The year before, Anti-Mason Thurlow Weed, who was helping push the outrage toward political action, had been chased up State Street by a supporter of the brotherhood. His friend Frederick Whittlesey had pummeled a fellow lawyer at the Eagle Tavern during an argument over Morgan.

Sam Patch set up a subscription at the Recess, inviting "gentlemen who feel disposed to witness the spectacle" to make contributions to help defray his expenses. Some of his supporters passed a hat at the site of his performance.

The Genesee River flowed over a mill dam, then plunged down an abrupt, ninety-six-foot precipice just north of the canal aqueduct. Patch borrowed a rowboat and explored the pool at the bottom of the falls. He made soundings, judged distances, and hunted for any underwater hazards. Above him, the walls of the gorge formed an amphitheater, green with moss and decorated here and there with scarlet fans of sumac.

Crowds swarmed into Rochester—more than ten thousand people, one visitor estimated. They came together "like an army drawn up in battle array." Why take the time? Why travel for hours in a creaking wagon? What impulse powered the allure of celebrity? What fear spurred the fascination with mortality?

Patch was scheduled to jump at two o'clock. He appeared an hour late. Bets had been placed whether he would have the courage to show up at all. The crowd buzzed with anticipation. He bowed, looked over the edge. The water hissed.

Then he was gone. A gasp. He plummeted feet first. He crashed beneath the surface. Disappeared.

The usual whispers sizzled through the mass of onlookers. "He's dead!"

Sam's head bobbed above the water. Cheers echoed around the gorge.

"This is the real Sam Patch," he told the first to greet him along the shore. "No mistake." The man handed him a bottle of rum.

To the consternation of Rochester's respectable citizens, Sam scheduled another jump one week later, Friday the thirteenth. He had a platform constructed to raise him even farther above the river, 120 feet. Word went out. *There's no Mistake in SAM PATCH*, his handbills read. *HIGHER YET! Sam's Last Jump.*

Again the great mass of spectators. The mills shut down. Watchers crowded the windows and roofs of the factories. The sensation, one viewer noted, was "between a horse race and an execution." The curious waited in the penetrating cold of a November afternoon under a slate-gray sky.

For his performances, Sam Patch always dressed in the white togs that were the uniform of textile mill workers. He stepped onto the platform. He had imbibed, yes. He had taken enough of the water of life to make him sway a bit as he looked out on all those looking back.

"Napoleon!" he said. He shouted it, knowing few could hear. "Napoleon was a great man. But he couldn't jump the Genesee." Sam paused. The wind bit through his cotton clothing and carried his words away over the housetops. "That was left for me to do. I can do it and I will." Some things could be done. "I will!"

Sam was kicking at the struts that held up the reputations of great men. Any man, even a wage slave, could do some things. Could be great. Could be celebrated. If he dared.

Behind him, he could hear words of caution from those who suddenly saw in the tremendous height sure death. *Don't, Sam. For God's sake. It's your life. Don't. Don't.*

The anticipation had built long enough. Time, like the water, was rushing, tumbling. The watching eyes rounded. A man in the crowd bit his thumb. Sam stepped to the very edge of the platform. Each spectator drew a breath and held it. Sam looked into all their eyes, into the abyss.

He jumped.

TRANSLATION

The Egyptian Pharaohs enjoyed sovereignty in the eastern Mediterranean for nearly three thousand years before Alexander the Great conquered them in the fourth century before Christ. Within a few generations, the Greek rulers had adopted many of the customs of the former kings. Soon after 200 B.C., Ptolemy V, an ancestor of the legendary beauty Cleopatra, was having difficulties controlling the country. Facing a rebellion by ethnic Egyptians, Ptolemy ordered his attendants to set up inscribed stones that declared him a god. The granite signboards also listed concessions to the priestly caste, a bit of political maneuvering by a hard-pressed potentate.

Carvers inscribed the message on these stones in three versions. The first was written in hieroglyphics, the priestly writing that harked back to Egypt's early history. A different script told the story in the colloquial Egyptian of the day. The third transcription was in Greek, the language of governmental administration.

Traditional Egyptian culture continued its decline under the Greeks, the Romans, the Byzantines, and finally the Muslims. The knowledge of hieroglyphics died out entirely. In the Mediterranean town of al-Rashid, Ptolemy's ancient proclamation stone was incorporated into the foundation of a fort and forgotten.

In 1798, Napoleon Bonaparte conquered the country's Ottoman rulers and their British allies. He brought scholars and antiquarians with him to study and to loot. They uncovered the inscribed stone at al-Rashid, a town they called Rosetta, and quickly saw its importance. This could be the key to reading the indecipherable hieroglyphics, within which knowledge of Egypt's vast history was locked. Scholars copied and began to study the inscriptions. They lost the stone itself to the British, who forced the French army's surrender in 1801. The victors shipped the Rosetta Stone to London.

An Anglo-French competition began to see who could first break the code. Thomas Young, a brilliant British scientist and physician, spent more than ten years unraveling the colloquial Egyptian script. He identified figures within the hieroglyphics that represented Greek names, including that of Ptolemy, spelled out phonetically.

In France, Jean-François Champollion, a language prodigy still in his twenties, strongly suspected that he could decipher all the hieroglyphics, not just the Greek names, into the components of words. The glyphs were a readable language, not a collection of pictographs. Taking cues from spoken and written Coptic, kept alive by Egyptian Christians, Champollion hammered away at the code. In 1822, he produced a table listing the meaning of some of the glyphs. It was a significant breakthrough. By 1828, he understood the system of writing well enough to travel to Egypt and read the history of the dynasties from the walls of the great tombs and monuments. The avalanche of discoveries thoroughly upset European ideas about the Egyptians. In the process, the new knowledge called into question Biblical accounts of the origin of the earth and of the timing of the great flood of Noah.

During the 1820s, as scholars were deciphering the Rosetta Stone, Joseph Smith Jr. had recovered the bundle of golden plates. The message he found inscribed on them, he declared in 1827, was written in "reformed" Egyptian. The year before, a local newspaper had reported the discovery of Mexican manuscripts written in hieroglyphics. This suggested that early Mexicans and peoples from the Middle East must have had some connection. The fact that an American artifact from western New York would be written in hieroglyphics was plausible to many.

Joseph and Emma had returned from Palmyra to Harmony. When Emma's father, Isaac Hale, demanded to see the plates, Joseph refused. Annoyed by the secrecy, Hale would not allow the couple to live with him, but allotted them a two-room house on his farm. Joseph set to work deciphering the "gold Bible." He hoped that he could enlist an expert to help him with the translation, or at least to verify that he was reading the markings on the plates correctly. To this end, he asked Martin Harris, who came to visit the young couple in February 1828, to find a scholar who could confirm Joseph's own intuitive interpretation. He gave Harris a sheet of paper on which he had copied some of the "Caractors" from the golden plates.

Harris traveled to New York City and met with one of the leading classicists of the day, Professor Charles Anthon of Columbia University. Harris said that Anthon verified Smith's correct translation of the characters, affirming them to be a mix of Egyptian, Chaldaic, Assyriac, and Arabic. Anthon gave him a certificate testifying to the characters' authenticity, but then destroyed it when Harris revealed the dubious source of the inscription.

Anthon told another story. He had only given Harris a letter stating that the marks on the paper appeared to be just imitations of various alphabetical characters. He said he wanted to keep Harris from falling victim to a fraud.

On discovering that no learned man would help with the translation, Joseph Smith cited a prophecy from Isaiah. It said that a sealed book would be read by "him that is not learned." He continued to interpret the plates himself. Shunning the methods of scholars like Young and Champollion, he translated by inspiration. The meaning of the hieroglyphics came to him as a series of divine revelations. He spoke, Emma wrote down his words.

Martin Harris returned to Harmony in April. Joseph allowed him to take Emma's place as scribe. He hung a blanket across the room so that Harris could not see the plates, which were formed into a book by metal rings. Joseph dictated on one side, Harris scribbled furiously on the other.

By June, they had managed to record 116 manuscript pages of the translation. Harris kept entreating Joseph: If he could not see the actual plates, could he at least take the manuscript back to Palmyra to placate his wife? She was convinced her husband was the victim of a dangerous hoax. Relenting, Smith granted his patron's request.

Emma gave birth to their son Alvin on June 15, 1828. The infant died the same day. Soon afterward, the spirit Moroni took back the plates and the magical diamond spectacles. He was imposing a punishment on Joseph for giving Harris the manuscript. When Harris did not return, an anxious Smith hurried to his family's farm to search for his scribe. Called to the Smith home, Harris slouched through the door to relate a sad tale. Having promised to show the papers to only five family members, he had instead revealed the manuscript to practically any curious local who asked to see it. Then, somehow, it had gone missing.

It was a fierce blow that meant months of work wasted. With the plates now gone as well, the whole project seemed, like so many treasure hunts, to have come to naught. But like his parents, Joseph Smith Jr. had a deeply resilient character. The Lord admonished him in a revelation to repent his casualness. He was promised that the plates and the translation keys would be returned. He did not lose his faith.

Back in Harmony, the sacred materials restored, he continued the translation, Emma writing down his words. They worked all summer during breaks in their arduous farm chores. Joseph had returned to his familiar seer stone as a means of deciphering the plates. "I frequently wrote day after day, often sitting at the table close by him," Emma would remember, "he sitting with his face buried in his hat, with the stone in it and dictating hour after hour."

He needed no screen when working with her. He did not even look at the plates, which lay on the table "wrapped in a small linen table cloth." Yet the words flowed. Emma said the plates were like thick paper, and would "rustle with a metallic sound" when she touched their edges through the cloth.

By September the couple were practically destitute. Joseph went begging to his friend Joseph Knight. The older man gave him food, a pair of shoes, and three dollars. Bad news kept arriving from Palmyra. In the autumn of 1828, Joseph's siblings Sophronia and Samuel both suffered serious and expensive illnesses. Early in 1829, the Smiths' landlord decided he wanted to move his daughter into their home, the frame house that Alvin had built for his mother and father.

The Smiths, with their five younger children, were forced to move back to the two-room log cabin, now occupied by Hyrum and his wife. In spite of the cramped quarters, they took with them their boarder, a young man named Oliver Cowdery. Hyrum, who served on the district education committee, had hired Cowdery to teach at the local school.

Cowdery was a native of eastern Vermont; his family had followed the same well-beaten path to western New York as the Smiths. His mother was a distant relation of Lucy Smith, and Oliver had won the family's confidence. Hearing their stories of Joseph's renowned abilities, he wanted to learn more about the gold bible.

When Samuel finally recovered from his illness and talked of visiting his older brother, Cowdery asked to go along. They departed on foot at the end of March 1829, just after school was out for the year. Along the way, they stopped at the Whitmer farm in Fayette, thirty miles east of Palmyra. David Whitmer, a friend of Cowdery, shared his fascination with Smith's purported treasure. Cowdery told him he would tease out the truth of the matter and report back.

Trudging along muddy spring roads, the two young men covered another hundred miles before they reached Harmony. They arrived at Smith's modest farmhouse on April 5. Joseph said he was not surprised to see them. An angel had let him know that a scribe "should be forthcoming in a few days." The greeting impressed Cowdery. He and Joseph "sat down and conversed together till late." Cowdery was also a diviner, with a "gift of working with the rod." Joseph, his head teeming with visions and ideas, found it easy to confide in this man, who was a year younger and of similar background and interests.

Cowdery prayed, asking the Lord if the plates contained a genuine revelation. He was assured they did. Almost immediately, he and Joseph began one of the most remarkable literary collaborations in history. Between April 7 and the middle of June, they would together translate, at a rate of almost ten pages a day, a complex, multilayered historical and spiritual record that explained the peopling of America and unfolded details of God's plan for the salvation of mankind. The text would run to nearly six hundred pages in book form.

Joseph Knight, who occasionally brought Smith and his wife provisions, said that the young seer translated the plates by putting the Urim and Thummim into his hat and staring intently. A sentence "would apper in Brite Roman Letters," Joseph would dictate it to Cowdery, then the next sentence would manifest.

Cowdery tried and failed to do some of the translating himself. The Lord had explained the process to Joseph: "You must study it out in your mind, then you must ask me if it be right, and if it is right, I will cause that your bosom shall burn within you . . . but if it be not right, you shall have no such feelings." Cowdery never acquired the knack. There would be only one prophet.

Yet the two men served as catalysts for each other. It was a marvelous time. On May 15, they went down to the Susquehanna River and experienced joint visions of John the Baptist. They declared themselves members of a new priesthood. They baptized each other as elders in a church of their own invention. "We experienced great and glorious blessings," Smith remembered. "Our minds being now enlightened, we began to have the Scriptures laid open to our understanding."

"These days were never to be forgotten," Oliver Cowdery concurred. "To sit under the sound of a voice dictated by the *inspiration* of heaven." The two young men worked tirelessly, in a kind of rapture. Cowdery said, "Day after day I continued uninterrupted to write from his mouth, as he translated . . . the history or record, called 'The Book of Mormon.'"

TIME

God and time. The relationship between the Almighty and the dimension in which He causes His creation to unfold is a deep mystery. God lives outside of time, but all His miraculous manifestations occur within the world of growth and decay. The Bible makes time human. Generation succeeds generation, each one comprehensible in relation to the reader's own limited lifetime. The process continues for hundreds, then thousands of years. Abraham, Moses, Jesus, the march of the Lord's years for eighteen centuries down to the present—a vast span, but one a man can feel in his bones.

In 1830, the year after Joseph Smith finished his translation, the Scottish scientist Sir Charles Lyell published his book *Principles of Geology.* The volume challenged readers to apprehend spans of time far beyond what they had heretofore imagined. Christian observers had long tried to reconcile what they saw in the natural world with the stories found in Scripture. Most religious authorities calculated the age of the earth, on the basis of Biblical evidence, at around six thousand years. If that were true, the forces that had gouged enormous canyons or thrown up mountains must have been catastrophic beyond imagining, events like Noah's great flood. Late in the eighteenth century, as a scientific view of geology began to emerge, the evidence increasingly supported a different theory.

Drawing on the work of other scientists, Lyell rejected a static natural world shaped by sudden, divinely engineered events. Familiar processes that could be observed in human time—erosion, sedimentation, volcanic eruptions—had determined the earth's face. They had acted gradually, not over centuries or even millennia, but across eons of time far beyond man's intuition—millions, even billions of years.

Lyell, although a devout Christian himself, introduced ideas that were as challenging to the Christian view of the natural world as were his friend Charles Darwin's theories of biological evolution. Lyell saw himself as the man who rescued geology from dependence on Biblical authority. The clash between systematic observation and religious belief, which continues in our own day, was particularly contentious in the early nineteenth century.

The engineers who were hurrying to finish the Erie Canal had no reason to concern themselves with such controversies. But hints about nature's continual change contributed to their view that man could impose his own changes on the landscape. God had shaped the earth, so could men. Humans could finish the divine work, make God's world their own.

No one as yet had a clear idea that during distant eons western New York had sat at the bottom of an inland sea, or that the skeletons of calciferous creatures had formed into limestone, which now stretched in a long, stony escarpment, like a wrinkle in a giant's brow, between Lake Erie and Lake Ontario. Water flowing from Lake Erie tumbled over the precipice of this Niagara Escarpment in spectacular fashion at Niagara Falls, the cataract that had inspired Jesse Hawley's initial vision of the canal. The ridge continued many miles eastward before finally tapering to nothing.

The Lake Ontario plain north of this ridge offered a convenient pathway for a canal. After the ditch left Rochester heading west, workers did not have to construct a single lock for sixty miles. But sooner or later, in order to reach Lake Erie and tap its waters, engineers needed to find a way to take the ditch up the ragged, eighty-foot cliff to the south. As early as 1817, the canal commissioners had reported that climbing the escarpment was "one of the most serious difficulties presented on the whole route."

Surveyor James Geddes, when sketching a potential route in 1808, had chosen to make this leap at a gorge twenty miles northeast of Buffalo, where Eighteen Mile Creek, flowing over the cliff from the south, had already worn down its edge. The ravine there would make the climb easier, but only slightly. At least eight locks would be needed, Geddes calculated. The engineers took to calling the site the Mountain Ridge, so menacing did the cliff appear.

Planners had not yet determined exactly how the ascent would be accomplished. Adding to the difficulty was the fact that the edge of the cliff was almost twenty feet higher than the surface of Lake Erie. The land did not reach lake level until it had descended for seven miles to the south. Bringing the canal past this wide lip would present another massive engineering challenge.

As the canal construction moved westward, the commissioners asked the project's engineers for detailed proposals about how to overcome this final obstacle. The flight of locks required was unprecedented in America. The commissioners chose a design submitted by Nathan Roberts.

Like most of the other canal engineers, Roberts had received neither a college education nor any formal training in his profession. Born of Puritan stock on a New Jersey farm, he had begun teaching school at sixteen. He saved his meager salary and, as soon as classes were out, purchased a hundred-acre plot of land in the middle of Vermont. This set a pattern for Roberts, who alternated teaching with buying, selling, and trading land.

During his travels, Roberts met Ansel White, who lured him to teach at a frontier school near his home at Whitesboro, a town along the Mohawk River between Utica and Rome. White sent four of his own children to the school, including Lavinia, eleven, and Canvass, thirteen. Roberts picked up some extra income surveying what was still a frontier region. Years later, at the age of forty, Roberts was hired by fellow Mohawk Valley resident Benjamin Wright to work on the canal. Roberts honed his craft during Wright's 1816 survey. He worked with his onetime student Canvass White, and married White's sister Lavinia, now twenty-four.

Roberts arrived at his idea for overcoming the daunting Mountain Ridge, a nineteenth-century historian noted, "without consulting any one; with but little aid from published works on the subject of engineering." His ingenious plan envisioned five locks, each of which would lift or lower a boat twelve feet, rather than the eight feet typical of the other seventy-eight locks along the canal. He designed the locks one after another in a kind of stairway, each one opening into the next. Because of the unlimited supply of water flowing from Lake Erie, the water that drained out each time the system was used would never leave the upper level too low. In fact, the same source of water that supplied the canal also could run mills in the town that everyone knew was sure to grow up around the great engineering project. The village would be named Lockport, yet another inland "port" to join Spencerport, Brockport, Fairport, Gasport, and other nautical-minded towns along the waterway.

Locks operated slowly, as the water gently lifted or lowered the barge. Roberts knew that his flight of locks would add to the time and cost of shipping on the canal. He planned to minimize the delay by incorporating two sets of locks into his design. At all other changes in elevation, a single lock had to carry traffic in both directions. Passing Lockport, a boat headed east could drop down to the long level while a westbound one was lifted to the top of the escarpment. Roberts basked in the acceptance of his plan, but he knew that constructing a trench to connect the topmost lock with the waters of Lake Erie would be the more formidable challenge.

The building of the canal was the largest public works project undertaken in the United States to that point. In fact, it was larger than any industrial enterprise on the continent. It required the organization of a large workforce, twelve hundred men at Lockport alone. Men in the eastern cities who had jobs were not likely to relinquish them to travel to the wilderness, however attractive the twelve-dollars-a-month wage. Workers had to be enlisted from among the poor and the unemployed. New York City's notorious Five Points slum was a prime recruiting area.

The arrival of this large body of hired laborers in what had so recently been a frontier wilderness was a shock to inhabitants of western New York. The yeomen farmers who populated the area worked hard, but if successful they received sustenance, a small cash crop, and an increasingly valuable piece of property. The daunting labor that the canal workers performed did not offer wealth or security, only dependence. They sold their time and put themselves at the command of contractors and overseers.

These rough men brought a clash of cultures to the frontier towns where they worked. Canal construction was a mobile version of the factory. The shanties provided by the contractors, "more like

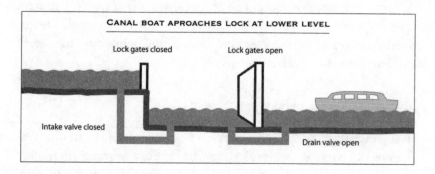

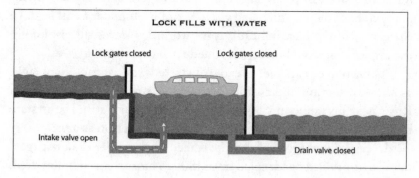

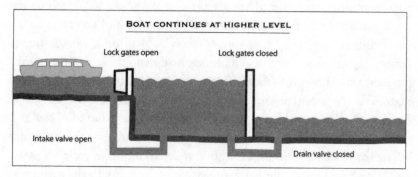

How a canal lock works   *by Joy Taylor*

dog-kennels than the habitations of men," resembled the slums that infected major cities. The squalor and violence unsettled established residents. The arrival of so many laborers accelerated the stratification of society. Working for wages, a contemporary essayist wrote, was "the very essence of slavery." It was in Lockport that the idea of a distinct working class found one of its earliest expressions. Laborers were different from permanent "citizens." A Presbyterian minister noted that "respect there is paid to *caste*, as if a man's rank in society was determined by dollars and cents."

MOST IMMINENT DANGER

In November 1822, Thurlow Weed became one of the first travelers to arrive in Rochester by canal boat. The construction project was still a work in progress. Weed had to disembark at the Irondequoit embankment, which had yet to prove itself under a full load. In the center of the bustling mill town, workmen were still fashioning the arches that would carry the aqueduct across the Genesee.

Twenty-five years old, Weed had started work at the age of eight as a tavern servant and a cabin boy on boats that plied the Hudson River near his home in Catskill, New York. After a stint in the state militia during the War of 1812, he found his vocation as a printer.

It was an exciting time for the trade. The number of newspapers in the country had quadrupled since 1800 to more than eight hundred, helped along by a similar proliferation of post offices. Novels, almanacs, pamphlets, tracts, and broadsides were being published to quench the expanding middle class's thirst for knowledge and entertainment.

Printers operated small shops, often publishing a weekly newspaper. Editors filled out local items with reprinted stories from other publications. The profession offered variety and travel: as a journeyman, Weed's peregrinations took him to New York City, where he developed a love of theater, and to Cooperstown, where he met and married Catherine Ostrander. A friend suggested that the booming village of Rochester might be a good place to look for opportunity.

Weed applied at the printing office of Everard Peck, who published the weekly *Rochester Telegraph*. Peck soon came to depend on Weed's energy and his incisive editorials. Weed got on well with the young and rising men of the city: lawyers, physicians, and merchants. He loved to talk and he loved to talk politics. He joined a "base-ball club" that included fifty members. They met every afternoon during the summer at Mumford's Meadow near the middle of town.

In 1824, Peck appointed Weed editor of the *Telegraph*. The paper supported John Quincy Adams in that year's election and favored the business-friendly principles of internal improvements and protective tariffs for which Adams stood. Weed's interest in politics paid off when he was hired by local merchants to travel to Albany and petition the state legislature to charter a bank for Rochester. Given a $300 expense account, Weed threw a $400 dinner for legislators and managed to secure the only charter issued that year. He loved the role of legislative solicitor, what we would now call a lobbyist.

Adams made it to the White House over Andrew Jackson. The Tennessee war hero racked up the most popular votes, but lost in the House of Representatives. Weed won his own election for the state assembly and took his seat in Albany in January 1825. He was as adroit at the game of politics as he was on the baseball diamond. He rewarded his friends and did favors for the influential. He traveled to Washington on behalf of New York lieutenant-governor James Tallmadge, who wanted a foreign diplomatic post in the new administration. Weed stood by at "a respectful distance" while President Adams took his daily nude plunge into the Potomac, but failed to secure the boon.

During 1825, Weed dared to taste one of the first tomatoes grown in Rochester—the fruit had long been thought poisonous. Although he was $250 in debt, he borrowed $2,500 to buy out Peck's interest in the newspaper. He gave up his Assembly seat and took another printer, Robert Martin, as his partner. With the finished canal now accelerating growth in town, the two men turned the paper into a daily.

The disappearance of William Morgan in September 1826 had all the elements of a newspaperman's dream: mystery, pathos, and the shadowy involvement of prominent men. Weed already knew the background of the story. For a time that summer, Morgan had lived next door to Weed while compiling his exposé. Weed's neighbor Russell Dyer had broached the possibility of his publishing Morgan's "revelation." Dyer insisted on secrecy, asserting that if the author's identity became known, it would be "at the peril of his life." Weed declined on the grounds that Martin, his new partner, was a Mason.

The influential Freemasons of western New York were not always subtle in applying pressure. Frederick Whittlesey, a young Rochester lawyer, was a friend and ball club mate of Weed's. He owned an interest in a rival newspaper. In November, after Morgan's abduction, he met with his minister, who was a knight templar in the local

Freemasons. If Whittlesey valued his reputation, the clergyman told him, he would ignore Morgan's disappearance. He was to understand that the Masons could easily ruin him, Whittlesey reported. Angered by the threat, he soon became a leader among the growing ranks of Anti-Masons.

During the first month of the controversy, Weed steered a middle course, expressing concern about Morgan's kidnapping but suggesting that abductors "must have been over-zealous members of the fraternity." He found that this moderate stance made no business sense. Both Masons and the swelling number of Anti-Masons were dissatisfied with the *Telegraph's* lukewarm coverage. He decided to choose a side in the growing imbroglio. He became an Anti-Mason.

Incensed citizens were organizing meetings up and down the canal district. Two weeks after Morgan's disappearance, a crowd in Batavia heard affidavits from persons involved, including Lucinda Morgan. The Canandaigua jailer's wife, who had released Morgan to his kidnappers, testified. Other eyewitnesses gave their accounts of the abduction. It was clear to all that Morgan had been kidnapped and that prominent Freemasons had been involved.

Across western New York, women took the lead in demanding action. In early November, "matron ladies" in Wheatland, halfway between Batavia and Canandaigua, declared that "the vultures of Masonry pounced on a defenceless man in the streets of Batavia." They sympathized with his wife, left with "the horrors of suspense and heart rending anticipation." The brotherhood, "though supported by High and Mighty names," should be suppressed, the Wheatland ladies declared. "Reason and religion equally demand its overthrow."

The Anti-Masonic phenomenon spread with stunning rapidity. Anti-Masons routinely exaggerated the threat from what was in fact a generally benign brotherhood. They labeled Masons "daring Banditti," who constituted a "most imminent danger." They were "a conspiracy more numerous and better organized for mischief, than any other," one of "monstrous power."

Anti-Masons were anxious that the still-fragile American experiment with republican government was drifting off its moorings. If Freemasons, who included justices of the peace, magistrates, and the governor himself, did not respect the rule of law; if they were bound by secret oaths; if they were unwilling to defend a principle as fundamental as freedom of the press; if an American citizen like Morgan could be apprehended, tried, and punished by secret courts outside the purview of elected officials; then how could citizens have confidence that they were living in a free society? If anyone doubted the Masons' perfidy, opponents need only point to the desolation of Morgan's wife and children.

Citizens at a public meeting in Batavia declared that the law itself had been used "for the purpose of giving an unholy sanction to the violence" against Morgan. They resolved to investigate and to lay the facts before their countrymen. A gathering at the town of Seneca, east of Canandaigua, asserted that "all secret associations are dangerous to freedom." Participants vowed not to vote for any Freemason for any public office.

In December 1826, three months after Morgan's abduction, Thurlow Weed joined a committee to raise funds to investigate the affair. If the state would not get to the bottom of the matter, citizens must. He also decided, perhaps under financial pressure, to sell his interest in the *Telegraph* to Martin. He elected to stay in Rochester and double down on his commitment to the cause. In early 1828, he found backers to start a new newspaper, the *Antimasonic Enquirer*. It would eventually be joined by 125 other Anti-Masonic papers.

Weed was genuinely concerned about the danger of Masonic power. But his penetrating political instinct allowed him to peer into the future and gauge the movement's long-range potential. Politics had entered the Morgan affair early. Governor DeWitt Clinton's proclamations following Morgan's disappearance had offered rewards of up to $2,000 to anyone bringing his abductors to justice. Clinton, like many Masons, was acutely embarrassed by the actions taken in the name of the brotherhood. He was one of Weed's heroes, but had lately allied himself with those backing Andrew Jackson. Jackson's faction would soon coalesce into the Democratic Party, while Weed's loyalty would veer toward the emerging Whigs.

State and national political alignments were passing through a muddled phase. Martin Van Buren and his supporters in the patronage empire that Weed had labeled the "Albany Regency," backed by members of Tammany Hall in New York City, held a majority bloc in the New York state capital. They too sided with Jackson. Looking ahead, Weed saw new political fault lines developing. Businessmen wanted internal improvements, strong banks, and protective tariffs. Populists and farmers favored limited spending, tight controls on the money interests, and low tariffs to hold down prices. To keep the Jackson–Van Buren party from dominating by sheer numbers, Weed needed to nourish a third faction. Anti-Masonry, he felt, held the key.

Meanwhile, the controversy spurred sales of Morgan's book to a gallop. An edition in Canada sold a hundred copies on the day it was issued. Whether any of the profits found their way to Lucinda Morgan is unknown. Anti-Masonic groups solicited funds to help her and her children.

The details of Morgan's abduction began to emerge from both official and informal investigations. The perpetrators had done little to cover their tracks. Following his kidnapping in Canandaigua on September 12, Morgan had been spirited in closed coaches to Rochester, then hurried west on the Ridge Road that stretched parallel to Lake Ontario north of the canal. The men had stopped at taverns along the way, finally reaching the town of Lewiston on the Niagara River. There, Eli Bruce, the sheriff of Niagara County and a Mason, had escorted Morgan down the river to the point where its waters poured into the lake at Fort Niagara. Masons imprisoned Morgan in the magazine of the disused fort. What happened to him after that, no one could—or was willing to—say. Month followed month with no sign of him.

In October 1827, thirteen months after the abduction, the case took a sudden turn. A man's decomposed body washed up on the rocky shore of Lake Ontario at Oak Orchard Creek, forty miles east of the fort. The coroner conducted an inquest, found that death was caused by drowning, and ordered the corpse buried near the lake.

But the coincidence was too great. When Weed heard about the find, he immediately set out for the spot. So did Lucinda Morgan and friends of the missing man from Batavia. So did many others. Was this the body of William Morgan?

BY THE HAND OF MORMON

Early in June 1829, Joseph Smith and his wife Emma, accompanied by Oliver Cowdery, left Harmony to return to the vicinity of the Erie Canal. They were brimming with excitement. The feverish translation of the gold plates was nearly complete. Hundreds of pages had accumulated in the past two months. Soon the entire revelation would exist in readable form for the first time in fourteen hundred years.

The Peter Whitmer family, eager to get in on the project, invited the Smiths and Cowdery to finish the book at their farm in Fayette near the northern tip of Seneca Lake. All that was left to translate was the account by Nephi, an early and crucial prophet of the Mormon revelation, of how his family had come to America from Jerusalem in 600 B.C.

The story had been included in the 116 pages that Martin Harris had lost a year earlier. In a revelation, God told Smith not to translate the plates again—doubters could point to minor discrepancies and cry hoax. Instead, he was to consult another section of the plates, which contained the same narrative in different words. In a strange warp of time, Nephi himself, all those years earlier, had been instructed by God to write his account twice—why, he did not know. Harris's carelessness had been foreseen.

Even as he worked on this final section, Smith applied for a copyright by submitting the title page to a federal court on June 11, 1829. He listed himself as "author and proprietor." He was required to claim authorship because copyright law afforded no protection to translators. In fact, he always insisted that the book was his transcription of the golden plates, not his own work. Future editions would refer to him only as translator. His family were adamant that Joseph did not dictate the book from his imagination. With barely any formal schooling, he simply did not have the grasp of literary technique required to write a long, complex narrative. The book was a true rendering of the plates into English.

The gold plates, Smith now knew, had been inscribed in the fourth century A.D. by the prophet Mormon and his son Moroni. They were a compilation of much older historical records and prophecies, which told a story heretofore unknown to the world. So far, Joseph Smith was the only man alive who had seen these marvelous artifacts. That knowledge, he said, made him feel "entirely alone." He wanted others to confirm the reality of the treasure he had found buried on Hill Cumorah.

On a warm summer day in July 1829, he told Cowdery it was time. They headed toward a wooded area of the Whitmer farm, taking Martin Harris with them. On the way, they picked up David Whitmer, who had been plowing a field. They walked in among the trees.

The four men prayed. Nothing happened. Harris, the man who did not want to be made a fool, had yet to put aside all his doubts. He was forty-six, the others in their early twenties. He suspected that his lack of faith was interfering. As much as he longed to see the plates, he offered to leave the others alone so they might have a chance. He walked farther into the forest.

Suddenly, an angel surrounded by an aura of blazing light appeared before the three younger men. In the midst of this light, Whitmer noted, a table materialized. Resting on it were the golden plates. He also saw the sword of Laban, the sparkling Excalibur that Nephi had used to kill his enemy. Beside it was a breastplate and Lehi's Liahona, a ball with spindles that had guided Nephi's father through the wilderness.

A voice out of the light flooded the grove: "I command you to bear record of what you now see and hear." Joseph had translated the plates correctly, the voice said. Cowdery later claimed, "I beheld with my eyes. And handled with my hands the gold plates from which it was translated. I also beheld the Interpreters."

When the vision faded, Joseph went to find the disappointed Harris. They prayed together. Then the older man also had his chance to see the plates. Ecstatic, Harris cried out, "'Tis enough; mine eyes have beheld." Later, Harris would hedge his account, affirming that he had seen them "with the eye of faith," but he never denied the reality of the experience. David Whitmer told an inquirer that "I saw them as plain as I see you now."

A few days later, Smith showed the plates to eight more witnesses. This was decidedly a family affair: four were David Whitmer's brothers, one his brother-in-law, Hiram Page. The remaining three were Smith's father and his own brothers Hyrum and Samuel. They saw the plates without the intervention of an angel. Afterward, Joseph told his mother, he felt "relieved of a burden." The witnesses, eleven in all, signed affidavits, which appeared in the first edition of the book. All testified to the plates' reality. "We beheld and saw the plates," the three said. The eight swore, "We did handle with our hands; and we also saw the engravings thereon."

The six-by-nine-inch plates were bound by three heavy metal rings. Altogether, the book weighed between forty and sixty pounds, Martin Harris estimated. All the witnesses agreed the plates had "the appearance of gold." Once the translation was complete, Joseph said, he returned the record to Moroni. Some said that Smith and Cowdery deposited the plates in a cave on Hill Cumorah, or perhaps another nearby hill. They have not been seen again.

Joseph was eager to publish his astounding book to the world. He first approached Egbert B. Grandin, who ran a Palmyra print shop and edited the local newspaper. Grandin, at twenty-three the same age as Joseph, was reluctant to take on the formidable project. The number of books to be printed was extraordinary. Smith wanted five thousand copies, all bound in leather. A few hundred copies would have been a more typical print run for the time. Grandin was also wary of the reaction of local people. He could imagine the type of retaliation now famously visited on David Miller, publisher of William Morgan's exposé of Freemasonry, three years earlier.

Aware that no printer would take the job on speculation, Joseph induced Martin Harris to mortgage part of his farm for three thousand dollars to cover the cost. Harris's wife, who saw her worst fears materializing, divorced him.

Smith next went to see Thurlow Weed, the Rochester printer and politician, who was planning to run for state assembly again, this time as an Anti-Mason. As Weed described it, he was approached by a "stout, round, smooth-faced young man." Smith described to him how he had found the "golden Bible" and how he wanted the text published. The young man read a chapter of the manuscript, which Weed found "so senseless that I thought the man either crazed or a very shallow imposter." He refused the job.

Eventually, Joseph convinced Grandin to change his mind. During the summer of 1829, the task began in Palmyra. Physical security was a concern. Grandin feared that his shop might be ransacked or his life threatened. Money-diggers still wanted the gold bible for their own. Orthodox clergy might try to block the publication. Joseph ordered Oliver Cowdery to copy his original manuscript and never to leave both copies at the print shop.

Cowdery took over management of the publication. The arduous duty of setting the type fell on John Gilbert, another printer, whom Grandin hired. It was Gilbert who had to supply all the punctuation for the book as he painstakingly set each letter in place to create a reverse image of the text. Cowdery checked proofs as the sets of pages came off the press. Once the work was under way, Joseph joined Emma at the Hale farm in Harmony.

A snag came in October 1829 when a man named Abner Cole, who hired Grandin's shop to print his own newspaper, *The Reflector*, began including excerpts of "Jo Smith's Gold Bible" in his paper. He ridiculed the revelation as humbug, the prophet as a "spindle shanked ignoramus." Joseph rushed back to Palmyra and confronted Cole, who wrote under the pseudonym *Obadiah Dogberry, Esq.*

"Do you want to fight, Sir," the forty-six-year-old Cole growled, removing his coat. Smith declined the offer of combat and calmly threatened the printer with the law, citing his copyright. Cole saw his point and the pirating ceased. Cole had entered history as the first critic of Mormonism. A year later, he would move to Rochester and turn his ridicule on the revivals of Charles Finney.

On March 26, 1830, Grandin published in his *Wayne Sentinel* a copy of the title page of *The Book of Mormon: An Account Written by the Hand of Mormon, Upon Plates Taken from the Plates of Nephi.* The notice advised that the work was "now for sale" at his shop.

Sales came slowly. Martin Harris and Joseph's brother Sam, going door to door around the region, sold few copies. Harris would soon have to dispose of 150 acres of his farm in order to satisfy the debt he had incurred to have the book printed.

But the mere existence of the book made Joseph Smith famous. Rochester newspapers picked up the story, then journals and weeklies in other cities. His notoriety spread across the country. "Blasphemy!" the papers howled. "Fanaticism!" A minister called it "the greatest fraud of our time in the field of religion." An editor declared that "it partakes largely of Salem Witchcraft-ism and Jemima Wilkinson-ism."

No matter. With the publication of the book, life for Joseph Smith accelerated. He had made himself into a full-fledged prophet and was already baptizing converts. In the weeks following the book's publication, he and his brothers Hyrum and Sam, along with

Oliver Cowdery and two of the Whitmer boys, declared themselves organizers of the new Church of Christ. Their first congregation included forty converts. A few years later, they would change the name to The Church of Jesus Christ of Latter-day Saints.

Mormonism had been born.

A BATTLEFIELD

The hydraulic machinery for Nathan Roberts's now famous flight of locks required a great deal of masonry and a complicated system of valves and channels to move the water. But the principles were known, and construction was simply a matter of converting the details into reality.

His other problem would be relatively simple but immensely difficult. If he stepped the locks to the very top of the escarpment, the canal would be about fourteen feet higher than the level of Lake Erie. He had to situate the top lock *below* the lip of the ridge, then carve a ditch southward at Erie level. At the peak of the escarpment, the bottom of the ditch would need to be thirty feet below ground level and would be passing through ultrahard dolomite limestone. The Deep Cut would continue for seven miles. Twenty miles to the west, the Niagara River had sliced a crevice of the same length through the same escarpment. That process of erosion had taken twelve thousand years. Roberts had only three years to meet the schedule set by the canal commissioners.

The Deep Cut, Roberts knew, would be impossible to construct with the tools workers had used to dig the canal: pickaxes and plows, shovels and wheelbarrows. The rock would have to be attacked with a form of concentrated energy, an explosive. He turned to gunpowder, what we know as black powder. Twenty years earlier, a French immigrant named Éleuthère Irénée du Pont had set up a gunpowder mill in Wilmington, Delaware. Du Pont mixed together saltpeter, sulfur, and charcoal to produce high-quality gunpowder on an industrial scale. The company offered a formulation designed specifically for blasting rock.

To fracture rock, Du Pont's powder had to be packed inside a narrow, closed hole. Drilling these holes using a steel rod and a sledgehammer was an arduous task—an inaccurate blow could smash the wrist of the man holding the drill. Drills worked well in coal mines, where the material to be penetrated was relatively soft. When workers tried them on hard rock, they found that the tip quickly flattened against the stone.

Roberts offered a one-hundred-dollar reward for a better tool. Experts in New York and Philadelphia tried and failed to find an improvement. A blacksmith from Buffalo named Botsford showed up in Lockport with his own idea. Judging by color, Botsford heated the steel red-hot before plunging it into a barrel of water. This changed the metal's crystalline structure, making it hard but subject to shattering. By heating it again and letting it cool slowly, he was able to retain the hardness but rid it of its brittleness. The process worked and was applied to all the drills used on the job.

Roberts had allocated the work for the cut to contractors in the usual way, assigning each a short section to excavate. But the effort was technically too demanding and progress too slow. This was the last obstacle to the canal's completion; cuts were already approaching from both east and west. Delays at Lockport threatened to interfere with the planned 1825 opening of the entire waterway.

In 1823, the canal commissioners admitted that the rock was "more difficult to remove, by blasting or otherwise, than was anticipated." They said that it had become "perfectly apparent that the work . . . would fail entirely if a new course was not adopted."

They decided that the state should take on the effort directly. The contractors were retained, but became state employees, assigned to implement orders from Roberts and his assistants rather than to act as independent agents.

Workers started at both ends of the cut. The farther they moved inward, the more difficult it became to clear the rubble. Roberts turned to another ad hoc invention, a horse crane invented by a local man named Orange H. Dibble. Wooden derricks with booms were constructed every seventy feet along the top of the excavation. Workers at the bottom dumped wheelbarrow loads of dirt and stone into baskets. Horses at the top worked treadmills to draw the half-ton load over the lip of the ditch. An operator swung the crane around and dumped the debris.

The blasting was what Lockport residents remembered most vividly. "The explosions (cannonading) were almost continuous during the day," one recalled. Another wrote that when a warning cry rang out, everyone "flew to a place of shelter." Then came the thud of a concussion and a hailstorm of small stones that were "anything but pleasant."

"One stone weighing eighteen pounds was thrown over our house and buried itself in the front yard," a doctor's wife remembered. A lawyer was seated in his Main Street office when a twenty-pound stone rolled through the front door and knocked the legs from his chair, leaving him seated on the floor "in a very dignified manner, and a surprised state of mind."

Local people took to protecting their cabins by leaning a protective wall of six-inch-thick logs against them to deflect flying debris. Pedestrians hearing a blast "would look upward so as to dodge any falling stones." Both workers and citizens were injured and killed by the rain of rocks. "The atmosphere," an observer noted, "was murky with the smoke of burning powder."

Disregard of danger was part of the culture of canal workers. Powder men went by jaunty names like "Hercules," "Bob the Blaster," and "Monster Manley." They made a point of handling the volatile material with insouciance. Other workers, warned of an impending blast, would simply hold their shovels over their heads to deflect the rain of stones.

Accidents involving powder were particularly gruesome. Sometimes, if a fuse burned slowly or went out, men unwisely approached to relight it. If exposed to the full force of the blast, a man could be blown to bits. Arms and legs were amputated. One resident noted that "on some days the list of killed and wounded would be almost like that of a battlefield."

The smoky struggle took much longer than anyone had predicted, but by 1825 the end was in sight. An observer who examined the Deep Cut marveled at "the rough perpendicular walls pierced in every part with drill-holes used for blasting the rock." He was astonished "at the perseverance, labor, and expense which it cost."

The cost was not just financial. The great project at Lockport held the first intimations that the nature of work in America was changing. Sam Patch had faced it firsthand in the factories of Pawtucket and Paterson. The same industrial principles governed the lives of Irish laborers at Lockport. During the 1820s, workers first began using the word *boss*. They were becoming alienated from their own labor.

New England intellectual and labor organizer Orestes Brownson saw wages as "a cunning devise" that allowed the employer to "retain all the advantages of the slave system, without the expense, trouble, and odium of being slave-holder."

If canal workers fell ill or conditions were unfavorable for work, they received no pay and their dependents were not cared for. An accident that left a man disabled also left him destitute. If wages were higher than in the cities, so were prices. Workers lived in squalor, contending with vermin and inclement weather, sleeping in makeshift hovels. One of the results of their marginal status was violence.

In 1821, a canal digger was beaten nearly to death by "freeborn Yankees as they are pleased to style themselves." On other occasions, the immigrant laborers "held the sober Yankees . . . in terrorism." The workers also fought among themselves. In Lockport, the Christmas Eve celebration of 1822 turned into a brawl. Men spilled from drinking establishments into the street. Citizens were alarmed—no city had a police force at the time. The workers "attempted to raze several buildings." Missiles flew, two men were killed and several seriously injured. One man ended the evening with a stone imbedded in his skull. It had to be "dug out with a jack-knife." Lockport, for a brief period, had become the definition of the Wild West.

The flight of locks was not quite finished in June 1825, when the town received its most famous visitor. Lafayette, one of the last living heroes of the Revolution, was making a grand tour of the nation he had helped to free from British control. He had sailed along Lake Erie by steamboat. Buffalo, which had been burned to the ground in the War of 1812, now had a new harbor and was about to be linked to the Atlantic Ocean. He was able to travel the canal as far as Black Rock, on the Niagara River. He detoured to make the obligatory stop at Niagara Falls before traveling to Lockport by carriage. Workers there filled hundreds of small holes along the Deep Cut with gunpowder and set them off simultaneously. This "extraordinary kind of artillery" delighted Lafayette, the more so when a spray of rock fragments "fell amidst the acclamations of the crowd." After a brief stay, the old warrior boarded a canal packet boat at the temporary terminal pool that marked the bottom of the flight of locks. He glided away on the long, smooth trip to Albany and beyond.

Three weeks after he left, workmen finished the stone framework of Roberts's flight of five locks. The great hydraulic lifting mechanism was, the commissioners bragged, "a work of the first magnitude on the line, and one of the greatest of the kind in the world."

Laborers worked feverishly all summer to prepare the locks and the Great Cut for operation. The long trench, with its walls of solid rock and the narrow towpath carved into its side, astounded all who encountered it. Workers had dug several wider basins along the way where boats could pass each other along the narrow channel. The Deep Cut, a tourist said, "staggers belief." She claimed that it "strikes the traveler with nearly the same awe and admiration he feels at the grandeur of the great falls." As Great Lakes water finally reached the top of the locks, Judge John Birdsall declared, "The last barrier is past! We have now risen to the level of lake Erie."

When the first boat mounted the finished locks, a passenger would describe it as an experience "calculated to bewilder the senses." Another said, "I was more astonished than I ever was by anything I had ever before witnessed." On visiting Lockport, Caroline Gilman, a noted children's book author and poet, marveled, "Here the great Erie Canal has defied nature, and used it like a toy; lock rises upon lock, and miles are cut in the solid stone."

After years of conjecture, years of doubt, and years of intense labor, the Erie Canal was ready to open.

MORGAN'S GHOST

On October 10, 1827, five days after the discovery of the mysterious corpse on Lake Ontario's rocky shore, the coroner reported it to be the body of a man of around fifty, five feet eight inches tall, with gray hair. Two teeth were missing and an unusual row of double teeth marked the front of the jaw. The dead man's frock coat pockets held four religious tracts, a scrap of paper with the words "September 24th, 1828, Mr. James Websa," and two plugs of tobacco. No identifying documents. Death had resulted from "suffocation by drowning."

Thurlow Weed was determined to investigate. If it was William Morgan, the discovery would be a sensational news item, the first solid evidence related to the disappearance in more than a year. With state and local elections looming, proof that Morgan had been murdered would boost the chances of candidates allied with the suddenly surging Anti-Masonic political movement.

Weed set off, accompanied by Dr. Ezra Strong, who had extracted two teeth from Morgan while Morgan was alive. He sent Russell Dyer, who knew Morgan well, to fetch anyone in Batavia who might shed light on the mystery, including Mrs. Morgan. Along the fifty-mile route to the site of the find, Weed spread the word. The case was now a national sensation, and a large crowd of the curious joined the procession.

The coroner exhumed the corpse. Before opening the crude coffin, he asked each potential witness separately to describe Mason's identifying features. Lucinda Morgan had saved and brought with her the two teeth that had been taken from her husband's mouth. She described a scar on his big toe, the result of a surgical operation.

The malodorous inquest was especially trying for her. With eighty people watching, she had to scrutinize a body that may have been that of the man she loved. Its time in the water and under the earth had left the corpse putrid and grotesque. The face was a mess. "No feature of it was distinguishable," Weed noted.

But the teeth fit, the scar was there, the hair, a smallpox inoculation mark, everything matched. Nine witnesses, including the man's partner David Miller, swore that it was Morgan. Lucinda had "no doubt but that this is the body of my husband." Only the clothes—the flannel shirt, coat, pants, and relatively new boots—did not match any that Morgan had owned, according to Lucinda.

The coroner declared the corpse to be the body of William Morgan. The great mystery had been solved.

But wait. Did it make sense that Morgan's body could have been drifting around Lake Ontario for a year and still be intact? Weed pointed out that a futile attempt in September to drag the mouth of the Niagara River must have dislodged the body from its weights and set it afloat. He organized a solemn procession to bring the corpse to Batavia. Thousands turned out for the funeral. "People left their busy occupations," a newspaper reported, "and in wagons, on horseback, and on foot, crowded to the village." Morgan was buried "amidst the tears of the widow, and the curses of the people."

Like Weed, candidates sympathetic to the Anti-Masonic cause saw the discovery of the body as a boon to their chances. Eulogizers spoke of "the majesty of the people," and the fact that "Morgan's ghost walks unavenged among us." Local Freemasons were not cowed. They denounced the parade and funeral as a mockery staged for political effect.

Enter stage right Mrs. Sarah Munro. She claimed that her husband, Timothy, had drowned in the Niagara River on September 26 or 27 of that year. The corpse could be his remains. She had traveled from her home in Canada to Batavia with her son and a friend of her husband. It was widely asserted that the Freemasons had paid her expenses.

Again, Masons and Anti-Masons gathered. Again the body was exhumed. The coroner had preserved the clothes taken from the corpse. Mrs. Munro described them perfectly, down to the different color yarn she had used to darn a sock and the buttons she had sewed onto the pantaloons to replace those lost. The timing fit. It was easier to believe that this was a corpse that had been in the water a few weeks rather than a year.

But not so fast. Timothy Munro had had a heavy black beard, but the corpse had none. Munro's hair was dark and short, that of the dead man long and chestnut. Munro was four inches shorter than the deceased. This raised what Weed called "the contradiction, if not the absurdity," that the clothes were Munro's, the body Morgan's. Or somebody else's.

More questions were raised than answered. How could the body have floated forty miles in only eleven or twelve days? Weather reports were checked: the wind had been from the east. As for the hair, accusations were now raised that the corpse had been shaved or the hair pulled out after the initial inquest. Fingers were pointed at Weed. And what to make of the comment that Weed had purportedly uttered referring to the corpse: "That is a good enough Morgan until after the election." He said he had been misunderstood. "My action in reference to the body in question," he demurred, "was influenced by a sincere and earnest desire for truth."

The coroner's jury was split. Relying on the exactness of Mrs. Munro's knowledge of the apparel, thirteen of the twenty-four jurors now affirmed the corpse to be that of Munro. Nine were unconvinced that it was either man. Two believed it to be Morgan. It was buried a third time under the name of Timothy Munro.

Just as the third inquest was winding up, a man named R. H. Hill came forward in Buffalo and confessed to the murder of William Morgan. The "stings of conscience" had prompted him to reveal his role in the crime, but he refused to name the others who had participated because of the "solemn and fearful oaths" that rule the Masonic brotherhood. A grand jury at Batavia listened to his evidence, declared him insane, and released him.

On October 5, Governor DeWitt Clinton, alarmed by the growing wrath of the citizenry, removed from office Eli Bruce, the sheriff of Niagara County. Called as a witness, Bruce had refused to testify to avoid self-incrimination. Clinton was persuaded that Bruce was a participant in the abduction.

As voters went to the polls in the autumn of 1827, Weed drove home his message, handing out Anti-Masonic ballots and proclaiming, "There is no blood on these tickets, gentlemen." To the surprise of everyone, voters in western New York sent seventeen avowed Anti-Masonic legislators to Albany. In March 1828, citizens from around western New York met in Le Roy for the first convention of the new Anti-Masonic Party. If the frontier politicians were looking for a fight, they had come together at the right time. The presidential election that year was destined to be the most extravagent mudslinging contest in American history.

The Anti-Masonic Party would add something new to American politics. The major parties, Andrew Jackson's Democrats and John Quincy Adams's National Republicans, dominated. The Anti-Masons were the nation's original third party, focused on one issue, pulsing with grassroots energy. The passions of the people, the Anti-Masons held, should be the rudder that steered the ship of state. "Public opinion is the law of this land," Frederick Whittlesey said at a party convention 1828. Anti-Masons made the most of their populist roots. They attracted support from those unsettled by the rising economic inequality. They led protests against absentee landlords and high rents. They campaigned against imprisonment for debt.

Anti-Mason zealots also brought religion into politics. Their cause was a crusade. "This Institution," they declared of Freemasonry, "strikes at the basis of all morality and religion." One campaigner labeled the Masonic brotherhood "an engine of Satan." It was, he said, "dark, unfruitful, selfish, demoralizing, blasphemous, murderous, anti-republican and anti-Christian."

Anti-Masons did not simply oppose Freemasons, they wanted to convert them. Newspapers listed the names of those who had left the order, some of whom became fervent Anti-Masons. With their knack for organizing popular enthusiasm and their embrace of moral certainty, Anti-Masons established a template for a parade of causes that would march through the 1830s, including temperance, Sabbath observance, opposition to slavery, and support for the rights of women.

As the election of 1828 loomed, the knives came out. Andrew Jackson had lived with his beloved wife, Rachel, for several years before she could obtain a divorce from her first husband. Such casualness was common on the frontier, but did not sit well with the new age of moral prudery. An Adams paper resurrected the story for the election. Jackson was livid, and his supporters returned fire, accusing Adams of having procured an American girl for the tsar when he was minister to Russia. They attacked the president's Unitarian religious affiliation, suggesting he was a closet atheist. Adams men dug deeper into the mud, even accusing Jackson's mother of prostitution.

Anti-Masons shared Jackson's regard for the authority of the masses and his antipathy to privilege; they were put off by his Freemasonry and his opposition to internal improvements—they were witnessing the benefits of canal-building firsthand. Thurlow Weed tried to steer them into the Adams camp, but there would be no second term for John Quincy Adams. The people spoke, and Jackson became the nation's seventh president.

The investigation of William Morgan's disappearance had kept the controversy about Freemasonry on a rolling boil in western New York. Twenty grand juries were empaneled in five counties. Some Masons paid a twenty-five-dollar fine for refusing to testify and were let go. The term "stone-walling" was invented to describe their obstruction. Fifty-four Masons were indicted for some connection to the Morgan affair, thirty-nine came to trial, but only ten were convicted.

Loton Lawson and Nicholas Chesebro, who had abducted Morgan in Canandaigua, denied knowing what became of the apostate after they passed him on to others of the brotherhood. Kidnapping was at the time only a misdemeanor in New York. Lawson received two years in the county jail, Chesebro one year. Another trial convicted the men who had kidnapped David Miller. All spent a year or less in the lockup. The sentences set off howls of protest among Anti-Masons.

Sheriff Eli Bruce at first escaped charges. After Clinton removed him from office, he was convicted of participating in the abduction and sat grimly behind bars for twenty-eight months. He came out a broken man and died two years later. Masons declared him a martyr to their cause.

In early 1828, several of the conspirators were sentenced by Judge Enos T. Throop. He acknowledged that a "strong feeling of virtuous indignation" among the people was what had brought the perpetrators to justice. He called it a "blessed spirit," a term the Anti-Masons took to heart. With the guidance of Thurlow Weed, now editor of the Anti-Masonic *Albany Evening Journal*, the movement continued to grow.

If Anti-Masons were charged with fanaticism, their leaders, many of them veterans of the Christian revivals, declared that "excitement is not fanaticism." Not when you were absolutely sure of your cause. "What great moral benefit, let me ask, was ever conferred upon mankind which was not produced by *excitement?*" a speaker at an Anti-Masonic convention said. "How was the Christian religion itself propagated but by *excitement?*"

STORY

The question of how the Western Hemisphere came to be populated was one that intrigued thinkers of the nineteenth century. Lacking hard evidence, they had to build their theories on the sand of speculation. A common idea was that the indigenous people had descended from the lost tribes of Israel. Following the Assyrians' conquest of the Israelites in 722 B.C., ten of the tribes, all but those of Judah and Benjamin, were lost to history. Whether they were exiled to wander the world or merely ceased to exist as distinct groups is not known. If it could be shown that they had reached America, two separate mysteries would be solved.

Religion has its roots in storytelling. The *Book of Mormon* explained the peopling of America in detail and gave the experience of the continent's early inhabitants a meaning that made sense to the generation of the 1830s and beyond. The book's core was a long and intriguing narrative. The writing was layered with flashbacks and flashbacks within flashbacks. Like the Bible, it also contained sermons and visions, prophecy and poetry.

According to the book, Lehi was a descendant of Manasseh, a leader of one of the lost tribes. In roughly 600 B.C. God warned him of the coming destruction of Jerusalem and told him to flee the city with his family. The Lord declared that He would lead Lehi's people to a promised land. They wandered across the Arabian desert, reached the Red Sea, built ships, and departed. They crossed the Indian and Pacific Oceans and reached the Western Hemisphere.

The families of Lehi's sons Laman and Nephi divided into two factions. Over the centuries, the Lamanites were given to idolatry, the Nephites to faithfulness, although the groups sometimes switched roles. The more numerous Lamanites waged almost continuous war on the Nephites. At one point the Nephites encountered and subsumed another group of Jewish exiles, the Mulekites.

After Jesus was crucified, he appeared in resurrected form to the New World inhabitants and established a church among them. Two centuries of peace ensued, but eventually both sides lost touch with Christ. The factions went at each other again. In A.D. 385, a battle near Hill Cumorah in what would later be western New York took the lives of more than two hundred thousand Nephites, leaving only twenty-four alive, including the last Nephite prophets, Mormon and his son Moroni. They had amassed a record of the thousand-year journey of their people. Much of it was a summary of events recorded by earlier prophets on metal plates. Moroni inscribed his testament onto his own plates and buried them on the hill. With the Nephites gone, the Lamanites evolved into American Indians.

Although Moroni's narrative stopped in A.D. 400, the saga was starting up again in the 1820s. The prophets in the *Book of Mormon* had foreseen that great revelations would come forth from a "choice seer" named Joseph. Now all would be fulfilled, including the gathering of believers, the establishment of the true Church, and the preparations for the imminent return of Jesus. These, indeed, were the latter days.

The stories in the fifteen books that made up the *Book of Mormon* were told by a variety of narrators. Some were transcriptions from ancient writers like Nephi or his brother Jacob. Some had multiple authors. Some were the direct writings of Mormon and Moroni. Some were Mormon's abridgements of earlier records. The book of Ether was passed on by Moroni from the records of the Jaredites, who had traveled to America two millennia before Lehi, around 3000 B.C., and who had also succumbed to internecine warfare.

Mormon's book is the very definition of an epic. It embraces vast stretches of time, is peopled by more than three hundred named characters, and relates family sagas, century-long rivalries, monumental battles, catastrophes, prophecies, transformations, crimes, betrayals, quests, and a steady stream of divine revelations. It tells how a single family, without riches, position, or glory, could change history.

Its language is reminiscent of the King James Version of the Bible, which itself combined the English of 1611 with the style of William Tyndale's 1525 translation. The King James Bible reflects its translators' attempts to convey the flavor and word order of the original Hebrew and Greek texts. Joseph Smith employed the scriptural language with which he was familiar to render the "reformed Egyptian" in which his golden book was recorded.

Skeptics quickly pointed out the book's historical inaccuracies. Horses, cattle, wheat, and honeybees are mentioned, yet all were brought to the New World by Europeans after Columbus. Nephites quote the New Testament directly, but they had left the Middle East centuries before it was written. Israelites fight with steel weapons and use compasses, neither of which existed in the ancient world.

Literalists on both sides have fought over the book's fanciful elements and its archeological foundation. What mattered in Joseph Smith's time was the very existence of a modern divine revelation. A prophet had produced a book, the book established the prophet's authority. The Almighty was speaking directly to men after a 1,500-year silence since the days of the early Christian Church. That was the big news.

Was it true? The truth of the *Book of Mormon* was not to be found in the book itself. In the same way that the translation was revealed to Joseph, the book's authenticity would be revealed to each reader: in his or her own heart. Converts were instructed not to try to comprehend its mysteries with their inadequate understanding. They should ask God if it was true. That was always Smith's answer to skeptics. Search your heart. Ask God.

Mark Twain famously labeled the *Book of Mormon* "chloroform in print." It was, he said, "an insipid mess of inspiration," very "tiresome to read." The nineteenth century was the era of the nine-hundred-page novel and of speeches and sermons that could go on for three hours and more. A man who knew Joseph Smith in Palmyra said, "He could never tell a common occurrence in his daily life without embellishing the story with his imagination." Where the King James Bible could be brilliantly succinct, Mormon scripture was wordy, padded with repetition and with empty constructions like *I say unto you; verily, verily;* and *it came to pass.*

The *Book of Mormon* emphasized that America was a promised land preserved for a chosen people. The New World was the site of the Garden of Eden. Smith eventually identified a valley in Missouri, which he called Adam-ondi-Ahman, as the very place where Adam and Eve had eaten of the forbidden fruit. Nearby, he planned to found his new Jerusalem, his Zion.

Readers of the book were warned of the dire consequences for any people who turn away from God. Again and again, unfaithful nations were chastised. To see the effect firsthand, one need only look at the remnants of the Indian tribes, the erstwhile Lamanites. Their dark skin and lack of civilization were their degrading punishment for unfaithfulness. Only by widespread repentance could a nation be saved. And what nation needed saving more than the chaotic, sin-ridden, blasphemous America of 1830?

The text included or reflected on many other themes relevant to the time. One minister said it weighed in on "infant baptism, ordination, the trinity, regeneration, repentance, justification, the fall of man, the atonement, transubstantiation, fasting, penance, church government." The Anti-Masonic fever then burning through western New York was alluded to repeatedly. The book was said to make an effort to treat "every error and almost every truth discussed in N. York for the last ten years."

Yet who could ignore this vast, awkward, monumental work of religious literature? Who could fail to marvel that a ditch-digging, barely educated, twenty-four-year-old farm boy had woven this fabulous word tapestry? He had tapped into a miraculous source of inspiration and had transcribed the whole thing without making a single revision. It was an achievement for the ages.

AWAKE

66 **I**t was a young city," Charles Grandison Finney said of Rochester, "full of thrift and enterprise, and full of sin."

Just past dawn on September, 15, 1830, Finney floated up the Erie Canal into this venal settlement. Somber forest gave way with breathtaking suddenness to a dense conglomeration of frame houses. The air was rich with the yeasty aroma of brewing, the smell of sawdust, and the rank odors of draft animals. The din of twenty-one flour mills assaulted Finney's ears. Looking up the river to his right, he could see the spot where Sam Patch had leapt over the Genesee Falls the previous November.

So quickly had Rochester grown that Hamlet Scrantom, its first permanent resident, still raised chickens on his State Street homestead even as paved sidewalks and office buildings crowded around him. The artist Thomas Cole judged Rochester "one of the wonders of the world," a city that "has risen in the midst of a wilderness almost with the rapidity of thought."

The city was a microcosm of America in a time of optimism and opportunity, of suspicion and rancor, of scrambling, grabbing, and greedy hurry. It boasted eleven churches, seven newspapers, hotels, libraries, a museum, and a glass-ceilinged business arcade. Three quarters of its ten thousand residents were under thirty.

Rochesterians defied piety. Lottery kiosks, which offered the promise of a splendid fortune to the lucky, made a mockery of Providence. Canal boatmen brawled along the wharfs. At the city's theater, "a noisome sink of immorality," strolling entertainers, ropedancers, pugilists, and hurdy-gurdy men entertained crowds of rowdies.

But Rochester was already developing a more staid element: mill owners, successful artisans, lawyers, physicians, bankers. All puckered their lips in distaste at the shenanigans of the lower classes. Respectability was their creed. Social order. Prayerful adherence to religion. They had little patience with those who rejected the cant of domesticity, who failed to show up for work after a weekend drunk, or who brazenly defied their betters.

The Erie Canal was the source of the city's enterprise, its phenomenal growth, and its sin. Millers had shipped ten thousand barrels of flour from the city the week the canal opened in 1825. Rochester had quickly become the greatest flour producer in the world.

The waterway had brought the atmosphere of a port to this inland town. Canal boatmen, footloose boys who served as mule drivers, wandering adventurers, prostitutes, swindlers, impostors, and cardsharps, all crowded the dramshops, gambling dens, and boardinghouses along the banks of the ditch. They were part of the most mobile generation in the nation's history. A steady stream of newcomers replaced those who decided to venture farther west. Seedy former canal diggers, mostly Irish, crowded into the slum neighborhood known as Dublin.

The moral license of the town went beyond what its respectable citizens could tolerate. The stiff-necked city fathers, fearful that their community was sinking into permanent debauchery, had called in the greatest evangelist of the day to put the city's moral house in order.

Although only thirty-eight, Finney had adopted the "dignity and majesty of one of the old prophets." He doted on his children. Helen, now almost three, could just peep over the gunwales of the canal boat. Charles Jr. was still in the arms of Finney's wife, Lydia.

Finney was determined to use his growing celebrity to accomplish God's work. It did little good to light a small fire of enthusiasm in a single church. Only a massive bonfire that set a whole city ablaze, that singed believers and nonbelievers alike, would accomplish his goal.

Winter was the ideal time for a revival. By December the canal would be shut down and drained. No way had been found to keep it free of ice, and the ditch needed yearly maintenance to repair leaks.

Farmers would have completed their harvests. A snowbound Rochester would become Finney's workshop.

His timing was perfect. Sinfulness had enjoyed a jubilee of sorts a year earlier when Sam Patch jumped over the falls. The young man had lost control of his erect posture halfway down. Waking into a nightmare, he panicked. His arms flailed. He tipped sideways. Some spectators covered their eyes. The True Sam Patch slammed into the river.

"When the bubbling water closed over him," wrote Thurlow Weed, who had witnessed the spectacle, "the almost breathless silence and suspense of the multitude for several minutes was indescribably impressive and painful." No one moved or spoke. Then, finally, "it became too apparent that poor Sam had jumped from life into eternity."

Soon afterward, Josiah Bissell, a leader of Rochester's respectable class, rose in the Third Presbyterian Sabbath School and warned that anyone who had "encouraged that soul to leap into eternity" would be held accountable on Judgment Day.

Eternity. The echoing word sounded an ominous note. A drunk and a sinner, Patch had lost his only chance for salvation. His soul was condemned to everlasting torment. Each spectator who had watched him perish bore a portion of the blame. Patch's death was the last straw. Bissell, in consultation with the pious citizens of Rochester, had begged Charles Finney to mount a revival.

Now local ministers were greeting the great evangelist as he stepped off the canal boat. Finney's blue eyes surveyed the curious, hard-faced mechanics, the merchants intent on the work of Mammon, the smirking jokers, the tipsy idlers. He had, he was sure, come to the right town. "Rochester was the place," he later asserted, "to which the Lord would have me go."

TELL IT TO THE WORLD

What do you do when you find out that the world will end within the lifetime of most people on earth? The knowledge left William Miller, the Low Hampton farmer, deeply conflicted. He immediately felt "the duty to publish this doctrine that the world might believe and get ready."

Yet he did nothing, alerted no one. At first, he blamed his failure on doubts. As he read the Bible, "texts would occur to me, which seemed to weigh against my conclusions." Speaking of the time heaven and earth would pass away, Jesus had said, "of that day and hour knoweth no man." Miller had faith in his intricate calculations, but should he presume to *know*?

Nor was he the type to draw attention to himself. "I told the Lord I was not used to public speaking," he wrote, "that I had not the necessary qualifications." Miller was a shy, simple man, not a preacher or an orator. "I was very diffident and feared to go before the world."

What was more, he had responsibilities. His wife and eight children, along with his mother, his sister, his brother's family, and a number of farm laborers, were all part of his extended household. He owned three farms around Low Hampton and was looked on as a man of stature, a war hero. He was an important figure in the Baptist church. He had enjoyed a very public role as a school trustee, town supervisor, and justice of the peace.

Why put his hard-earned reputation on the line? Why risk being labeled a fanatic? During the late 1820s, he saw how much animosity religious and political controversy could generate. The Anti-Masonic fervor resulting from William Morgan's disappearance was tearing churches apart. Six Baptist congregations in eastern New York had split from the local confederation over the issue, barring all Freemasons from fellowship.

Miller was himself a Mason. The brotherhood's enlightened rationality appealed to him. He had risen to become a Grand Master. But more and more evangelical Christians had turned against the Masons as reprobates. Miller reluctantly decided that he must resign from the order. He did so, he said, to avoid "any practice that may be incompatible with the Word of God."

As years passed and he kept his awful secret locked in his heart, Miller told himself that someone else would surely raise the alarm. He hoped that the Bible's prophecy, so clear to him, would inspire some established minister to speak out. He sent one clergyman "a few Evidences of the time of the 2nd coming of Christ," hoping he would take up the message.

Many preachers did cite the end times. They raised the specter of destruction mentioned in the Bible in order to spur their listeners to greater piety. But they generally did not point to a specific date.

Miller "began to speak more clearly my opinions to my neighbors, to ministers, and others." He was dismayed by their reaction. "To my astonishment, I found very few who listened with any interest."

He had acquired, he said, "no little celebrity" locally as a man with unusual and striking views about the end of time. In 1831, Miller was approaching his fiftieth birthday, no longer a young man. Time was short. Thirteen years had passed since he had learned of the imminent end of the world. In twelve more, the awful event would descend on an unsuspecting human race. One Saturday afternoon, he felt a sudden urgency. A voice told him to raise the warning, the midnight cry.

Still he hesitated. He vowed to God that he would preach the awful truth, but only if someone invited him to. That same day, his nephew arrived at Miller's farm. Miller's sister lived in the tiny hamlet of Dresden, New York, sixteen miles away on Lake Champlain. The Baptist church there lacked a regular minister and the faithful were interested in Miller's ideas about the millennium. They wanted him to preach to them. He honored his vow and went.

The next Sunday morning, he mounted the pulpit and talked for the first time in public about the coming last days. The isolated Baptists found the notion fascinating. They induced him to stay for a week, as he explained in detail his celestial arithmetic. He returned again and again, for a year serving as the lay leader of the small congregation. He baptized twenty new members.

Now, finally, Miller was determined. He would continue to heed the inner voice that had so long whispered to him: "Go and tell it to the world!"

LATTER DAYS

The crucial nucleus of Joseph Smith's new faith was his own family. "We are a visionary house," his brother Hyrum had told a visitor. When, soon after the formation of his new Church, Joseph witnessed the baptism of his father in a stream near the cabin, he cried, "I have lived to see my father baptized into the true church of

Jesus Christ." He broke into an ecstasy of sobbing. He was "the most wrot upon that I ever saw any man," Joseph Knight said.

The Smiths had long been accustomed to the curled lip and averted glance. But now they had arrived. The success of the Church had vindicated them. Joseph had found them a path to greatness. His family's loyalty was clannish and unwavering. Confidence was swelling in Joseph's own breast. "Criticism," an admirer noted, "even by associates, was rarely acceptable, and contradiction would rouse in him the lion at once."

The Church Joseph invented shared much with the sects he had long scorned. Like Methodists, Mormons believed that salvation was open to all. Like Baptists, they practiced adult baptism by immersion. Like the Shakers, they were open to Pentecostal powers—visions, healings, speaking in tongues—and encouraged believers to gather together, separating themselves from the larger society. Like many evangelical sects, they expected the literal return of Christ and the establishment of his kingdom on earth.

After formally organizing the Church in April 1830, Joseph returned to his home in Harmony. His family, the Whitmers, his financial backer Martin Harris, and a few others formed the core of his followers along the canal. The Knight family and Josiah Stowell were among the cadre of believers in the Pennsylvania border region. These outposts were the seeds of a church that was intended to restore the earliest Christian faith. The members were Latter Day Saints. Some called them Mormonites—they would later be known simply as Mormons.

Joseph hurried back and forth between the two groups of believers. Unlike Charles Finney and other masters of the pulpit, Joseph was not a fluent sermonizer. He was to be "a seer, a translator, a prophet, an apostle of Jesus Christ." His church pivoted on the fact that God was speaking to his people *now*. Revelations vital to these latter days were issuing from Joseph's mouth.

In June, he held his Church's first conference back at the Whitmer farm in Fayette. Thirty members gathered to kick off the new religion. Joseph Smith Sr. was licensed as a priest, Joseph Jr. and Oliver Cowdery were made first and second elders.

A few weeks later, back at the Knight farm, Joseph and Emma, accompanied by Cowdery and two of the Whitmer boys, dammed a stream to form a baptism pool. The next morning they found it smashed by vandals. Trouble was brewing. They rebuilt the dam and Cowdery baptized Emma, Joseph Knight, and Knight's wife, Polly, along with eleven friends of the Knight family. The ceremony was barely over when fifty men, "raging with anger" at what they considered blasphemous services, surrounded Knight's farmhouse.

A local doctor named A. W. Benton brought charges against Joseph Smith Jr. Constable Ebenezer Hatch arrested the prophet and transported him to a court in South Bainbridge. A mob followed. Hatch grew apprehensive that Joseph would be taken from him and lynched. He had been won over by the young man's sincerity and regretted his role in the case. He guarded his prisoner at a tavern by sleeping with his feet against the door and a loaded musket by his side.

Joseph said the trial had to do with his "setting the country in an uproar by preaching the Book of Mormon." Others claimed it was about his pretending to see underground. Josiah Stowell, the farmer who had hired him five years earlier to find a silver mine, was called as a witness. Dr. Benton said the trial was to "check the progress of delusion." The judge in the case returned an acquittal.

Smith was immediately rearrested and carried fifteen miles south to stand trial in Broome County. Witnesses in this case followed each other until two in the morning. Joseph was again acquitted. He snuck out the back door to avoid danger. He and Cowdery escaped by night, fearful of pursuit.

In spite of the persecution, the Church was taking off. Joseph moved to solidify his power. The first person he subdued was the one who knew the most about him, his wife Emma. In July, he had a revelation from God that addressed her directly. "Let thy soul delight in thy husband and the glory which shall come upon him," the Lord said. "Murmur not." If she worried about his ability to provide for his family, she must "lay aside the things of this world, and seek for the things of a better." As consolation, God named her "an elect lady," who was to create a selection of hymns for the Church.

Bumps in the road were unavoidable. One convert left in disgust when his name was misspelled in a revelation. A mission to Canada to try to sell the copyright to the *Book of Mormon* in order to raise money for the Church, prompted by a direct order from God, failed.

Oliver Cowdery wanted his share of the glory. From the Whitmer farm, he wrote to Smith in Harmony objecting to one of the prophet's revelations. Joseph wrote back to demand "by what authority" Cowdery commanded him to "alter or erase, to add to or diminish" any revelation from God? In September Smith journeyed to Fayette to confront Cowdery and the Whitmers, who had joined in questioning him.

Joseph's divine revelations, as much as the *Book of Mormon*, were the bedrock of the growing movement. Some of these revelations occurred quite casually. Joseph decided matters in church council meetings by issuing sudden edicts from God. Some he wrote down, most he dictated. A witness who watched him receive one saw "his countenance change [and] he stood mute . . . there was a search light within him, over every part of his body. I never saw anything like it on earth." Smith himself said the process was "light bursting upon the world."

After disciplining Cowdery and the Whitmers, he faced down Hiram Page, the Whitmers' brother-in-law. Page had announced his own revelations, which he said were given authority because he had achieved them by means of a seer stone. At the next quarterly conference of the Church, Smith established his dominance as prophet. "Brother Joseph Smith Jr. was appointed by the voice of the Conference to receive and write Revelations and Commandments for this Church."

Now firmly in control, Joseph was on the verge of his most consequential revelation yet. The Latter Day Saints were about to move toward their destiny.

ALL ROCHESTER

The black evening air that drapes the church glitters with snowflakes. Congregants nod to acquaintances as they enter the sanctuary. The candles and oil lamps emit a nervous, ghostly light. Shadows dance in the church's corners and ascend to the gloomy ceiling. The pews are packed, the smell of wet wool pervades.

Everyone is alive with excited expectancy. They are accustomed to a calm and decorous church experience. Tonight the atmosphere is unfamiliar. The air crackles with electric tension. The alert congregation frets. The prayers have a secret listener, the hymns a new meaning. The whole gathering seems aimed toward a grave and ominous purpose. Anticipation mounts.

A rustle of excitement shoots through the dark cavern. A man walks in from the wings and mounts the pulpit. The renowned Charles Grandison Finney is tall and slender, dressed in an ordinary gray suit rather than in clergyman's black. He exudes a majestic confidence. Those who expected either a studious ecclesiastic or a wild man are disappointed. Energetic, somber, he grips the sides of the lectern and looks out at the congregation. The craggy dome of his forehead, the gaunt face, the patrician nose, all testify to his authority. His eyes, frightening in their intensity, stare silently, roaming the faces, as if taking the measure of each person's soul.

"If ye will hear his voice," Finney intones, "harden not your hearts." A long pause. He cites the source of the verse: Hebrews, chapter 3. Speaking without notes, he begins his sermon. It is not the expected hellfire. He does not harangue. He defines his terms, builds his argument. What is the heart? It is a man's will. Why do sinners harden their hearts? Prejudices. Habits. Erroneous beliefs.

He uses logic like a knife to stab the resistant minds of sinners, to lacerate those unwilling to throw themselves on the mercy of the Almighty. He does not need hysterics. He speaks like a lawyer, appealing irresistibly to the mind and the reason of each hearer.

Why do you harden your heart? he demands. Is it procrastination? You will follow Jesus, but not now? You have more important things to attend to? Or is it because you will have to lead an upright life if you become a Christian? You fear what will be required of you? You fear to be humble, to mend your ways?

His pace increases.

One time, you have one reason, at another, another; and you have, in fact, as many reasons as occasions.

He claps his hands.

Your excuses come up whenever you are pressed immediately to surrender your heart to God. I ask you if you do not know that it is true, as well as you know that you exist?

He throws words with grand gestures that make congregants duck. His voice thunders, then drops to a whisper. He paints heaven and hell in vivid colors. He makes listeners hold their breath.

The veriest sinner in the world will make some excuse for what he is doing. It is remarkable to see how a man will evade conviction.

The future feminist leader Elizabeth Cady Stanton remembered him describing sinners plunging "into the burning depths of liquid fire." *There*, he demanded, *do you not see them!* So vivid was his imagery that young Elizabeth jumped up to look where he pointed.

God never forces you against your will. If he cannot gain your own consent to be saved in his own way, he cannot possibly save you at all.

Each person feels the sting of his *you*. He is not accusing but questioning, not condemning, but pleading. Jesus is going to give his life for you. Right now, tonight.

The evangelist makes each person see the need to let go. If you can relax your grip on yourself, God will do the rest. The Lord will receive you into his bosom.

All your merciful saviour asks is for you to remember his struggle, his agony, and his death. Will you obey? Why do you turn your back upon him? Would you not rather say, This night, Lord, I give thee a solemn pledge that, by thy grace, I will remember thee always! Always!

Finney keenly remembers his own embarrassment when, as a young lawyer, he endured his spiritual crisis. He understands the importance of making a physical commitment. He needs to include "some measure that would bring sinners to a stand." It is as simple as that. Stand up.

Stand up and walk forward and acknowledge that you are a sinner in need of God's loving grace. Don't be ashamed. Don't be proud. Come forward now.

He sets aside pews at the front for those whose minds are torn between sin and redemption, between the old life of selfishness and the new life in Christ. If a sinner removes himself to this "anxious bench," it is an invitation for the whole congregation to pray for his or her conversion.

Women play a large role in the revival. In general, men go to church as a matter of show; women out of faith. Finney enlists them to help convert their husbands. He organizes women's prayer groups. He sends them door to door to visit potential converts. At church services, groups of women gather around the anxious bench murmuring for the salvation of the struggling sinners. The participation shocks some, but it gives Christian women a sense of their power and importance.

Everything about Finney's revivals is meant to make commitment public, to enlist the members of a community to help each other toward salvation. When he is not preaching, Finney brings Rochesterians together. Inquiry meetings welcome those who feel a stirring in their hearts. Home visits target those who have taken steps but needed further exhorting. Finney is not beyond knocking on the doors of skeptics who he knows will not receive him. He welcomes their rebukes. His acolytes circulate the story of this or that proud man who rejected his appeal. Anything that encourages talk promotes the revival.

It worked. "All Rochester was moved that winter," a resident remembered. "You could not go upon the streets, and hear any conversations, except on religion." Religion became the rage. Every person who was converted instantly became an evangelist. You could not believe and keep the good news to yourself. You took on an obligation to spread the Word.

Prayer groups roamed through the city seeking the unconverted. Students at a high school administered by a skeptical teacher became anxious about their souls. They refused to continue their class work. Many wept, terrified of damnation. Their master was "confounded." He called on Finney. When the famous man strode into the school, the effect among the teenagers was electrifying. "The revival took a tremendous hold of that school," Finney related. The teacher was himself converted. Many of the students resolved to devote themselves to the ministry.

Finney had engineered many revivals, but none like this one. He gave credit to the Holy Spirit, but he was the one who made it happen. Up at dawn for prayer meetings. Wading through snow-packed streets to visit house after house. Preaching every night, three times on Sunday. He wore himself to exhaustion, then pushed on.

From the beginning, Finney targeted for conversion members of Rochester's upper and rising middle classes: men of property, manufacturers, physicians, mill owners. He had barely stepped down from the canal boat when he was introduced to a "lady of high standing," the wife of a lawyer. She was "a gay, worldly woman, and very fond of society." She was afraid the revival would interfere with her high-toned pleasures. Conversing with her, Finney saw that under her haughty demeanor, she was wrestling with doubt, with the suspicion that she was a sinner.

"I pressed her hard," he remembered, "to renounce sin, and the world and self." He emphasized the line from Matthew that had troubled him so deeply in his own time of doubt: "Except ye be converted, and become as little children, ye shall not enter into the kingdom of heaven." The words took hold of the woman's mind. As little children. Finney closed his eyes and prayed for her to embrace Jesus in this way—as little children. When he opened them he saw "tears streaming over her face." She accepted the faith from that moment and became "zealous for the conversion of her friends."

Finney directed his energy toward the "highest classes of society" for a tactical purpose. If they were converted, others would follow their example. Accepting Jesus would become fashionable. He did not leave the matter to chance. He identified likely targets among the town's elite, visited their homes, pressed them to attend services, exhorted them by name during sermons, and soon had them sweating on his anxious bench. Each conversion was newsworthy.

With the passing months, Finney's efforts in Rochester bore more and more fruit. Word spread through religious circles around the country. Something miraculous was happening in western New York.

WEDDING

It would be a grand experiment in telecommunication. Governor DeWitt Clinton thought that scientists might "by the use of accurate chronometers" take advantage of the occasion to determine the speed of sound, but no one took him up on the idea. On the Buffalo waterfront, a 32-pounder cannon, one of the largest in the American arsenal, stood ready. At exactly 10:00 a.m. on October 26, 1825, the gun sent out an enormous blast that rippled the waters of Lake Erie. Farther along the canal line, cannoneers waited at intervals of ten or fifteen miles. Each team of gunners listened intently for the signal from the previous firing. On hearing it, they immediately ignited their own piece.

Onward the message went, gun after gun, for an hour and twenty minutes until it reached the Atlantic, more than five hundred miles away. It was the first time that news of an event in the interior had arrived at the coast in an approximation of real time. Now the signal was relayed back, reaching Buffalo just after 1:00 p.m. The speed hinted at the earth-shrinking technology, the telegraph and the steam locomotive, that lay just over the horizon.

The first thunderous peal marked the departure of a flotilla of boats down the Grand Western Canal, afterward known as the Erie Canal. The vessels were to travel the length of the waterway, from the shore of Lake Erie to Albany, then down the Hudson to New York City. From a luxury packet boat, James Geddes could examine the transformation along the route he had first surveyed in 1808. Benjamin Wright could inspect the technology that his team of self-taught engineers had made possible. Governor Clinton could revel in the project on which he had staked his political fortunes and which had catapulted him to his exalted position.

Before the boats left, Jesse Hawley gave one of the celebratory speeches. In July, he had finally unmasked himself as the "Hercules" who had, eighteen years earlier, penned the essays that had helped set the whole grand project in motion. He noted how he himself had "by laborious industry, attained from bankruptcy to a comfortable moderate competency." The fact that three thousand barrels of flour were now flowing down the canal every day afforded him deep satisfaction. The opening of the canal, he said, was "among the greatest events of our Nation." New Yorkers had built "the longest Canal—in the least time—with the least experience—for the least money." In fact, they had spent just over $7 million. When the canal matured, it would take in more than that in tolls every year.

The dignitaries rode the boat called *Seneca Chief*, but the Seneca tribe of the Iroquois Confederacy, through whose ancestral land the canal had been carved, was represented only by two Indian boys aboard the last boat in line. This vessel, designated *Noah's Ark*, carried curiosities in the form of a bear, a couple of fawns, two eagles, and numerous "creeping things." The undisturbed habitat of these creatures, along with the Indians themselves, had now faded into a bucolic and irretrievable past. *Noah's Ark* later fell behind the other boats and had to drop out of the parade.

After passing the Deep Cut and the amazing flight of locks at Lockport, the boats ambled eastward. Along the way, the celebrants hailed a group of nineteen travelers headed west, who answered in an unfamiliar language. They turned out to be the first Norwegian immigrants to America. Having crossed the Atlantic on a fifty-four-foot fishing sloop, they had purchased land on the Lake Ontario plain. Their settlement became a way station for the thousands of Nordic immigrants who traveled the canal to populate the Great Lakes region.

Just outside Rochester, the *Seneca Chief* met a boat that bore the city's nickname, the *Young Lion of the West*. The captains of the two boats went through some ritualistic rigmarole with a Masonic flavor. "Who comes there?" "Your brothers from the West. . . . By the channel of the Grand Erie Canal."

Farther east, having stopped briefly at Palmyra, the flotilla paused for speeches at Lyons. A local editor noted that in previous years "coarse epithets, and vulgar sarcasms were heaped upon the abbettors of this project." Now, all the canal's opponents were chewing diligently on humble pie and singing the project's praises. A month before he died, Thomas Jefferson admitted that "this great work will immortalize the present authorities of N.Y."

In Weedsport, west of Syracuse, the festivities had been marred when an old cannon exploded, killing two men. They might have stood in as a symbol of the hundreds of workers who had died from illness and accidents during the eight years of the canal's construction.

The boats arrived in Syracuse, a town brought into existence by the waterway. Joshua Forman, who in 1808 had introduced the bill in the state legislature to get the project started, said its completion "marks a new era in the history of man." He and his fellow citizens had "broken down the old barriers of nature."

Then they were passing into the Hudson River at Albany. More ceremonies, more speeches. Two powerful steamships took over from the mules to tow the fleet of canal boats the 150 miles to New York City. Cannons fired from towns along the shore to welcome the fleet. Fireworks set the sky ablaze.

They reached New York on November 4. A city of 25,000 during Clinton's youth, the metropolis was now crowded with 166,000 citizens. They were determined to celebrate "in a manner suited to the character of our City." And they did. Tens of thousands turned out to line the shore and pack the Battery. All were eager to view the Grand Aquatic Procession. A mass of ships and barges accompanied the canal boats to Sandy Hook, at the mouth of the harbor.

Rocked by the waves of the ocean, his eyes wet with tears, Clinton "wedded" the waters of the Great Lakes with the Atlantic by pouring Lake Erie water from a gaudily decorated cask. The governor gave a nod to the Almighty, asking Him to "smile most propitiously on this work." But he also sang the praises of Mammon, telling New Yorkers there were now "no limits to your lucrative extensions of trade and commerce."

The celebrants returned to Manhattan to join the greatest parade ever staged in North America. Cordwainers (shoemakers), hatters, and shipwrights by the hundreds marched to honor their professions. Tinsmiths towed a float containing a replica of the Lockport lock system, complete with pumped water. Fire companies hauled decorated engines. Volunteers of Company Number 41, whose founder and once most active member was DeWitt Clinton himself, had painted theirs with canal scenes.

Two working printing presses were towed through the streets, stamping out broadsides of treacle-saturated verse for immediate consumption. Of course there had to be a book. Promoters marked the occasion by commissioning a four-hundred-page *Memoir* of canal scenes sketched by such noted American artists as Asher Durand. Citizens dined on Canal Beef, wrapped their heads in Canal turbans, and that evening crowded into the Grand Canal Ball, where a canal boat modeled from maple sugar slowly dissolved in Erie water. The city's buildings were ablaze with oil and gas lights. Overhead, sky-rockets blazed. Through it all, the future whispered in every ear.

BIG THINGS

Parley Pratt had grown up in central New York, son of a poor farmer. His education was limited, but, he said, "I always loved a book." He hired out as a farm laborer before traveling west in search of brighter prospects. In 1827, at twenty-one, he married and settled with his bride in northern Ohio. Always a spiritual seeker, he put his faith in a frontier Baptist exhorter there named Sidney Rigdon.

In 1830, Pratt felt the call to become a missionary himself. He and his wife took passage along the Erie Canal to visit her home in eastern New York. Along the way, Pratt was prompted, for what reason he did not know, to get off the canal boat near Palmyra. He sent his wife on to her people.

He preached only once before a farmer alerted him to what he called "a very strange book." He loaned Pratt a copy of the brand-new *Book of Mormon*. Pratt went to the Smith homestead and met Hyrum. The two men stayed up all night, talking about the new religion. Pratt read the book and was entranced. He walked twenty-five miles to Fayette, where Oliver Cowdery baptized him. He was immediately ordained an elder of the new Church. He met Joseph and was impressed by his affability and by "the serene and penetrating glance of his eye, as if he would penetrate the deepest abyss of the human heart."

In October, Joseph sent Cowdery and Peter Whitmer westward on a mission to the Lamanites, his term for Native Americans. Pratt went along. As they traveled through northeast Ohio, Pratt introduced his companions to his former pastor. At thirty-seven, Sidney Rigdon was a dynamic preacher, a self-taught scholar of history, and an expert on the Bible. He had become a Baptist minister in Pittsburgh, and soon gravitated to the ideas of Alexander Campbell, who advocated a return to the simple faith of the original Apostles. Rigdon's oratory and his notion of a church cleansed of extraneous doctrines helped grow his Ohio congregation.

With the zeal of a new convert, Pratt urged Rigdon to consider the *Book of Mormon*. The minister was impressed and devoted several weeks to studying the text. He could hardly believe that a twenty-four-year-old farmer had produced such a scripture, yet the authenticity of the story took hold of him. Smith's idea of a pending millennium resonated with his own beliefs. So did the idea that believers were not to live in isolation but to gather together in a community they forged for themselves. Rigdon asked Pratt to baptize him into the new religion. He urged members of his congregation to convert as well. Many of them followed him into the Mormon faith.

In the winter of 1830, as gray snow clouds descended on western New York and the revival fires burned brightly in Rochester, Joseph Smith received news of a development almost miraculous in its scope. Cowdery sent back word that an entirely new Mormon congregation had materialized in Ohio, nearly doubling Church membership overnight. Rigdon, he said, was eager to meet the young prophet.

On December 10, Rigdon and his friend Edward Partridge arrived at the Whitmer farm looking for Joseph. Rigdon was thirteen years older than Smith and better educated than any of his rustic followers. He was a practiced orator, eager to turn his talents to the promotion of Mormonism. David Whitmer, although peeved by the warm embrace Smith offered to the new convert, called Rigdon "a great and mighty man."

Joseph was determined to keep a firm grip on the reins of the accelerating project. He assigned Rigdon to take over the role previously performed by Cowdery. He would act as a scribe and important assistant, but always secondary to Smith himself. Rigdon agreed. He and Joseph made the rounds of the tiny Mormon communities in New York State. When Rigdon rose to preach in Palmyra, "the people stood trembling and amazed, so powerful were his words."

Rigdon later remembered Church members meeting in a house twenty feet square. "We began to talk about the kingdom of God as if we had the world at our command," he wrote. "We talked such big things that men could not bear them."

The church that Joseph was establishing, like many frontier congregations, favored the downtrodden. In the *Book of Mormon*, the prophet Nephi said that churches "rob the poor." The learned and the rich "are puffed up in the pride of their hearts." Almost all the early Mormons knew poverty and hard work intimately. Parley Pratt said that employers "treated a laborer as a machine; not as a human being." The new religion would promote "an equality among all men." It would eschew an idle clergy; preachers would work like everyone else.

Facing opposition from nonbelievers both in the Palmyra area and along the Pennsylvania border, excited by the prospects farther west, Joseph received a stunning revelation. All members of the Church were to move to Ohio. They would have to sell or rent their farms at distressed prices, pack up, and get on the road as quickly as possible. The gathering was beginning.

Smith was demanding a radical commitment. Leave behind familiar surroundings, friends, and economic prospects. Head toward the western frontier. It was more than a test of faith. He was turning his Church into a community. The Latter Day Saints would not exist in isolated congregations like members of most churches. They would come together, live together, share their property, establish a holy nation in the American interior. Speaking with the voice of God, Joseph told his followers to go out from among the wicked. "Hear my voice and follow me and you shall be free people, and ye shall have no laws, but my laws."

The revelation was ratified at a Church conference in early January 1831. By the end of the month, Joseph and Emma were ready to leave. Like so many Americans in those days, the Mormons were heading west.

WORK OF GOD

During a revival service in Rochester, Charles Finney asked congregants to rise if they could accept the conditions of salvation. "Simultaneously hundreds arose from all parts of the house." It was an evangelist's dream.

Converts were pouring into Rochester churches. All denominations saw increases in membership. The Methodists had to build a large new church to accommodate the influx. Two nondenominational churches were created to house those not inclined to affiliation. Conversions and satellite revivals broke out up and down the canal and began to spread to nearby states.

What did conversion mean? It always began with a split. A person believed in a benevolent God worthy of love and obedience, yet he saw in himself a sinner. He wanted to be close to the divine, yet he keenly felt his distance from the holy presence. William James, analyzing the phenomenon later in the century, would call this "the divided self." Such a condition created unbearable anguish.

The evangelist's role, Finney felt, was to make this dual state as clear and as painful as possible. His goal was not to soothe, but to trouble his listeners, to make them uncomfortable in their own skin. "All sin consists in selfishness," Finney insisted. What was needed for conversion was a spiritual sleight of hand in which the self chose to relinquish the self.

As the Rochester revival proceeded, the opposition to Finney's new methods faded. Lyman Beecher, once his staunchest enemy, admitted that the transformation Finney effected in Rochester "was the greatest work of God, and the greatest revival of religion, that the world has ever seen in so short a time."

Basking in his own success, Finney began to envision something truly grand emerging from the revival. If Christians made the effort, if they gave up sin, embraced the Bible, devoted themselves to good works, spread the Word to the unsaved, something magical could happen on earth. They could bring on the millennium, the thousand-year reign of Christ's terrestrial kingdom. It was a hope that went back to Jonathan Edwards, the great Puritan clergyman prominent during the first Christian "awakening," the Great Awakening of the 1740s. He too had looked forward to the coming millennium.

If a new order was about to engulf the earth, it was only natural to imagine that it would have its origin in the New World. Edwards had thought it probable that "this work will begin in America." Finney agreed. Lyman Beecher envisioned a time when "nation after nation, cheered by our example, will follow in our footsteps till the whole earth is freed."

The evangelical millennium was not William Miller's catastrophic view of the end times. Finney, like most Protestants, believed the thousand years of peace on earth would be a *preparation* for Christ's arrival. The world would enter a state of spiritual perfection. Believers could hurry the millennium by erasing sin from the world: drinking, cursing, violence, slave-driving, desecration of the Sabbath—it all held back God's glorious plan.

The possibility of living to experience the enchanted world of the millennium gave Christians a gleaming hope. All they needed to do was to reform the world. Conversions, Finney saw, especially mass conversions, were the first step. Newly active Christians then had to fight against sin. The spirit of the saved, he asserted, is "necessarily that of the reformer." Believers must go beyond individual virtue. They must make others virtuous. The reform impulse predated the Rochester revival, but in Rochester it became increasingly central to evangelical doctrine. The initial target was an obvious one: whiskey.

In March 1830, four months after Sam Patch had dared the devil by jumping over the Genesee Falls, a workman watering horses near the mouth of the river broke the ice and discovered Sam's frozen body, still dressed in white. Over his grave, someone mounted a wooden plaque that read: "Sam Patch, Such is Fame." In death, Sam had entered the national consciousness. "Why do we call him a madman or a fool?" Nathaniel Hawthorne asked. "Was the leaper of cataracts more mad or foolish than other men who throw away life?"

By the time of Finney's revival, it was no longer disputed that Sam was drunk when he leapt the Rochester falls. Strong drink had literally killed him. Anyone could see that the national predilection for the jug generated crime, lust, poverty, illness, insanity, and death. It generated sin. Seen as a booster of productivity during canal construction, whiskey drinking now was depicted as an extravagant waste of time. It clouded a man's mind and eroded his moral judgment. The tide of American drinking, after years of rising, was about to go out with a rush.

Emotionally exhausted by the end of December, Finney decided to briefly make temperance the focus of the revival. He called on the young man he had converted in Utica four years earlier, Theodore Dwight Weld.

Weld was a born fanatic. After his encounter with the evangelist in Utica and a period in which he helped Finney engineer revivals, the younger man had continued his education at the Oneida Academy in central New York, still hoping to become a minister of Christ. The unusual school he attended was overseen by Finney's old pastor, George Gale, now an advocate of Finney's revival methods. Gale felt that manual labor must be part of education. The regime he imposed was designed to promote health, and it also connected the seminarians to the lives of working men and women. It suited the hyperactive Weld. "Whether in exercise or in study," he noted, "I felt continually hurried. Every nerve was strained."

The young men at Oneida were Christian revolutionaries. They identified with the Jacksonian common man; they were preparing for the millennium by pursuing a primitive Christianity. They dressed like peasants, rose at four in the morning, milked cows before breakfast. They studied Latin and Greek, cut wood, memorized orations, dug ditches.

With the millennium shining in his mind, Weld understood the urgency of reform. Alcohol killed the body and set the soul on the road to hell. He recognized that a corrupt and changing society drove men to drink by creating a "universal insecurity of life and property." His answer was to induce drinkers to shun the bottle entirely.

Weld agreed to put his studies aside once again and went to work for the cause. In Rochester, with Finney's encouragement, he began to hold meetings promoting temperance. On New Year's Eve he mounted the pulpit of the packed Third Presbyterian church and launched into a four-hour oration that electrified his audience. Those who had made a decision for Christ must not touch a drop of whiskey, must not do business with any merchant who traded in the stuff, must not even sell grain to a distiller. A local minister, caught up in Weld's plea, rose during his sermon to demand that all alcohol vendors cease dealing in the devil's brew. Ten liquor dealers stood to take the pledge. In the morning, Albert and Elijah Smith, who ran the city's largest grocery, ordered their clerks to move casks of whiskey into Exchange Street. Church members applauded as the barrels were opened and the liquor gurgled into the gutters. Others were astonished at the waste.

It did not stop there. Some wealthy converts went to groceries and grog shops, bought out the merchants' entire stock of booze, and destroyed it. Repentant liquor dealers poured their wares into the canal. Only a few retailers dared defy the mania and continue in the trade. With the scent of spilled whiskey tinting the winter air, Weld, Finney, and many a pious Rochesterian could taste the millennium.

Finney had formed a bridge from stale orthodox Calvinism to a new, dynamic, hopeful faith that would become a mainstay of American religion. He drew energy from the frontier. He created a religion of can-do self-reliance, of hope and good works. His eyes shining, Finney declared: "If the church will do all her duty, the millennium may come in this country in three years."

SHARP SICKLE

William Miller was preaching a message far more ominous than Finney's hopeful tidings. He began to receive invitations from ministers in the surrounding area, usually from Baptists, sometimes from Methodists or Congregationalists. Like Finney, he was sure his news transcended denominations. At both regular services and revivals, his grim prediction served as a lash to encourage congregants to convert.

Miller's intricate proof of Christ's second coming took time to explain. In a series of lectures, he walked his listeners through the Biblical prophecies and the complex calculations that proved his conclusion. Proved it—this was not guesswork or speculation. His certainty was based on centuries of prophecy. Like Joseph Smith's *Book of Mormon*, Miller's story reached back in time to bring a potent message to the present. It kept churchgoers coming back for more. Little by little, interest in Miller's startling news grew. "There is an increasing anxiety on the subject in this quarter," Miller noted with satisfaction. His reputation spread. The term *Millerites* entered the language. Preachers came to his farm to "talk Bible."

Miller was tapping into a widespread millennial fever that would peak in the coming decade. A woman in Oswego, New York, said in 1831 that she only waited "to hear the cry 'Behold the bridegroom cometh!'" All kinds of natural phenomena—the cholera epidemic of 1832, a pyrotechnic meteor display in 1833, comets, eclipses, storms—were seen as harbingers. Almost all Christians sensed that *something* was going to happen.

Short and squat, his round face ruddy with outdoor work, Miller was not an imposing figure in the pulpit. The doubts that had induced him to hold his tongue stayed with him. His habitual self-deprecation helped deflect the criticisms that learned clergy and scholars inevitably directed at him. He referred to himself as a "dry old stick," and described his performance in the pulpit as "cold, dull & lifeless."

In fact, he was a fluid speaker, able to lay out his ideas in a logical, easy-to-follow manner. But he did feel a burden. "I sometimes feel as though I can do all things through Christ," he said, "and sometimes the shaking of a leaf is a terror to me." His popularity as a preacher surprised him and boosted his confidence. Some might scoff at the "end-of-the-world man" or label him a monomaniac, but many others listened, drawn to his urgent pleading.

He jolted over bad roads in stagecoaches, negotiated muddy lanes on horseback, slept two to a bed in remote inns, occupied tents at camp meetings. He addressed country people who knew that life was precarious. Babies routinely died, epidemics swept like scythes, eternity was always hovering.

At an evening service, amid the flicker of candlelight, with the wind sighing through fir trees outside and rain tap-tapping at windows, Miller rose to speak. In a very orderly progression—he had a passion for numbering each of his points—he unfolded the danger that was marching toward every inhabitant of the planet.

He did not assert that a single calculation proved his case. He had found more than a dozen Biblical formulas, all of them pointing to the same conclusion. For example, from the decree of Artaxerxes I in 457 B.C., count 2,300 days—that is, years—and you find that Daniel's vision ends in 1843. Or extract numbers from Exodus, Leviticus, and Deuteronomy. Seven times seven times fifty gives 2,450 years until the great Jubilee of Jubilees. Start from 607 B.C., the close of Josiah's reign, when the Jews stopped keeping God's Sabbath. Take 607 from 2,450, it leaves 1843. And so forth.

All of this required careful listening over several sessions. He supplemented Biblical verses with references to "profane history," events in the world that corresponded to and proved the validity of ancient prophecies. The "fall of the Western Empire," the Napoleonic wars, Joan of Arc, the restoration of the Bourbon dynasty in France, the decline of the Ottomans—it all made sense in the grand scheme. It all fit with the hallucinatory imagery of the Book of Revelation.

Miller had enough of a showman's instinct to know that he had to make the numbers real. He described Daniel's interpretation of Nebuchadnezzar's dream. The king had seen a creature whose "head was of fine gold, his breast and his arms of silver, his belly and his thighs of brass, his legs of iron, his feet part of iron and part of clay." These, Miller said, were the various ages of celestial history. He explained each one. He spoke of the ram and the goat, interpreted the significance of the four-faced beast: lion and sheep, man and eagle.

"See," he whispered, "see, the angel with his sharp sickle is about to take the field." Listeners could indeed see "victims fall before his pestilential breath." Miller awakened the senses of people whose lives included so much that was monotonous and drab. "Hark, hear those dreadfull bellowings of the angry nations," he shouted. He painted for them the "horrid and terrific war." He made "carnivorous fowls fly screeming through the air." He pointed to the pale moon, the hail, the "stream of sulphros flames." And just as the horror reached a crescendo, Jesus appeared. The "great white throne's in sight. Amazement fills the universe with awe—he comes."

His prediction first saw print in 1832. The editor of the *Vermont Telegraph*, a Baptist newspaper, published a series of articles in which Miller was asked questions and explained the details of his notion. "It will start some queries if nothing else," Miller wrote.

A year later, the Baptist authorities saw fit to issue him a license to preach. He became Reverend Miller, but because of his age he was already being called Father Miller. He published a detailed pamphlet that laid out his argument. He called it *Evidences from Scripture and History of the Second Coming of Christ About the Year A.D. 1843 and of His Personal Reign of 1000 Years*. It proved so popular that another Baptist preacher republished it in book form.

Realizing that time was short, Miller responded to the growing urgency of the invitations. From 1835 to 1837, he preached more than two hundred times, traveling as far as Canada. In 1838, his pace quickened further. A few other ministers were taking up his theme, preparing the ground. The enthusiasm spread into western New York. Miller spoke at Troy, the thriving city opposite the mouth of the Erie Canal. In 1839 he commenced a grueling five-month tour of Massachusetts.

The more he repeated his prediction, the surer he became that it was beyond all doubt. His own popularity proved to him that he was on to something. Some critics suggested that if his forecast failed it would hurt the cause of Christ. Miller brushed off the possibility. Every prophet back to Noah had stared into the uncertain future. What if, when the ark was finished, no rain had come? His stark answer to critics was: "Time is precious."

But as time ran through the hourglass, Miller failed to gain the kind of momentum he thought his message demanded. He continued to lecture in isolated churches. Too few preachers were picking up his banner. Rumors circulated that Miller was dead or, even worse, that he had made a hundred-year error in calculation. He began to suffer from dropsy, a swelling of the ankles that suggested he was developing congestive heart failure. He was closer to sixty now than to fifty, and the end of the world was only four years away.

Preaching in Groton, Massachusetts, in 1839, Miller met a thirty-four-year-old man of God named Joshua V. Himes, pastor of a small church in Boston. Himes invited Miller to address his congregation. Miller went to Boston in December and gave his usual series of lectures. Himes's eyes were opened. He could not deny or ignore the man's disturbing but utterly convincing revelation. He grilled Miller after his talk: Do you believe this message? Certainly. What are you doing to spread the Word? All I can. Then why have so few heard the message?

"No time should be lost," Himes said, "in giving the church and the world warning, in thundertones."

Miller was, as usual, self-deprecating. "What can an old farmer do?" he rejoined. "I was never used to public speaking." He confessed to Himes that the relentless, seemingly fruitless effort, the growing resistance from orthodox clergy, and his failure to spark a self-perpetuating movement were wearing him down. Most of all, he felt alone. "I have been looking for help—I want help!"

Himes had the soul of a reformer. His Boston chapel had housed an early pacifist organization. Like many attracted to Miller's teaching, he was an active abolitionist. He decided he would be the one who would help Father Miller. Together, they would warn the world.

Himes was sure he could convert one man's crusade into a historic mass movement.

He was right. Before long, thousands of voices would be proclaiming the Advent message. They would be singing hymns praising the destruction of the entire earth and proclaiming that when the end came they would "smile to see the burning world."

ZION

During the first week of February 1831, Joseph and Emma Smith arrived in Kirtland, Ohio, accompanied by Sidney Rigdon. Joseph strode into a mercantile store there and said to one of the proprietors, "Newel K. Whitney! Thou art the man!"

The thirty-five-year-old Whitney was at a loss.

"I am Joseph the Prophet," Smith said. "You've prayed me here, now what do you want of me?" It was the type of dramatic gesture that made a lasting impression. Smith may have delivered his grandiose announcement with a touch of sly humor. He admitted to a "native cheery Temperament." One of his followers who later left the Church complained of "a spirit of lightness and levity" in the young man not appropriate for a prophet. Joseph had a "habitual proneness to jesting and joking."

Kirtland stood between the shore of Lake Erie and the inland hills. Sparsely populated, only partly cultivated, now linked to the East by steamer and canal boat, it was rapidly attracting settlers. Most came from New England. Many, like their western New York counterparts, were religious seekers.

The mix of fields and woods, the wheat growing amid stumps, the tiny isolated villages, all was familiar to Joseph Smith. What was different was the reception he received. Local families converted to Mormonism by Cowdery and Whitmer joined Rigdon's followers in a community of faith. Mormons moving from Palmyra and the Colesville area arrived to fill out the ranks. Rather than animosity and threats, Joseph was met with respect and cordiality bordering on awe.

Even in this welcoming environment, Joseph and Emma continued to endure precarious finances and a string of bad luck. For lodging, they at first depended on local followers. Then Joseph had a revelation that a new house should be provided, and convert Isaac Morley built them a one-room cabin on his farm.

At the end of April, Emma gave birth to premature twins, Thaddeus and Louisa. Both died the same day, just as the Smiths' first child Alvin had perished three years earlier. Married four years, Emma had buried three children. She had also suffered a break with her parents and had been uprooted from two homes. But Joseph's mother Lucy wrote about Emma, "I have never seen a woman in my life, who would endure every species of fatigue and hardship . . . with that unflinching courage, zeal, and patience, which she has ever done."

The wife of another Mormon follower died in childbirth the day after Emma's heartbreak, leaving behind twins of her own. Their father offered the babies to the Smiths, who took them in and raised them. Lucy Smith arrived soon afterward from New York, joining her husband, who had preceded her to Kirtland. The older couple moved in with Joseph and Emma and the two infants, taking again to the farming life they knew so well.

Joseph Jr. also returned to translating. He was revising and adding to the Bible. He did not, like the seventeenth-century translators of the King James Version, refer to the original Greek and Hebrew texts. His alterations and supplements were inspired directly by God. He related how Moses, who had lived thirteen centuries before Christ, had experienced a vision of Jesus. Meeting God face-to-face, Moses pressed the Almighty to reveal the meaning of his creation. God told him the heavens "are many, & they cannot be numbered unto man."

Later, Smith and Sidney Rigdon recorded a joint revelation that Church members could become "gods, even the sons of God." They could "be made equal with him." In their exaltation, they would dwell in a "celestial kingdom." Heaven had two other, lower realms, which they called "terrestrial" and "telestial." The idea of a multiplicity of heavens was a strange new take on traditional theology. Mormon doctrine was spinning ever further beyond the confines of orthodox Christianity.

Joseph was also devising a novel structure for the Church. Rather than a professional clergy, he incorporated all male members into the various offices of the church. Breaking down the division between lay and clerical was almost unknown in Christianity; only the Quakers had come close to it.

In June 1831, he took an even more radical step, ordaining five men into the priesthood. He made the hierarchical office an essential part of his Church. Eventually, almost all Mormon men would have the chance to enter the Aaronic or the higher Melchizedek priesthood. The Mormon emphasis on priestly functions marked a distinct break with the tradition of Puritan Protestantism, which had dominated American faith since the seventeenth century. The idea that every person could have a direct relationship with the Divine was an axiom of evangelical Christianity. Joseph returned Mormonism to an earlier concept, still enshrined in Roman Catholicism, in which priests served as intermediaries. A Mormon was initiated into the faith not by his own efforts alone but through the intercession of another. Smith based the doctrine on the ancient Hebrew priesthood. Ingeniously, he had found a way to fuse hierarchical and democratic principles to yield a Church structure that was both innovative and practical.

Continuing to look westward, Smith sent fourteen pairs of elders to join Oliver Cowdery, who was teaching the "Lamanites" in western Missouri. A few weeks later, he followed them. The purpose of the trip was to select a site for Zion, the new Jerusalem where all Latter Day Saints would eventually gather. Revelations from God led him to Independence, a tiny village in Jackson County, on the opposite side of the state from St. Louis. The Saints already there were joined by a group who had journeyed directly from New York State. This was to be the Mormons' sacred refuge.

Their reception in Missouri was chillier than the Mormons' welcome in Kirtland. Locals here were not visionary Yankees but hard-eyed southern backwoodsmen. They were not inclined to join the new religion. Nor did they welcome a group of strangers who declared their town the promised land and who appeared to be the vanguard of an invasion of fanatics.

Joseph selected a lot where the Saints were to build their temple in "Zion." He then returned to Kirtland to manage the larger body of Church members there.

He must have felt an immense satisfaction to reflect on how far he had come. Less than four years had passed since he had climbed

Hill Cumorah and returned with the gold plates. In that time he had translated a major new scripture, published a six-hundred-page book, started a church, revised part of the Bible, established a new and enthusiastic base in Ohio, set up the crucial community on the edge of the western frontier, and sent missionaries to gather new members from around the country. A year later he would write a history of his life, calling it "an account of his marvilous experience and of all the mighty acts which he doeth."

FORT NIAGARA

When a loved one goes missing, hope becomes a bitter thorn. William Morgan was the most intelligent, insightful, and intriguing man that his wife Lucinda had ever met. Her love had made her overlook his age, his hollow ambitions, his heavy drinking, and his unreliable breadwinning. After September 11, 1826, each day of dwindling hope made her heart ache.

Each day, each week. A year passed. She endured the macabre burlesque of the rotting corpse found in Lake Ontario. Wanting, yet not wanting it to be him. Wanting to end hope and know he was at rest. It was him; it was not him. The torture continued.

Her husband had become the focus of a great excitement sweeping western New York. To the increasingly organized and avid Anti-Masonic forces, Morgan was an icon, a proof of Masonic treachery. Morgan's blood cried from the ground. The circumstances of his death, an observer noted, were the "rallying signals of a political party; and the still small voice of reason and reflection was drowned amid the universal din."

Freemasons dug in their heels against the onslaught of hatred and mistrust. But the tide kept rising, and their footing washed away under them. Thousands of Masons left the order. Almost four hundred lodges in New York State closed. Many in neighboring states fell inactive as well. The number of Freemasons in the United States dropped by 60 percent in ten years. Masonic ceremonies at public events largely ceased.

"Antimasonry is bottomed upon rank political hatred and bigoted intolerant sectarianism," wrote the editor of the *Masonic Mirror* in 1831. Hatred proved a solid foundation for a suddenly potent political movement.

The Anti-Masons saw an affront to their newly muscular religious sensibilities. A Massachusetts preacher roared that Freemasonry was the "darkest and deepest plot that ever was formed in this wicked world." Cooler heads saw that Freemasonry, rather than being sacrilege, was an elaborate form of make-believe. Masons incorporated all kinds of hocus-pocus into their rituals in order to add mystery and "zest" to the play.

But to opponents, Freemasonry's secret reach made it a truly terrifying enemy. "Why are six hundred thousand men united together by mysterious ties," a convention speaker demanded, "the nature of which are studiously concealed from their countrymen?"

A story emerged from all the testimony, investigations, rumors, and confessions surrounding the case. It began the night before Morgan's arrest in Batavia. Masons in Canandaigua met to discuss the imminent publication of Morgan's book. They sent Loton Lawson, who would participate in Morgan's actual abduction, to arrange for relays of horses and drivers along the route from Canandaigua to Lewiston, 125 miles away on the Niagara frontier.

After the Masons hustled Morgan into a closed carriage the evening of September 12, a man named Hiram Hubbard drove him ten miles to Victor and pulled in behind a tavern kept by Dr. Thomas Beach. Beach purportedly said of Morgan, "Damn him, he ought to be drawn and quartered."

The men had some drinks and proceeded onward to Hanford's Landing, a settlement on the west side of the Genesee River north of Rochester. Ezra Platt, a Royal Arch Mason, provided a new carriage from his livery stable. The abductors continued westward, stopping at various taverns to water or change horses. At every stop they "took drinks all around." By sundown on the 13th they had reached Wright's Corners, just north of Lockport, twenty-five miles east of Lewiston. Sheriff Eli Bruce joined them there and took charge of the prisoner.

In Lewiston, Bruce recruited a driver, Corydon Fox, who was not a Mason. Fox watched a man being led by the arm to the carriage. Bruce told Fox to drive six miles north to Fort Niagara. Fox pulled up his horses at a graveyard a quarter mile from the fort. He observed four persons descend from the carriage and proceed arm in arm toward the disused bastion.

Almost all the men involved in this strange trip were Masons. A few days later, Corydon Fox was inducted into the brotherhood as well, the usual fees being waived. "Morgan's abductors," a witness noted, "were respectable men." Some held important offices. They were a decorous mob that felt confident in taking the law into their own hands.

Fort Niagara had been left in the charge of Colonel Ezekiel Jewett, who lived in one of the buildings. Jewett, a Mason, entrusted the fort's upkeep to Edward Giddins, who also ran a ferry across the river. He had not been allowed to testify in court because he was an atheist. He told those interested that he had observed Morgan "bound, hoodwinked and under guard" on the night of September 13.

Later, Giddins said, he helped row the prisoner across the river to Canada. The Canadian Masons who were to take charge of him did not show up. The American Masons returned Morgan to the fort and imprisoned him in the magazine. Giddins supplied Morgan with food. At one point, the prisoner created a disturbance that alarmed a black woman who looked after Giddins's daughter. Giddins distracted the nanny by telling her it was the sound of ghosts.

At some point during the next four days, Giddins said, he joined a group of Masons who talked about what to do with Morgan. They finally agreed to take him out on the river, tie a stone to him, and sink him. But each in turn declared he could not go through with such a plan. Giddins proposed releasing the prisoner. After quarreling with others, he handed over the key to the magazine because he had to be away for a few days. He returned to find the building empty.

The story of Morgan's abduction could be traced in great detail up to his imprisonment in Fort Niagara. All of the characters in the drama were accounted for. But then what?

What was to become a semiofficial Masonic version said that their plan all along was to take Morgan to Canada. There he was given a farm and five hundred dollars on the promise that he would never return to the United States and never try to publish his book. His wife and children would be allowed to join him later.

If this or something like it happened, it exonerated the Masons of murder. If, as they held, Morgan agreed to the compensation from the beginning, there was no kidnapping. To explain the apparent force used in Canandaigua, they suggested that the abduction was a ruse, designed to get Morgan out of obligations to his publisher, David Miller. But Morgan's family never saw him again, his imprisonment in the magazine does not suggest a ruse, and his book was published and widely read, all facts that argue against this innocuous explanation.

Other stories, mostly from Freemason sources, concluded that Morgan emerged from the incident alive and well. In one, he was delivered to a member of the brotherhood who commanded a British man-of-war in Montreal, or maybe Quebec, and removed to some unknown destination. Or he was impressed into the British navy—a reprise of Morgan's purported stint in the American army during the War of 1812.

A persistent story set him down in Smyrna, on the west coast of Turkey. The port was a prosperous Greek outpost within the Ottoman Empire. A report in the *New-York Evening Post* placed Morgan there as early as 1828. Forty years after the event, a Captain Andrew Hitchcock said he saw a man there in February 1830. Although the stranger looked like a Turk, he told Hitchcock he was the missing Morgan. A year later, Joseph Bloom, a traveling scientist, met an American Mohammedan in Smyrna whom he was convinced was Morgan.

Another detailed story had Morgan going to Canada. He took the money and land the Freemasons offered, but sold the farm to start a new life. He went to sea on the *Constance* and was shipwrecked in a storm off Cuba. Fishermen picked him up and took him home with them to the Cayman Islands. There he married a woman named Catherine Ann Page. They had six children beginning in 1829. Ten years later, Morgan was caught in a storm while fishing for turtles. His dismasted boat drifted for weeks. Three Americans rescued him this time and towed him to Utila Island, off Belize, where he harvested turtles and sold coconut oil. When he managed to repair his boat, he went back to the Caymans and brought his family to live on

Utila. He later sent his daughter to school in Philadelphia. He died around 1864, when he would have been ninety.

No, some said, he escaped his Masonic captors and made his way west. He joined a band of Apache Indians in Texas, married an Indian maiden, became a chief. No, he was forced into the British navy, all right, but he jumped ship in Australia and started a newspaper called *The Advertiser*. He married a beautiful woman and became rich. No, he traveled to northern Maine where he lived as a hermit, quite content in his wilderness hut.

In other stories, his fate was grim. Some said that Masons had sliced open his throat, cut out his tongue, and buried him in sand at the edge of Lake Ontario, fulfilling the penalty for breaking his oath. Others were sure that his abductors did not stop until they reached a remote region of southwest Alabama, where they killed Morgan and buried his body. A rumor spread that, having taken him to Canada, the Masonic brothers handed him over to Captain John Brant, son of the Mohawk chief Joseph Brant, a feared warrior during the Revolutionary War. The Mohawks were said to have subjected Morgan to baroque native vengeance. Brant himself denied that he had ever heard of the man.

A number of men came forth in later years who claimed to have participated in Morgan's murder. In 1848, Doctor John L. Emery of Racine, Wisconsin, said that a remorseful Canadian Mason named Henry L. Valance had confessed to him. Valance said that a Masonic council had resolved that Morgan must die. A group of Masons drew lots to see who would serve as Morgan's executioners. Valance was required to go to the Fort Niagara magazine and tell the prisoner of his fate. The other brothers bound and gagged the victim, attached weights to him and rowed him to the middle of the river. The night was dark as pitch. They set Morgan on the boat's gunwale. Valance pushed him overboard. Another Canadian Mason named Samuel Chubbuck told a similar but conflicting story years later, suggesting that Morgan had been killed on land, his wrapped body tossed into the Niagara River.

Thurlow Weed chimed in with yet another confession. John Whitney, who was known to have participated in the abduction, told Weed that the Masons had intended to settle their recalcitrant brother in Canada, but that the Canadian Masons refused to take charge of him. Five enthusiastic Masons from the Lewiston Royal Arch decided to bind Morgan with chains, weight him with a stone, and drown him in the river. Whitney himself had been dead for six years before Weed first recounted this version of the crime fifty years after the event.

Even today, nearly two centuries after Morgan's disappearance, Freemasons take umbrage at the unproven accusation that their long-ago brothers murdered a man for writing a book. Certainly it's possible that Morgan, desperate for money and seeing little prospect in his publishing venture, had decided to abide by his oath, accept a bribe, and forsake his family. It's also possible that the Freemasons of western New York did in fact murder him.

None of the stories or rumors could bring anything but sorrow to Lucinda Morgan. She apparently saw little of the profits from William's book, in spite of the brisk sales. One who helped her financially was George Washington Harris, the silversmith who kept a shop below her apartment in Batavia. Harris had been a Freemason for twenty years before being expelled from the Lodge in August 1826, a month before Morgan's abduction. His friendship with the Morgans might have been the cause.

In 1828, Harris's wife Margaret died. The next year he began to court Lucinda. They were married in November 1830. Harris was fifty then. Morgan had been fifty-two when he disappeared. Lucinda had just turned thirty.

The wedding disappointed the Anti-Masons. Lucinda lost much of her value as the aggrieved symbol of their cause. Shortly after they became man and wife, the couple left Batavia and moved to Terre Haute, Indiana. Some years later they encountered a roving missionary named Orson Pratt. He was the younger brother of Parley Pratt, who had introduced Sidney Rigdon to Mormonism. Orson preached the doctrines of Joseph Smith to the Harrises. They were convinced. He baptized them into the Church of Jesus Christ of Latter-day Saints in the autumn of 1834.

SALVATION

"The waters of salvation had risen so high," Charles Finney wrote about the aftermath of his Rochester revival, "that men were afraid to oppose them." The sudden efflorescence of religion—a hundred thousand, maybe two hundred thousand citizens had joined churches—was unprecedented. It must, many thought, mean that the millennium was at hand. Finney thought so. The thousand-year reign of Christianity, heaven on earth, could be imminent. "In 1831," one observer noted, "the whole orthodox church was in a state of ebullition in regard to the Millennium."

But if Christians were to bring about the millennium, they needed to do more than bask in their own conversions. Preachers were the catalyst, but every Christian, Finney held, "is either gathering for Christ, or scattering abroad."

During this period of high enthusiasm, evangelical Christianity took a fateful turn. Christians, reveling in what a modern writer has called "the ecstasy of sanctimony," became soldiers in one of the earliest American culture wars. Charles Finney reinforced both the moral courage and the prying meddlesomeness of American religion.

Sin was sin. He would lead his flock in a war against the evening sip of wine and against the sexual degradation of women. They would march to eliminate the Sunday afternoon canal boat ride and to abolish the cruel enslavement of human beings. Finney condemned every self-indulgence, from coffee and pastries to the ribbons on women's dresses. He directed his censure at the "secular novel," and lumped Byron, Scott, and Shakespeare with "triflers and blasphemers of God."

Theodore Weld had shown the way with his absolutist and highly successful temperance campaign. Evangelicals worked to enforce observance of the Sabbath. They condemned all theatergoing. Christians bought one Rochester theater and turned it into a livery stable. A circus building was transformed into a soap factory.

The Rochester Christians recruited by Finney from the elite classes directed their benevolent gaze at the poor. They started a savings bank to encourage thrift. They set up schools for needy children. They established the Boatmen's Friend Society, which tried to bring the men and boys who worked the canal into the Christian community. They set up Bethel churches along the canal route to welcome transients.

But the soft glove of concern covered an iron fist of coercion, ready to strike those who persisted in sin. Soon, jobs advertised in

Rochester came with the proviso, "none need apply except those of moral habits." A Rochester maker of fire engines demanded that his workers never touch the bottle, at home or at work, on penalty of dismissal. Workers were strongly urged to attend revivals and join a church. One clerk forced to sit through a revival said, "I don't give a d—n. I get five dollars more in a month than before I got religion."

Entrepreneurs dared not cross the forces of evangelism. One printer seen joking and drinking with salesmen in a Rochester hotel was excommunicated. A few months later his newspaper was taken over by pious owners and he was ruined. A silversmith who over-imbibed before witnesses was suspended from his church and lost his business.

Finney's reforms attacked the time-wasting leisure activities of the working class. Sunday was a workman's only day off, whiskey his cheap escape. Theater, circuses, prostitution, all brought relief from the grind that commercial culture made of men's lives.

It seemed all too convenient that the moneyed mill owners, who profited from an orderly work force, were eager to promote religious dogma that imposed just the kind of discipline they wanted. The new world of factories and wage labor needed new social norms. The religion that Finney helped integrate into American culture facilitated moral compulsion and a bourgeois discipline that benefitted one class over another.

The great evangelist wound up his Rochester revival in late February 1831 with a "protracted meeting," a four-day prayer fest in which Finney and other preachers hammered home their message in all churches from dawn to midnight. Most businesses in the city closed. All stops were let out in a mighty effort to save those souls who had not yet fallen to the revival's prolonged pressure.

By the end of it, Finney was sick. Six months of unrelenting proselytizing had left him exhausted. Worse, a doctor diagnosed consumption and gave him only a few months to live.

He brushed off the warning and set off in a stagecoach over mud-clogged spring roads to continue stirring excitement along the canal. "Once get that region thoroughly soaked," Theodore Weld urged, "and all hell can't wring it dry." The doctor's diagnosis proved wrong, Finney's health rebounded.

He next set his sights on New England. Four years earlier, Lyman Beecher had threatened to call out the artillery to keep him from Boston. Now, Beecher could not help being impressed by the young clergyman's miraculous successes. But he and his colleagues still did not want the western barbarian barging into their territory and giving the skeptical Universalists a perfect excuse to mock Christian fanaticism.

Finney could not be stopped; his celebrity trumped opposition. He arrived in Boston in late August 1831 and stayed for eight months, preaching in every orthodox church. He found that the reserved Bostonians lacked a certain "strength of faith." He urged them to make a decision for Christ, but they remained cold. Attendance at revival meetings, which usually increased, dropped off. "This was something new to me," Finney admitted.

In Beecher's own church, Finney exhorted the congregants "to renounce themselves and their all, and give themselves and all they possessed to Christ." Beecher jumped up and assured them they need not fear giving their all to Christ, for "he will give it right back to you." Finney believed this was "the direct opposite of the truth," but politely refrained from contradicting his host.

Finney's next stop was New York City, where he was embraced by two business magnates, the successful silk importers Arthur and Lewis Tappan. The taciturn Arthur and congenial Lewis were both committed to philanthropy and reform. They supported the Anti-Masonic cause and were veterans of the Sabbatarian movement. Temperance fanatics, they had been mocked for importing alcohol-free Burgundy wine and pushing churchmen to substitute it in communion services. Their zeal for saving prostitutes through their Magdalen Society led them to label New York a city of "ten thousand harlots." Lower-class New Yorkers, the objects of the accusation, threatened to mob their home.

Arthur in particular was becoming an avid proponent of the abolition of slavery. In June 1831, the brothers organized a convention of "People of Color," planned a national antislavery society, and started an abolitionist newspaper called the *Emancipator*. The Tappans argued to Finney that his great influence would be wasted in the more sparsely populated west. Influential men from all over the country now regularly visited New York. "Measures adopted here thrill the nation," Lewis noted.

Finney was acutely aware of his own power, of the power of the Holy Spirit working through him. He could not resist the metropolis. He and Lydia arrived in the city in May 1832. The brothers ensconced the preacher in the Chatham Street Chapel, a 2,500-seat converted theater located near the notorious Five Points slum. Lydia was delighted to have a permanent home after eight years roaming the country. They slept on the floor while they waited for their furniture to be delivered. Finney's upstate friends worried that New York City would dull the evangelist's edge.

That autumn, cholera hit the city. It was an epidemic that would spread with particular virulence along the Erie Canal, accommodated by transients and primitive sanitation. The disease was known as *the destroyer*: victims could show signs of illness in the morning and be dead before the sun set. The Five Points, teeming with immigrants, was hard-hit. Carriages loaded with coffins could be seen on the streets. "The City is in great consternation," Lydia wrote her parents, "and multitudes are fleeing in every direction." She and her husband considered joining the refugees but decided it was their duty to remain. In September, Finney was "seized by the cholera," and spent weeks in bed.

His association with the Tappan brothers made it impossible to dodge the question of slavery. Finney opposed human bondage, but did not want to "divert the attention of the people from the work of converting souls." He allowed blacks to attend his church, but required them to sit in a special section.

In October 1833, Arthur and Lewis Tappan established the New York City Anti-Slavery Society. A newspaper called the rising abolition movement a "most dangerous species of fanaticism." A mob of 1,500 attacked a society gathering. The organizers switched the meeting to Finney's Chapel, which already had a reputation in the press as a "common focus of pollution." Rioters burst in and stampeded through the building. The Tappans barely managed to escape out the back door.

Finney's revivals had planted seeds among the nation's Christians, the seeds had produced trees, the trees were now bearing fruit. But the path away from sin was not yielding the era of peace and holiness that Finney had envisioned. Instead, the campaign against slavery was touching off a storm of unprecedented contention. No one in the 1830s could know that the great event slouching toward them was neither Finney's golden age nor William Miller's dream-like fulfillment of prophecy. It was instead a very real apocalypse of blood.

DEEP PREJUDICE

Joseph Smith Jr. never met Charles Finney, but the men had two close encounters. While Finney was lighting his revival fires in Rochester early in 1831, Smith was fifty miles down the canal in Fayette, organizing his Church for the move to Ohio. A year and a half later, with his Latter Day Saints established in Kirtland, Smith decided to make a trip to New York City. He traveled with Newel Whitney, the Kirtland store owner, who had business in the East.

The two men stayed at a hotel on Pearl Street, not far from the Five Points district where Finney was preaching at his Chapel. Finney, in spite of his rural upbringing, had taken to urban life. Smith did not. He wrote to Emma that the city's buildings were "truly great and wonderful." But he found the crowds hard to endure. He observed "something in every countinance that is disagreable." After a brief sightseeing tour, he rushed back to his room "to meditate and calm my mind and behold the thaughts of home." He soon returned to Ohio, arriving just in time for the birth of his son Joseph III on November 6, 1832.

Smith's home was not a peaceful place. Church membership had topped a thousand and was growing daily, but not everyone was content with Joseph's leadership. Joseph, Emma, and their children had been living with a follower named John Johnson in Hiram, a town thirty miles south of Kirtland. In March 1832, a mob had broken into the Johnson home and dragged Smith out. They stripped him naked, beat him, and broke his tooth trying to force a vial of poison between his lips. They brought a doctor along with the intention of castrating the prophet, but the medical man lost his nerve. They settled for cracking Joseph's ribs and pouring hot tar and feathers on him. They found Sidney Rigdon in a nearby house, roughed him up, and left him unconscious.

The presence in the house of seventeen-year-old Marinda Johnson, along with the castration threat, led to a persistent rumor, probably untrue, that the incident was a consequence of Smith's having made advances on the girl. It's more likely that the attackers were dissident Mormons concerned about Smith's efforts to acquire the property of his followers through a process known as "consecration," a command to give over all possessions to the stewardship of the Church.

Rumors would later circulate that as early as 1831 Joseph had spoken of polygamy as a correct principle. The prophet emphasized that "the time had not yet come to teach and practice it." That same year, Joseph told convert Mary Elizabeth Rollins, twelve years old, that, as she later recorded, "I was the first woman God commanded him to take as a plural wife." He would indeed "marry" her eleven years later. And although Marinda Johnson denied any sexual affair with Smith in the 1830s, she too became his "wife" in 1842.

After the attack, Joseph and Emma moved into rooms in Newel Whitney's store in Kirtland. In 1833, Joseph taught a class there that he called the School of Prophets. He was preparing missionaries to return east and to travel to England. Following the fashion of the day, the men smoked and chewed tobacco during these sessions, spitting liberally on the floor. Emma, who had to clean the mess, complained. Joseph received a revelation from God that "tobacco is not for the body neither for the belly and is not good for man." The lord of the universe also condemned alcohol. For added measure, He included "hot drinks," tea and coffee, a rule that, some said, was meant as a dig at women who enjoyed these tamer vices. The proscriptions were in line with the growing temperance movement and the dietary fads of other religious groups. Mormons have observed them ever since.

More serious issues weighed on Smith in 1834. The Mormon settlement in Independence, Missouri, which Joseph had blessed as the new Zion, was facing growing opposition from local settlers. To the Missourians, Mormons were fanatics intent on grabbing political power and "tampering with our slaves." They had already tarred and feathered Bishop Edward Partridge and destroyed the Mormons' printing press. Vigilante mobs now attacked Mormon farmers and townspeople, burning their homes and ransacking their stores. Most Saints fled from Jackson County to the more remote Clay County on the north side of the Missouri River.

Alarmed by the news and guided as always by revelations from God, Smith formed an armed band in Kirtland and planned a march to "redeem Zion." He called the expedition Zion's Camp. Numbering about a hundred volunteers, the group left Kirtland in May 1834. They walked across Ohio, Indiana, and Illinois. In Missouri they met a similar contingent, which Hyrum Smith had recruited among Michigan Mormons.

Joseph quickly saw that recovering Mormon land in Jackson County by force was hopeless. Legal remedies also failed. In spite of his rhetoric, in which God commanded him to "break down the walls of mine enemies; throw down their tower, and scatter their watchmen," his military force was really just a play army. Its only effect was to spook Missourians, who armed themselves and burned even more Mormon homes. In late June, realizing he was unprepared for real violence, Smith disbanded the camp. The Missouri Mormons would eventually settle even farther north in Caldwell County, where they created the town of Far West as their new headquarters.

The disappointed members of Zion's Camp dispersed to make their own way back to Ohio. Cholera chased after them, killing fourteen. Trudging back almost a thousand miles in summer heat was a disheartening ordeal. The venture had achieved nothing; the guiding revelations had proven empty. Yet the comradeship of shared adversity bound the believers even more firmly to their faith. The Mormons, like their leader, proved remarkably resilient.

Back in Kirtland, Joseph further elaborated the structure of the Church. He incorporated some of his colleagues from Zion's Camp into a powerful body known as the Twelve Apostles. Along with another group, the Seventy, they were "to go forth and gather the Elect," undertaking a wide-ranging campaign to proselytize among the gentiles, as the Mormons referred to those outside the fold.

Evangelical churches of the day tended to be simple and democratic. Following the lead of Charles Finney, more of them were open to active roles for women. The Latter-day Saints' organization was to be hierarchical, complex, and decidedly patriarchal. To the original system of elders, teachers, and deacons, Smith added bishops, who were responsible for administering Church property. Overseeing all was the Church presidency, consisting of Smith himself and two counselors.

Endowed with innate charisma, his mind crowded with ideas, young Joseph could not resist the force of his own creative nature. He spun further and further from orthodoxy. "The religious tenets of this people are so different from the present churches of the age," a newspaper in Clay County, Missouri, noted, "that they always have and always will, excite deep prejudices against them."

When the itinerant preacher Nancy Towle met Smith in Ohio, she said, "Are you not ashamed, of such pretensions? You who are no more, than any ignorant, plough-boy!" Joseph answered, "The gift, has returned back again, as in former times, to illiterate fishermen."

Impressions of the prophet varied. "His language and manner were the coarsest possible," a genteel visitor noted. A convert admitted that "he was a quear man for a Prophet." But, he added, "I found him to be a friendly cheerful pleasant agreeable man. I could not help liking him." Others were even more impressed. "On shaking hands with Joseph Smith, I received the Holy Spirit in such great abundance that I felt it thrill my whole system," said the newly baptized Mary Hales.

Smith published a volume of the revelations that flooded his mind. The book, *Doctrines and Covenants*, became, in its various editions, Mormon scripture. For Church members, the continued revelations were extraordinarily exciting. After centuries of silence, the Almighty was speaking to mankind as He had to the patriarchs.

In 1835, Joseph gathered $2,400, once an unimaginable sum for the Smith family, to purchase four Egyptian mummies and some papyrus scrolls from a traveling showman. He declared the scrolls to contain the Book of Abraham, an elaboration of stories in the Bible. He set about translating the hieroglyphics, creating more scripture to supplement the *Book of Mormon*. But while the gold plates from Hill Cumorah remained elusive, a fragment of this papyrus survived. It turned up in 1967 in the Metropolitan Museum of Art in New York. Scholars judged the document a routine funerary inscription unrelated to Smith's "translation."

In addition to his multitude of Church-related activities, Joseph started a store, an echo of his parents' ill-fated venture of 1802. A lack of business acumen ran in the family: ordering merchandise on credit, Joseph soon found himself heavily in debt.

The idea of family was at the heart of the Mormon experience. Joseph had made his father the Church's first patriarch, an official whose primary duty was to bestow formal blessings. This lovable underdog, so long scorned by his betters, was finally a somebody, a revered official in a burgeoning new religion. Hyrum was made a top counselor and would later succeed his father as patriarch.

Smith's continued emphasis on the Biblical patriarchs drew his attention to the fact that many of them had married multiple wives. A verse in 1 Kings said that Solomon "had seven hundred wives, princesses, and three hundred concubines." The *Book of Mormon* had rejected polygamy, calling multiple marriages "wicked practices" that were "abominable before me, saith the Lord."

Joseph Smith was thirty years old, at the peak of his manhood, trembling with energy and endowed with enormous power within his Church. Soon after the move to Ohio, rumors about sexual unorthodoxy began circulating inside and outside the faith.

Fanny Alger and her family were among the earliest Ohio converts to the Mormon faith. In 1833, when she was sixteen, Fanny moved into the Smith home to help with the housework. Emma was caring for two small children at the time. Fanny was "a varry nice & Comly young woman," convert Benjamin Johnson observed. Everyone was partial to her, he wrote, but "it was whispered eaven then that Joseph *Loved her.*"

Emma was fond of Fanny and looked on her as an adopted daughter. One story said that Emma discovered her husband engaged in a sex act with the girl by peeping through a crack in the door of the barn. Maybe. In some manner, she discerned that the relationship was "by no means a paternal affection." On discovering this treachery within her own home, "Emma was furious," a Kirtland convert reported, "and drove the girl, who was unable to conceal the consequences of her celestial relation with the prophet, out of her house."

A torrent of gossip swept the close-knit community. The Church high command approved a revelation, usually attributed to Oliver Cowdery, affirming that all marriages "should be solemnized in a public meeting." This "Article on Marriage," noted that "this Church of Christ has been reproached with the crime of fornication and polygamy." It declared that one man should have one wife, and one woman one husband.

Joseph was playing a deeper game. He began to couch his sexual liaisons in the language of "plural marriage," which would become accepted Mormon doctrine. Adultery in any form was clearly a sin. If Smith was to indulge his desire for women, it had to be in the context of marriage, however ad hoc the ceremony, however secret the banns. Over time, Joseph constructed an elaborate rigmarole to justify and regulate polygamy. For now, he was improvising and trying his best to keep Emma in the dark.

Sexual license would have the most profound consequences for Smith and for the Church as a whole. In addition to Emma's fury, Joseph had to contend with Oliver Cowdery, his early collaborator and boon companion in the priesthood. Cowdery looked on the prophet's intercourse with Fanny as "a dirty, nasty, filthy affair."

The momentum of Joseph's visionary mind and his unquenchable appetite for experience would continue to grow. This particular transgression seemed ordinary and petty, but the sex issue would become more complex and more grave as time went on. It introduced a dark secret into Smith's Mormon program that would fester until it became fatal.

VELOCITY

DeWitt Clinton died suddenly in 1828 at the age of fifty-eight, only three years after the completion of the ditch that would be forever associated with his name. On August 9, 1831, an excited crowd gathered in Albany to confer on him a unique and fitting honor.

The lucky few who had purchased tickets climbed either into carriages "of the old-fashioned stage-coach pattern" or took seats on benches mounted on open flatbed cars. They eagerly, nervously waited to take the "first ride on a railroad drawn by a locomotive." In town and country alike, hundreds of spectators lined the sixteen-mile route to Schenectady.

The conductor blew his horn, the engineer put the four-wheeled engine into motion. Because cars were connected by chains, each gave a mighty jerk as it started, throwing passengers around the carriages. Tall beaver hats were knocked asunder. As the train proceeded at a "considerable velocity," smoke and sparks from the wood-fired boiler rained down on the passengers. They quickly put up umbrellas, which quickly caught fire. So did straw hats and summer coats.

Passengers flapped at each other to extinguish the smoldering fabric. Spectators' horses bolted at the novel sight and sound. Gaping farmers watched as a new era materialized before their eyes. The name of the engine was the *DeWitt Clinton*. The canal's great proponent would have beamed had he lived to see the huffing, relentless engine, which was in perfect harmony with his interest in science and his determination to push into the future.

Passenger steam locomotive service made its first appearance in America as an adjunct to the Erie Canal. The Mohawk & Hudson Railroad, which completed its debut run that day, was intended as a convenience to canal passengers, saving them the tedious, all-day passage up the many locks that marked the first thirty miles of the waterway. They could zip to Schenectady in an hour by rail and transfer to a packet boat for the ride west.

John Jervis, who had started his career as an axman laying out a course for the ditch in 1817, was the railroad's principal designer. Like many American engineers weaned on the canal, he was coming into his own and eager for a new challenge.

In the first six months after this maiden trip, twenty-five railroad companies applied for incorporation in New York State alone. Canals were useless in winter, expensive to maintain, and limited in the routes they could cover. They would not quickly die out, but this short rail line was the harbinger of an entirely new mode of transportation.

SPIRIT

In the wake of the Morgan affair, Freemasons were widely denounced as "un-American." Mobs broke into lodges to expose the brotherhood's secrets. Masons made an effort to fight back. They attacked former brothers who publicly denounced the order. They sent their own mobs into the churches of ministers who preached against them. Masons packed Anti-Masonic meetings and shouted down speakers. Animosity ruled.

The success of the Anti-Masonic movement proved the power of paranoia. A conspiracy was a perfect target for citizens' anxieties. This was a second war of independence, aimed at freeing Americans "from the yoke of Masonic tyranny." The answer to anyone who doubted the movement's truths was simple: "The violence done to Capt. Morgan."

The ideals of the Revolution were indeed fading. But it was the reality of capitalism, not the fantasy of an aristocratic plot, that was bringing change. Riches, many suspected, were no longer a product of honest labor but of clever speculation. There had appeared in America, a Massachusetts congressman noted, "a race of non-producers, who render no equivalent to society for what they consume." Independent citizens were becoming dependent. Conspicuous consumption was captivating the middle class. The lucky were amassing wealth, the unfortunate falling into poverty.

Ironically, these same jarring factors had also encouraged men to join the Freemasons. In the lodges, they could find a refuge from the competitive market. They could find conviviality, mutual aid, benevolence. Both sides clung to a nostalgic dream of a time when American society was kinder, purer, more united in its devotion to republican principles.

The revivalists and the Anti-Masons formed an alliance that injected a pious, religious impulse into political action. "There is a union between religion and politics in all this region of the country," newspaper editor James Gordon Bennett said of Rochester. Anti-Masons stood with Christians to defend traditional ideals.

Thurlow Weed, the publisher and political operator, along with other Anti-Masonic activists, pushed their party to overcome its conspiratorial roots and embrace wider issues. Internal improvements were high on the list. Protection of domestic manufacture through tariffs. The repeal of imprisonment for debt. The abolition of militia duty. The party attracted support from political giants like Daniel Webster and Henry Clay.

"We are all becoming anti-masonick," William Seward, a lawyer based in Auburn, New York, wrote to his father in 1828. Seward became a close friend of Thurlow Weed. An early supporter of the cause, he was elected state senator on the Anti-Masonic ticket in 1830, beginning a meteoric political career. The most prominent of any politician to emerge from the Anti-Masonic movement, he would challenge Lincoln for the presidency in 1860, then serve as his secretary of state.

In 1830, the Anti-Masons were just beginning to feel their political oats. Weed hoped to gain national credibility and visibility by sponsoring a candidate in the presidential election of 1832. Up until that time, U.S. presidential candidates had been chosen by the members of Congress from each party. Lacking such a caucus, the Anti-Masonic Party needed another method. Having established their strength through public meetings, they decided that the best way to nominate a candidate was to do it during a convention. It would be a political camp meeting to rally their followers and ratify the nomination.

On September 11, 1831, the fifth anniversary of William Morgan's disappearance, they came together in Baltimore in the first national presidential convention in U.S. history. They chose as their candidate William Wirt, a sixty-year-old Marylander who had served both James Monroe and John Quincy Adams as attorney general. His gravitas helped counteract charges of fanaticism against the Anti-Masonic zealots. Although Wirt had once been a Mason, he now saw that the brotherhood was "at war with the fundamental principles of the social compact."

The other parties quickly followed the Anti-Masonic lead. Adherents of the fading National Republicans met in December to nominate Henry Clay. Jackson supporters, who would soon call themselves Democrats, held their own convention the following May.

In the 1832 election, Wirt won only Vermont. He may have taken some votes away from Clay, but it did not matter: Jackson won reelection in a landslide. With their defeat, the Anti-Masons lost cohesion. They were victims of their own success. As Freemasons closed their lodges, the exaggerated Anti-Masonic rhetoric rang hollow and the basic absurdity of their claims began to show. In the years after 1832, many Anti-Masons joined with other opponents of Jackson to form the Whig party. The political convention, that quadrennial amalgam of circus and speech fest, proved to be the most lasting contribution of the Anti-Masonic Party, which, born in 1828, would last barely ten years.

Anti-Masons mixed conservative and populist impulses into a potent ideological stew. Fueled by fear, they were sure of their principles, reluctant to compromise, resistant to change. They lived in a world fashioned from stark moral contrasts. The themes and style they introduced have echoed down the corridors of American politics ever since, from the Free Soil and Greenback Parties to the modern Tea Party.

EXTERMINATION

Brigham Young had much in common with the prophet Joseph Smith Jr. Both were born in Vermont. Both came from families that had been drawn by "York Fever" to western New York. Both had grown up poor. Young's family had headed for the frontier in 1804, when he was three, settling in the remote center of the state before trekking farther west into the Finger Lakes region. His father, like Smith's, was a failed farmer who worked as a day laborer. Young and his siblings knew real hunger.

When Brigham reached the age of sixteen, his father turned him out of the house to find his own way in life. The teenager settled in Auburn just as the canal was being built and apprenticed himself to a carpenter. Like the Smiths, the Youngs were more visionary than acquisitive. A Lorenzo Dow revival was one of Brigham's early memories. His younger brother, like many frontier babies, was named for the Methodist exhorter. Other brothers became itinerant preachers themselves.

Young tried unsuccessfully to catch hold of the prosperity the Erie Canal was bringing to the region. In 1828, he joined his extended family in Mendon, south of Rochester and a few miles from the canal's famous Irondequoit embankment. There he made a good friend in fellow craftsman Heber Kimball. Neither Kimball's pottery nor Young's furniture-making could quite pay the bills. Both men struggled with debt.

In 1830, Joseph Smith's brother Samuel introduced Young's brother Phineas to the "Golden Bible." Brigham thought deeply about the book. After two years of contemplation, he embraced the new religion. His father and siblings joined him. On a chilly day in April 1832, Brigham was baptized in a mill pond. He was made an elder in the Church "before my clothes were dry."

Brigham Young's wife died in September of the same year. He, his brother Joseph, and Heber Kimball made a pilgrimage down the canal and along Lake Erie to meet the author of the book that had won them over. They expected to encounter a holy man "in his sanctum dispensing spiritual blessings." Instead, they came upon a vigorous wood chopper a few years younger than themselves, a man who liked to laugh. Brigham, who had spent his boyhood at such work, picked up an ax, felled a tree, and formed a lasting connection with the smiling prophet.

Less than a year later, Young had settled in Kirtland with his two daughters. He strengthened his bond with Smith when he marched to Missouri as a soldier in Zion's Camp. In 1835, as Smith created his presidency, councils, priesthoods, and other Church structures, he raised Young to the Quorum of the Twelve Apostles, a group he intended as his primary proselytizers.

Early in 1836, Young joined Joseph's inner circle for Pentecostal visitations of the Holy Spirit. The men practiced the laying on of hands and anointings known as endowments. Foot washing gave way to the washing of each other's bodies "with whiskey, perfumed with cinnamon." Smith reported that "the heavens were opened upon us."

In March they dedicated the Kirtland temple, a church three years in the building, with fifty-foot walls and a tower more than a hundred feet high. Smith declared that "the angels are coming to visit the earth." Some who could not fit inside the building saw angels looking out the temple windows. Soon afterward, Smith and Oliver Cowdery saw "the Lord standing upon the breastwork of the pulpit." Brigham Young spotted forty angels "in white robes & caps."

Glorious times, but in 1837 it all fell apart.

Construction of the temple had left Mormons deeply in debt. The settlement in Missouri soaked up assets. So did caring for the poverty-stricken converts streaming into both Far West and Ohio. Smith and the Kirtland leaders thought that starting a bank would help firm up the settlement's shaky finances. The group possessed plenty of good farmland but little cash. With the land as collateral, they could issue banknotes to pay their debts and fuel the local economy. They joined the many others around the country who plunged into private banking during the Jackson years. The practice was being encouraged by policies set in Washington.

Andrew Jackson, following his hard-money ideology, had vetoed a bill to recharter the Second Bank of the United States. He moved federal funds to favored state banks. States in turn authorized hundreds of private banks, each of which issued its own notes. The nation's paper currency became a crazy quilt of bills with varying and often dubious value.

In the autumn of 1836, the Mormons formed the Kirtland Safety Society and applied for a state charter. Investors, mostly Mormons, were allowed to buy stock in the company by pledging land. Heber Kimball was granted a $50,000 interest; he put up only $15 in cash. Brigham Young received 2,000 shares for a $7 investment. The result was a disastrously undercapitalized enterprise.

Ohio authorities refused to charter this feeble institution. The Mormons decided to turn the Safety Society into an "anti-bank," whatever that meant. They stamped "Anti-" before the word "Bank," on all of the $100,000 worth of the notes they issued.

The anti-bank opened for business January 2, 1837. As customers came in to redeem notes, the bank's reserves of gold and silver coins quickly evaporated. "Mormon money" was trading for twelve cents on the dollar before February was over. By summer, the bank was largely insolvent. Anyone who had accepted the notes at face value lost heavily. Many Mormons harbored deep grievances against Church leaders.

Facing financial ruin that year, the Mormons had plenty of company. The flood of notes from state banks undermined currency all over the country. Big New York banks, stripped of federal deposits, cut back on lending. President Jackson decreed that western public lands could only be purchased for specie—gold or silver. His action jabbed a pin into the bubble in western real estate, which the Erie Canal had pumped to bursting. All of these factors combined to create a severe financial panic. Credit froze, banks failed, businesses went broke, and the country descended into its first serious economic depression, a slump that would not lift for six years.

Currency and prophets both depend on confidence. The value of a dollar bill requires faith in the issuing party. A revelation is worth as much as one's belief in its source. Brigham Young understood this.

"If I was to harbor a thought in my heart that Joseph could be wrong in anything," he noted, "I would begin to lose confidence in him." In particular, he would find it hard to believe in "his being the mouthpiece of the Almighty."

Young, Rigdon, and other loyalists kept their faith. Others did not. Joseph had promised glorious things in Kirtland, yet the local economy was collapsing. Doubt shot through the community. Whispers about sexual antics spread. By the summer of 1837, Heber Kimball estimated, the vast majority of Mormons had lost faith in their prophet. Parley Pratt publicly accused Joseph of "great sins."

By autumn, dissenting Mormons had virtually taken over in Kirtland, and Joseph was rapidly losing control. He excommunicated forty men, but the dissenters claimed to represent the legitimate authority of Mormonism, and they insisted on holding their own services in the temple. Joseph Smith, they said, was the one who had strayed from the faith. Harassed, denounced, threatened with violence, Joseph gave up on Kirtland. He relinquished the temple. A third of the high officials of his Church turned away from him. So did a large portion of his followers.

On the night of January 12, 1838, Smith and Sidney Rigdon mounted fast horses and fled from Kirtland. The Mormon printing office in town went up in flames. The perpetrators were not hostile gentiles but disillusioned Mormons.

Emma and Rigdon's wife, Phebe, along with their children, joined their husbands. The small caravan continued through the dead of winter toward Far West, the Mormon settlement eight hundred miles away on the Missouri frontier.

Along the way, the prophet became reacquainted with poverty. He begged for work chopping wood and threatened a tavern keeper who turned his ragged family away. Five-year-old Joseph III, for whom the journey was a combination of romp and nightmare, clung to his mother's hand as he marched through the cold. His father might have told the story of his own winter journey from the fairytale land of Vermont to Palmyra, where visions of angels awaited him.

In early March, after two months on the road, the party encountered a welcoming committee from Far West. As they neared the town, a brass band waited along the road. Crowds rushed out to celebrate the arrival of the prophet.

"We were immediately received under the hospitable roof of George W. Harris," Joseph later wrote, "who treated us with all kindness possible."

Harris was a high priest of the Church and a member of the Far West city council. His wife had, for a time, been one of the most famous women in America. Lucinda Pendleton Morgan Harris was the widow of William Morgan. The disappearance of her husband more than a decade earlier had rattled the country and remained fresh in many minds.

At thirty-seven, Lucinda was four years older than Joseph. Small, blond, her face lit by intelligent cornflower eyes, she was still a striking beauty. She had married two men, each twenty years her senior. She now stood face-to-face with the man who would become her third husband.

The Smiths stayed at the Harris home for two months before moving to their own house in the center of Far West. Years later, Joseph Smith would make a sexual proposition to Sarah Pratt, the wife of the missionary Orson Pratt, who had baptized the Harrises. With her husband off on a recruiting mission, Sarah expressed her concern to her good friend Mrs. Harris. "To my utter astonishment she said, laughing heartily: 'How foolish you are! I don't see anything so horrible in it. Why I am his mistress since four years!'"

Mormons had built the city of Far West on the open Missouri prairie after being forced from Independence, their original Zion. From Jackson and Clay counties, they had trekked thirty miles north to Caldwell County, where they established towns and farms. Missourians continued to mistrust them. "They are Eastern men," one said, "whose manners, habits, customs and even dialect, are essentially different from our own."

While the animosity of outsiders grew, internal dissension followed Joseph from Ohio. Now it broke out even among his closest supporters. Oliver Cowdery had taken up the practice of law and was accused of "selling his lands in Jackson County contrary to the Revelations." Cowdery felt that personal business was not a Church matter. He would not subject himself to "any ecclesiastical authority or pretended revelation."

Cowdery came before the Far West High Council, charged with "seeking to destroy the character of President Joseph Smith jr by falsely insinuating that he was guilty of adultery &c." It was a reference to Smith's seduction of his young servant Fanny Alger. Smith did not deny a relationship with Alger, but he insisted he had committed no sin. Cowdery was excommunicated.

Soon David Whitmer was expelled as well. Martin Harris, who had bankrolled the printing of the *Book of Mormon*, had not followed Smith to Missouri. All three of the original witnesses to the gold plates had separated themselves from the prophet. Other departures followed.

Some of the dissenters still owned land in Far West, and felt they had a right to live where they pleased. One of them, George Robinson, said that in a republic, he felt free to "oppose his own Judgment to the Judgment of God." Sidney Rigdon declared in a sermon that those who had been excommunicated had no rights among the Mormons. He called on the people to rise up "and rid the county of such a nuisance." Shortly afterward, eighty-three of Far West's leading citizens signed what amounted to an ultimatum. Cowdery, the Whitmers, and others dissidents were to leave voluntarily or "we will put you from the county." The apostates cleared out, the Church confiscated their property.

Ready to back up the threats against the rebels was a Mormon brotherhood known as the Sons of Dan. These Danites, like Freemasons, were bound by oaths and bonds of secrecy. The shadowy brotherhood served as enforcers within the community and as a counterpart to the mobs that were rising among the non-Mormon settlers of Missouri.

By all accounts, Joseph Smith had an aversion to violence. But in Missouri the law was weak and vigilante mobs strong. He and Rigdon may have tolerated the paramilitary Danites as a force that could protect the Saints from gentile nightriders.

Mormons had been pouring into the county all year, and few farm sites now remained available. Settlers were beginning to eye property in surrounding counties. Their presence alarmed non-Mormons. The wary locals were afraid that theocracy could replace democracy, that the kingship of Joseph Smith might supplant republican government. They were not about to tolerate it.

On the Fourth of July 1838, the Mormons mounted a parade and raised a liberty pole. Danite leaders marched with members of the Mormon militia of Caldwell County. Rigdon again rose in the pulpit to issue a challenge, this time to gentiles who had been menacing them. "From this day and hour we will suffer it no more," he said. "That mob that comes on us to disturb us; it shall be between us and them a war of extermination."

PACKET

The muddy ditch is only four feet deep, but on stepping aboard, the passenger feels the soft, teetering sensation of a water craft. Breathes the rancid smells. Is jostled by forty other passengers crowding onto the boat. Some climb to the deck on the roof of the long cabin, others find places on the benches or easy chairs inside.

A menagerie of people. Europeans come to get a taste of the exotic American west and not incidentally to experience the canal itself. They start their tour at New York City, take a steamer to Albany, absorb the always changing sights along the canal, and wind up at Niagara Falls. A local resident is going down the line to visit relatives, a Troy merchant is traveling to contract for wheat, a Rochester lawyer to see about a case. Laborers head down the canal to find work, the odd runaway slave to reach Canada, an itinerant preacher to spread the Gospel, a thimble-rigger to cheat the rustics.

The crew casts off. The boatmen have a "brigandish guise" and bold swagger, with bright ribbons decorating their slouch hats. They are "a terror to the smiling innocence of the villages." So observed Herman Melville, who traveled and may have worked on the canal.

Two mules, driven by a barefoot boy, strain against the two-hundred-foot-long tow rope. The helmsman guides the craft away from the wharf. The speed limit is walking pace, four miles an hour. The canal commissioners, hoping to limit erosion, fine captains for speeding.

Yet because of the silence and the nearness of the banks, the boat at first seems to be moving rapidly. "Commending my soul to God," said a Rochesterian of his first ride, "I stepped on board the canal boat, and was soon flying toward Utica." The travel is miraculously smooth, no bouncing in a stagecoach or jogging on horseback.

Most passengers opt for a seat on deck. In fine weather, everyone wants to take in the scenery, first the bustling town, then a bucolic landscape of fields and farms. They skim in and out of the shadows of trees. Indifferent turtles, nervous frogs, and inquisitive dragonflies observe their passing.

The names of the boats echo the times. *Old Hickory* honors the president. A passenger might catch sight of the *Anti-Masonic Republican*. The *Temperance* and the *Clergyman* nod to the revivals, the *Frolic*, the *Crazy John*, and *Cleopatra's Barge* to the youthful zest of canal denizens. At every stop, children leap aboard to offer apples or cakes for sale. The vessels are painted bright orange, green, and yellow. One is the home of E. E. Wilcox's Bookstore and Lottery Office, another of a mobile grocery store. Knife sharpeners, dentists, barbers, all ply their trades from boats. One old barge holds a carousel to delight children in remote towns. A floating museum offers "a fair collection of natural and artificial curiosities and wax works."

Skirting the Mohawk River, the boat heads for the gap at Little Falls. The mountains crowd in on either side until it seems impossible the canal can make it through. "We often passed between magnificent cliffs," wrote the English traveler and writer Frances Trollope (mother of the Victorian novelist Anthony Trollope), who made the tour with her two daughters. "The rocks over which the river runs are most fantastic in form. The fall continues nearly a mile."

Riding up top, passengers have more than the hot sun to contend with. "Low bridge!" It's already a catch phrase, but no empty warning. Injury and even death awaited the unwary. Hundreds of bridges have been thrown over the canal—farmers need to cross to till their fields on the other side. They do not build them any higher than necessary; most spans hover only a few feet above the packet's deck.

At first it is amusing, one passenger recorded, "to hop down and then to hop up again, but by and by this skipping about became very tiresome." On average, a passenger has to duck "every quarter of an hour, under penalty of having one's head crushed to atoms."

At dinnertime the passengers gather in the main cabin. Canal boats are America's first cruise ships, and the food is plentiful and palatable: ham, boiled beef, potted pigeons, lamb chops, venison, potatoes, calves' feet jelly, pudding, apple pie, cider, brown stout, coffee. Diners spend little time savoring the fare—the American habit is to eat quickly, downing a heavy meal in ten minutes or less.

Afterward, patrons can relax with one of the books or periodicals in the small library. In the newspapers, even four years after the event, column inches are still devoted to the Morgan disappearance. Advertisements recommend items ranging from anti-dyspeptick elixirs and Prosser's Liniment for spavined horses to bonnets, bridles, dancing academies, literary magazines, and lotteries ("Who wants a Fortune?"), all suggesting the growing prosperity of what was so recently a frontier. A notice says that a Reformed Church near Little Falls wishes to obtain a Minister, "one who will regard the flock more than the FLEECE."

Weary of reading, one might get up a game of whist or backgammon, doze in an armchair, or debate with fellow travelers the latest outrages or heroics of President Jackson.

Passing the locks is a thrill at first. The process is almost magical: engineers had found a way to use the gravity acting on water to effortlessly lift a boat and a hundred tons of cargo. All they needed was a stone chamber with gates at each end and a system of sluices and valves to let in water from the upper level or release it to the lower.

The boat clunks against the sides of the chamber—it's been constructed to fit with only inches of clearance. The closing doors create a damp box. Then the sound of rushing water, passengers catch their breath, and the boat rises. Long levers allow the lock-keeper to open the doors in front once the levels are equalized. The craft heads off on the higher plane.

But the novelty soon wears off. During the wait, many passengers hop off the boat to stretch their legs. They can be pretty sure of a chance to grab a glass of whiskey. Locks are favorite spots for locals to set up small grocery shops that sells drinks and sundries.

Reformers insisted in 1835 that there were some 1,500 drinking establishments along the canal, an astounding average of one every quarter mile. In Lockport two dozen bars crowded together within fifty feet of the locks.

The pugnacious character of canal workers is legendary, but the violence along the artificial river is sometimes real. Rough boatmen do not like having to wait in line to pass a lock. They fight other crews for position. The insolent youths who drive the mules scrap with local farm boys.

Gradually, the sensation of speed is replaced by the itch of impatience. In hot weather, the trip can be downright wearing. "Iced-water (without sugar) kept us alive," Trollope wrote. "But for this delightful recipe, feather fans, and eau de Cologne, I think we should have failed altogether; the thermometer stood at 90 degrees."

Nathaniel Hawthorne, who traveled the canal a few years later, was another who fell victim to Erie ennui. He had imagined an enchanted waterway, but found instead "an interminable mud-puddle." The jaded New Englander saw only "dismal swamps and unimpressive scenery." He wrinkled his nose at the "dull race of money-getting drudges" he met along the way.

After the evening meal, the boat's steward makes the cabin benches into beds. He hangs additional sleeping accommodations from the ceiling until the bunks are stacked three or four high. Charles Dickens, when he made his canal journey, pretended to mistake the narrow berths for bookshelves. The women's quarters are curtained off and the passengers bid good-night. To sleep while traveling is a fascinating novelty, assuming the travelers can accustom themselves to the snoring, the crying of babies, and the occasional thud and gurgle while passing a lock.

Frances Trollope relied on her cologne for a reason. The smell of all those bodies, the lingering aroma of cooking, and the fetid air of the canal itself create a memorable miasma. A tourist assigned to an upper berth noted that "the air was so foul that I found myself sick." He had to move. A Scottish traveler also found the "stench and effluvia from such a collection of human beings" intolerable. With the water a repository for human waste and the towpath for mule and horse droppings, canal air often takes on a villainous smell.

On close nights, the deck provides little relief, the ruffling of air not enough to keep off the clouds of mosquitoes. Hawthorne peered into the dark and saw an eerie land "whither dreams betake themselves when they quit the slumberer's brain."

But each day holds promise of new sights. Once the boat passes the settled Mohawk Valley, passengers are seeing the real western part of the state. Travelers from crowded eastern cities are amazed by the emptiness. Here Europeans encounter the novelty of virgin forests, trees that seem to scrape the sky. Tocqueville referred to the majesty of New World forests that "fills the soul with a sort of religious terror."

The boat glides over the towering embankment at Irondequoit. Passengers look down at trees and people below, virtually sailing through the sky. The Rochester aqueduct never fails to impress. The magnificent stairway of lifts at Lockport inspires awe. Navigating the man-made canyon of the Deep Cut, passengers stare in wonder at the sheer rock sides, which leave the boat in shade at the bottom. "You are actually sailing through a mountain," a traveler noted.

The five-day trip to Buffalo cuts the stagecoach time in half, and the fares are "so low that no man who consults economy, *can afford to go on foot!*" The cost averages four cents a mile with board, three without, fourteen dollars from Schenectady to Buffalo. Competition among packet companies will drive the price to $6.50 by the mid-1830s. With three meals a day it is "cheaper than staying at home," one company boasts.

Line boats, which carry a combination of freight and passengers, charge travelers a third less than the packets. Although slower, they offer immigrants a cheap way to reach new homes in the west. Package deals let them travel for as little as a penny a mile. Buffalo is inundated by a tidal wave of pioneers. In 1826, nearly twelve hundred, all headed west, arrived in a single day, clogging the city's hotels. They arrange for steamboat passage up Lake Erie and onward as far as Michigan Territory, present-day Minnesota.

Before the transportation breakthrough, those who ventured beyond the Appalachians were true pioneers. The move put them out of touch with family and friends in the East. The canal made it much easier for the venturer to return for a visit. Mail service westward became more reliable. Regular letters were a comfort that broke the isolation. The Erie Canal gave settlers courage. It facilitated a mobility that was to become a permanent characteristic of the American population.

UNUTTERABLE MAGNITUDE

In 1835, a former newspaper editor and shopkeeper invested a thousand dollars in the rights to a theatrical exhibit. Phineas Taylor Barnum became the manager of Joice Heth, a black woman who was both slave and experienced stage performer. Barnum took her to concert halls, taverns, pleasure gardens, and saloons, charging customers to see "the greatest curiosity in the world."

Heth had been born in Madagascar in 1674. Kidnapped into slavery, she had become the property of a Virginia planter named Augustine Washington. When Washington's wife gave birth to a baby boy in 1732, Joice served as nurse to "little Georgy." She practically raised the lad, she said, and taught him to sing hymns. All these years later she could relate many intimate stories about the youth who went on to become the father of his country.

Heth was 161 years old, toothless, remarkably wizened, paralyzed in both legs, and blind. Her long curving fingernails resembled claws. Yet she was bright, could hear perfectly, and was able to answer questions with practiced eloquence. In Barnum's promotional pamphlets, he mentioned that her pipe and tobacco were her greatest pleasure—she had been smoking for 120 years. Her pulse, he notified the curious, was between sixty-five and seventy, "full, strong, and perfectly regular."

Barnum and a partner reportedly made $30,000 by exhibiting Heth six days a week. When business lagged, Barnum sent a letter to a newspaper under a pseudonym, claiming that Heth was a fraud. She was not General Washington's nurse. She was not even human—she was an automaton constructed by "some of those cunning fellows who deal in gum elastick overshoes." Previous customers hurried back to see if they had been hornswoggled by a machine.

Heth died barely a year after Barnum acquired her. He charged fifty cents a head to watch a prominent New York doctor conduct her autopsy. When the doctor pronounced her to be about eighty years old, Barnum offered an exclusive interview to the *New York Herald* in which he explained that the corpse was a ringer; the real, ancient Joice was still alive. It was all pure humbug.

Barnum was one of the earliest Americans to fully grasp the dynamics of publicity, advertising, ballyhoo, and hype. Citizens were just beginning to amalgamate into a mass society and Barnum helped foster the national addiction to fame and spectacle.

The religious and political leaders of the era did not deal in humbug. They were sincere in their convictions. But many of them understood that to reach a large audience effectively required what

Charles Finney called "methods." Joseph Smith's golden plates, Thurlow Weed's drowned corpse, William Miller's lurid predictions, all contained a hint of Barnumesque promotional hoopla.

Like Lorenzo Dow, successful preachers and politicians were "cosmopolites." They had the capacity to believe wholeheartedly in their message even as they dressed it in glad rags to appeal to simple-minded listeners. Like Barnum, they knew the elements of bally-hoo: Spectacle never fails. Hyperbole pays. Details stymie skeptics. Controversy creates newspaper stories. If caught out, up the ante. Welcome attacks. Offer documentation, however dubious. Give the people exactly what they want: fantasy, novelty, the unusual, the miraculous.

William Miller, prompted by his new partner Joshua Himes, put many of these maxims to work to spread the news of the coming end. Miller's claim that the entire world would go up in flames in a few short years was more unthinkable than anything Barnum ever pro-moted, yet he convinced tens of thousands of its literal truth.

Miller had been a voice crying in the wilderness for eight years when he met Himes in 1839. Himes was a veteran of the reforms that grew out of the revivals. He had worked tirelessly for temperance and against slavery. He threw himself into promoting Miller's message because he saw that it injected urgent excitement into religion.

Miller learned from Himes that successful promotion required people and money. Himes invested his own funds in the cause, rounded up wealthy donors, and organized a campaign to elicit con-tributions. Miller's Advent message aided fund-raising. If his predic-tions were correct, all wealth would soon be superfluous. To hold on to your money was a sign you doubted Christ's imminent coming.

Himes had connections. He recruited a number of prominent preachers to help spread the word. In the manner of the Anti-Masons, he organized conferences where followers—increasingly called Adventists rather than Millerites—could meet, share experi-ences, and encourage one another. Scheduled to take place every six months, these meetings offered a chance to educate new cohorts of Adventist preachers. In 1842, devotees formed the Second Adventist Association.

To drum up attention, Himes turned to a familiar revival fea-ture: the camp meeting. The Quaker poet John Greenleaf Whittier remembered observing one of these gatherings on a lovely summer morning. He was impressed by "the white circle of tents . . . the up-turned earnest faces" listening to preachers warn of the nearness of the end. "How was it possible," he wondered, "in the midst of so much life, in that sunrise light . . . that the idea of the death of nature—the baptism of the world in fire—could take such a practical shape?"

Himes encouraged the use of images to depict the horrors of the last days. Whittier saw a painted "Apocalyptic vision" that included beasts, dragons, and "the scarlet woman." Elaborate charts made Miller's complex calculations easier to understand. He had the Adventist motto "The bridegroom cometh" printed on sheets of paper seals so that believers could cut them out and paste them on letters and envelopes.

Adventists tried to bar fanaticism from their meetings. Himes and Miller were staunch opponents of faith healing, wanton prophecy, speaking in tongues, and sexual escapades. Young people, tempted to taste forbidden fruits before it was too late, were thought vulnerable. Strict decorum was enforced at Adventist gatherings.

In a Barnum-like move, the Adventist leaders commissioned the largest tent in North America. As high as a five-story building, 120 feet in diameter, the enormous canvas enclosure could hold up to six thousand congregants. Circus tents were a novelty at the time, and the Great Tent drew crowds.

Taking another page from the Anti-Masonic campaign, Himes started Adventist newspapers. He invested his own money in *Signs of the Times*, the movement's flagship publication. When Miller appeared in New York City, the Adventists handed out thousands of copies of another paper, *The Midnight Cry*, which continued as a weekly. When the road-show traveled to Rochester, local Adventist Joseph Marsh published the *Glad Tidings of the Kingdom to Come*, which he announced in the first issue would run for thirteen weeks, "if time continues."

Miller was taken aback by the frenzy that was building around him. Himes, "a radical and an enthusiast by temperament," ordered him around quite imperiously. "I am coming on," he wrote to Miller in 1840, "and when I come—look out."

Himes, like Barnum, understood the power of celebrity. The crowds who attended Adventist services wanted more than ideas.

They wanted Miller. They needed to see the humble farmer who had made the astounding discovery. To enhance the personality cult, Himes hired Nathaniel Currier, the preeminent lithographic artist of the day (he later became half of Currier & Ives), to create a portrait of Miller that could be reproduced by the thousands.

As unlikely as it seemed, Miller developed charisma. His very diffidence attracted attention. He was "distinct in his utterance, and frequently quaint in his expressions," a Maine reporter wrote. Miller sometimes produced a smile from his listeners with his homespun wit. Himes and others could explain the millennial ideas adequately, but it was Miller's presence that mattered. "You can have no idea of the thrill of joy it produced when I told them you would come," Himes wrote Miller about a scheduled appearance.

Unused to strict schedules, Miller frustrated Himes by arriving late at engagements or failing to show. Miller was plagued by a painful skin condition, by worsening dropsy, and by the aches and ills that attend any sixty-year-old. His ailments sometimes sidelined him for months. Himes, who had genuine affection for Miller, grew concerned about his mentor's health.

Miller's unorthodox views generated a backlash of criticism. Anti-Miller preaching became rife. One pamphlet proclaimed *The End of the World Not Yet*. Another was titled *The Theory of William Miller, Utterly Exploded*. Millerism, preachers insisted, was the work of Satan, and Miller was amassing a fortune from sales of his books. Churchmen blasted Miller's theories as "a new edition of Mormonism." Opponents sent spies to Miller's home. They reported that his children were living in luxury and that he had bought a new stove and erected new stone walls, curious behavior for a man who asserted the world was about to end.

The mild-mannered farmer had another side to his personality, which further fueled the criticism. A Portland reporter said that Miller was "disposed to make but little allowance for those who think differently from him." He freely denounced his opponents as "dumb dogs," "wiseacres," or "Priestly dandies."

In 1842, Charles Finney attended several Adventist lectures in Boston and met privately with Miller, who was ten years his senior. His purpose was to "convince him that he was in error." Miller nodded his head in agreement as Finney listed the ways he had misread

Scripture. But when they were finished, Miller presented the famous clergyman with an autographed copy of his book. He assured Finney that if he read it, he would see the truth of the matter.

Many Adventists were "come-outers," who rejected fellowship with any church that denied the validity of the prediction. A Millerite preacher proclaimed: "If you intend to be found a Christian when Christ appears . . . come out *Now!*" Adventists took their worship to private homes and camp meetings. They formed breakaway congregations. In the process, they drew even more venom from churchgoing neighbors.

The more the Millerite excitement spread, the more its adherents were scoffed at and criticized. Newspapers called them deluded, ignorant, ridiculous, illiterate, blind, fanatical, and weak-minded. They were assuredly humbugs. William Lloyd Garrison in the *Liberator* said the frenzy was "an event scarcely paralleled in the history of popular excitements," but one soon to be "ignominiously exploded."

Like Barnum, Miller saw that opposition fueled the fire. When a clergyman traveled to Newark to preach against him, Miller said he had "done us so much good that I'd cheerfully pay all his expenses if he'd come again. We want the people aroused."

Miller had begun by saying the curtain would fall "about 1843." For most of his preaching career, he resisted making the date more specific. But the engine of the movement was the countdown. In May 1842, a conference of the Adventist Society in Boston endorsed the notion, first, that God had revealed the end time in the Bible, and, second, that it would come in 1843. Miller went along.

In August 1842, Himes too embraced the date. He declared, "I am confirmed in the doctrine of Christ's personal descent to this earth, to destroy the wicked and glorify the righteous some time in the year 1843." Three months later, Miller refined his computations. Taking into account the Hebrew ecclesiastical year, which began in the spring, he said that the end would come between March 21, 1843, and March 21, 1844.

PAGANS

The Erie Canal stimulated in Americans a new view of nature. Romanticism was steering sensibilities toward a greater awareness of the sublime. God and nature became nearly synonymous. Through God's "undefiled works," the artist Thomas Cole observed, "the mind is cast into the contemplation of eternal things." Theodore Weld was convinced that God had furnished every human with a revelation. "It is written in the language of nature," he said, "and can be understood without a commentary."

The canal made wilderness and natural wonders conveniently available to middle-class travelers. A tourist at Little Falls said, "such scenery is too sublime for my dull pen." The actress Fanny Kemble wrote that the canal was "beautiful from end to end."

But the works of man were challenging and replacing God's creation. A "vulgar and worldly throng," Hawthorne thought, was encroaching on the wilderness. He imagined of the canal that "in time, the wondrous stream may flow between two continuous lines of buildings, through one thronged street, from Buffalo to Albany."

"Nature is fairly routed, and driven from the field," Frances Trollope wrote. The factory, "the rattling, crackling, hissing, spitting demon," had taken possession of the land. Cole expressed regret that the "sublimity of the wilderness should pass away."

In the canal era, it was easier to reconcile these conflicting views. The wild would always be with us. Man's works, too, could invoke wonder. A Lockport visitor wrote that "as Niagara Falls are the greatest natural wonder, so Lockport, its Locks, and the portion of the Canal adjacent, are considered to be the greatest artificial curiosity in this part of America."

The vast majority of those who lived along the canal cared little about nature or sublime sights. Their interest was gold and the getting of it. So anxious were they to turn a profit, an observer noted of the residents of early Syracuse, that "every man moved as though he had just heard that his house was on fire." In Brockport, just west of Rochester, merchants toasted, "Pork and Flour coming down—Tea and Sugar coming up!" Commerce was exploding along the great waterway, which had brought the market to remote villages. Writer Walter Edmonds referred to the scene along the Erie's banks as "the bowels of the nation . . . the whole shebang of life!"

Passengers on the canal saw barge after barge loaded with barrels of flour headed east. Farmers were growing wheat to their doorsteps. Pork and beef, raw whiskey, lumber, potatoes, ashes, wool, dried fruit, cheese, lard—it all flowed cheaply down the Erie. Transportation costs dropped to one-tenth of what they had been. Consumer demand for tea and sugar, silk and perfume, fresh oysters and fine furniture fueled westward traffic.

Tolls on the canal exceeded debt interest in the very first year of operation. By 1837, the construction loan had been entirely repaid. Except for maintenance and operating costs, the rest would be gravy for the state. Even the most optimistic canal proponents had not dared to imagine such success.

If the canal brought a dynamic market to the interior, it also brought a risky one. A profit could turn to a loss overnight. Many businessmen took the terrifying plunge from prosperity to sudden failure. A young man named Lyman Spalding left Canandaigua to seek his fortune in Lockport while the canal was under construction. "I think for us young folks," a friend wrote to him, "we shall find a little better pickings on the confines of the great ditch!" In a few years, Spalding owned a flour mill. He went into debt to build another. It burned down, the market fluctuated, and Spalding was ruined. It took him years to climb back into the middle class.

The canal gave permanent employment to tens of thousands of workers. Entrepreneurs and their families lived on and operated freight barges. Farmers and small businessmen set up groceries and grog shops along the canal's banks. Poor folks, like the Smith family, hawked birch beer and cakes. Blacksmiths shoed the thousands of draft animals. Along-shore-men, or "longshoremen," worked the wharfs. Gamblers and confidence men sniffed for opportunities among the gullible.

The captains of packet boats contracted for teams of mules or horses, which were kept in barns about fifteen miles apart. Cargo boats were most often pulled by a pair of mules while a second pair rested on board, the animals working in shifts. Mule handlers, among the roughest of the canal workers, routinely mistreated the animals and sometimes worked them to death.

Boys known as hoggees drove the mules, riding on their backs as they plodded the towpath. Children were being exploited in the factories, too, but here the abuse was in the open. As many as five thousand young people worked on the canal, and harsh, Dickensian conditions aroused censure. The boys, sometimes as young as six, were routinely kicked or beaten. Barefoot and clothed in cheap cotton, they worked in the rain, slept in the barns, occasionally went hungry. One who came down with cholera was abandoned by his boat's captain to die on the towpath. Only some had a home to return to in winter when the canal closed. A Syracuse newspaper of 1843 reported many canal boys "loafing about the city, without a place to sleep, or money to purchase food or clothing."

They picked up bad habits. One offended citizen wrote to the Canal Board that "the Boys who Drive the horses . . . are the most profain beings that now exist on the face of this hole erth without exception." Another observer noted that "they are only specimens of a larger budget of evil rolling thro our land & among us."

Women hung around groggeries or took jobs as cabin girls and gave men the knowing eye. Drivers and boatmen pilfered farmers' fruit and eggs. Vandalism and assaults were common, rapes and murder not unknown. No passenger dared leave his belongings unattended. Within a decade, a quarter of the inmates of the prison at Auburn were men who had "followed the canal."

Herman Melville called the ditch "one continual stream of Venetianly corrupt and often lawless life." The Erie brought to America's interior the crime, double-dealing, and moral license of port cities everywhere.

"There howl your pagans," Melville wrote.

WAR

Mormon converts kept arriving in Missouri, gathering as commanded, drawn to the new religion. They spilled over from Caldwell County into Daviess County to the north and into Carroll County to the east. Missourians watched with growing apprehension as the newcomers threatened to grab political control of the region.

By August 6, 1838, Mormons already made up more than a third of voters in Daviess County. They went to the polls that day in Gallatin, the county seat. A local citizen announced that they had no more right to cast a ballot "than the negroes." A brawl broke out.

The Mormons defended themselves with oak staves and fought the locals to a draw.

Sidney Rigdon's loose talk about "extermination" a month earlier had put tensions in the region on a hair trigger. By the time word of the fight flew the twenty-five miles to Far West, it had become a frantic report of two Mormons killed and an army of Missourians gathering to clear the rest of the Saints from Daviess County.

The Danites saddled their horses, Joseph Smith swung onto a mount, and the Mormons galloped north to protect their people. Rumors flashed around the state. Insurrection. Mob chaos. Missouri authorities issued a warrant for Smith's arrest. Governor Lilburn Boggs called out six companies of state militia.

On arriving in Gallatin, the Mormons discovered that it was a false alarm. They forced a sheriff to promise protection for local Church members. Hearing of the governor's arrest order, Smith agreed to surrender. He put up bail and was ordered to appear in court in November. A tense peace settled on the state.

But Missouri was raw frontier with minimal law enforcement. In the vigilante West, the lynch mob was an instrument of rough justice. Poorly trained militia units were often hard to distinguish from outlaws.

Rumors of the Mormons' nefarious plans did not stop. A nervous Governor Boggs activated several thousand men in state military units. Non-Mormons organized armed bands. On October 1, raiders besieged the Mormon outpost of DeWitt in eastern Carroll County and burned the property of farmers there. Refugees trudged to Far West.

As October progressed and wintery weather swept the grasslands, Mormons retaliated. They marched into Daviess County in a show of force. Local non-Mormons, spooked by tales of an invasion, left their farms. The Mormons grabbed the property of gentiles. They drove their cattle, horses, and hogs back to Far West. "Lawlessness prevailed," a Mormon observed, "and pillage was the rule."

The mob violence on both sides grew ugly. Men with blackened faces attacked and burned outlying Mormon farms. Houses were burned. Women were raped.

Mormon militiamen rode out to disperse the mobs. They raided the farms of non-Mormons, burning buildings, intimidating settlers, and stealing supplies. On October 25, seventy armed Mormons encountered a company of state militia on the banks of Crooked River, mistaking them for vigilantes. A firefight broke out. The Mormons attacked with swords. Three Mormons and one militia soldier died in the skirmish.

Outrage now galloped at full speed through the region. Killing a member of the state militia was treason. Two days after the fight at Crooked River, Governor Boggs issued an order stating that "the Mormons must be treated as enemies, and must be exterminated or driven from the State if necessary for the public peace."

Joseph Smith encouraged Mormons to abandon their outlying settlements. Jacob Haun, who had just finished building a gristmill eighteen miles from Far West, was loath to leave it to gentile arsonists. Local Mormon families stayed with him. On October 30, following the governor's extermination order, two hundred gentile militiamen rode down on Haun's Mill. Some residents fled. Many took refuge in a log-built blacksmith shop. The non-Mormons hid behind trees and aimed through the cracks between the logs. They picked off the Saints one by one.

So toxic had feelings grown between the two sides that the militiamen fired at women running toward the woods. Having shot the occupants of the shop, they entered to finish off the wounded. They fired a bullet into the head of a nine-year-old boy. Of thirty-eight Mormon men and boys, seventeen were shot dead and fifteen wounded.

The same day, several thousand militiamen surrounded the Mormons in the barricaded town of Far West. With only eight hundred poorly armed fighting men, Joseph Smith and Church leaders understood that the extermination that Governor Boggs had ordered had become a serious possibility. When more state troops arrived on October 31, Smith, Rigdon, and Parley Pratt walked out of the town under a flag of truce to negotiate a surrender.

Major General Samuel D. Lucas, the state commander, was not there to talk. He arrested Smith and dictated terms. Those accused of crimes would give themselves up. The Mormons would surrender their arms. The state would confiscate the Saints' property to pay Mormon debts. Every Mormon was to leave the state of Missouri. Period.

That evening, Lucas court-martialed Smith and four other Mormon leaders. He ordered their execution in the Far West town square at nine the next morning. The men slept on the ground in the rain, surrounded by armed soldiers gleeful at having captured the fabled Mormon prophet. The prisoners were "about as badly scared set as I ever saw," a Missourian noted.

With daylight, Brigadier General Alexander W. Doniphan, who was to carry out the execution order, judged it to be "cold-blooded murder." He flatly refused. A military court, he pointed out, had no jurisdiction over ordinary citizens. The men were criminals, not prisoners of war. Lucas backed down.

Smith, Rigdon, and Pratt, accompanied by about fifty other Mormon prisoners, were forced to walk four days to Independence, where they would be out of range of any attempt by Mormons to free them. Threatening, curious crowds lined the roads to watch and jeer. General Moses Wilson was determined that his prisoners would not be grabbed by a lynch mob along the way.

"I carried him into my house a prisoner in chains," the general was recorded to have said about the prophet. "In less than two hours my wife loved him better than she did me." If the quote is accurate, it is high testimony to Joseph Smith's deep and alluring charm.

At a preliminary hearing, probable cause was found to try the prophet and five others for "overt acts of treason," an offense punishable by hanging. The men were taken in chains and shackles ten miles north to Liberty. Joseph, his brother Hyrum, and four other men were imprisoned in the fourteen-foot-square basement of the jail there, with a trapdoor above and straw bedding on the dirt floor. Local citizens made a habit of gawking through the narrow iron grates and abusing the prisoners with blasphemous obscenities. Sidney Rigdon became so ill that he was released on bail. He fled Missouri to avoid the mobs.

In the cold, reeking dungeon, Joseph Smith had reached yet another low point. Although the governor had given the remaining Saints until spring to clear out, most left that winter, moving north to Iowa or across the Mississippi to Illinois. Finding refuge in the Illinois river town of Quincy, Emma wrote to her husband, "I hope there is better days to come to us yet."

In March, after four months in prison, Joseph wrote back, "my nerve trembles from long confinement," but he assured her that "not one of us have flinched yet." He allowed himself a hint of self-pity. "Dear Emma," he wrote, "do you think that my being cast into prison by the mob renders me less worthy of your friendship?" Perhaps concerned about rumors of his infidelity, he wrote of himself, "fools may tell you he has some *faults*."

During the difficult incarceration, Joseph thought deeply about what had brought on this calamity. He was probably thinking of Sidney Rigdon when he warned in a letter against a "fanciful and flowe[r]y and heated imagination." He could well have applied the counsel to himself.

As spring began to sweeten the air, state authorities in Missouri were also having second thoughts. A fair trial was impossible. Any litigation would raise the question of the many crimes committed by

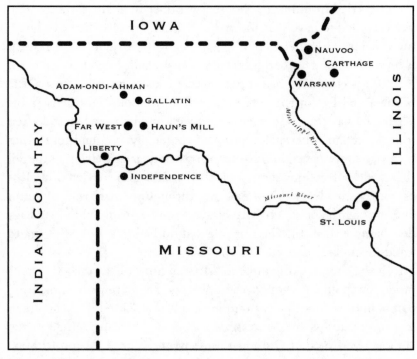

Mormon Missouri and Illinois   *by Joy Taylor*

vigilantes during the brief war. Governor Boggs's "extermination" order was an additional embarrassment.

In April 1839, the men were to be transported to Columbia, in the southern part of the state, for trial. On the way they broke free—Hyrum said the sheriff accompanying them allowed the escape. Using assumed names, they traveled back roads to Illinois. Two weeks later, they reached Quincy. A Mormon diarist noted that when he arrived, Joseph "was frank open & familiar as usual." He said, "Sister Emma was truly happy."

Wherever they had gathered, the Mormons had come into conflict with local residents. Many Mormons began to question whether it made sense to again congregate in a single location, especially since it seemed impossible to reach Zion. The land of promise that God had revealed to Joseph Smith eight years earlier now lay in the forbidden state of Missouri. Smith's followers had refrained from buying land until they could consult the prophet.

The principle of gathering made any sect distinctive. Others, including Jemima Wilkinson's followers and Mother Ann's Shakers, had found coherence by separating themselves from the larger society. Joseph did not hesitate. He asked the Lord and the Lord commanded: "Build up a city & call my saints to this place!"

The place was a tiny village called Commerce, a day's journey north of Quincy, Illinois, on the east bank of the Mississippi River. Commerce sat at the upstream end of a fifteen-mile rapids in the river. Its founders thought it had potential as a port for steamboats on the upper river, but it had yet to live up to its name.

The settlement was more wilderness than town. Surrounded by wetlands, it was "so unhealthy, very few could live there," Smith wrote. Nevertheless, he directed the Mormons to purchase the land on twenty-year mortgages. Ever the optimist, he renamed the place Nauvoo, a transliteration of a Hebrew word for "beautiful place."

Here the Saints would again gather. They would suffer under the scourge of mosquitoes and endure an epidemic of malaria, but they would keep coming, by the hundreds, and then thousands. Here they would build yet another massive temple. Here, in Nauvoo, the final act in the life of America's most creative and consequential prophet would be played out.

PUBLIC PROSPERITY

The Erie Canal's astonishing success created problems. Former chief engineer Benjamin Wright admitted that "in the size of our canal, we have made great errors." A forty-foot-wide, four-foot-deep channel could not cope with the burgeoning flow of barges. Boatmen waited for hours to get their craft through the single locks. Failures in the canal banks that were not repaired quickly resulted in delays lasting weeks.

Feeder canals, which extended from the Erie to serve other parts of the state, added to the traffic. Jesse Hawley, back in 1807, had correctly predicted that the Finger Lakes region would one day be "laced with canals." The Erie became a tree trunk with branches veering north and south. They were part of a countrywide canal-digging mania that extended from the late 1820s well into the 1830s. Many of these projects failed to yield a penny in profit, leading a modern historian to label canals "the country's first technological bubble and bust."

In 1835, only ten years after the Erie Canal's opening, state fathers decided to enlarge the channel. The plan was to expand the ditch from forty to seventy feet wide and to dig it seven feet deep rather than four. The work began in 1836 under the direction of John Jervis, a humble axman on the canal in 1817, now one of the country's leading engineers.

In addition to widening the channel, Jervis's mission was to make the canal straighter to speed travel. He reduced the number of locks from eighty-three to seventy-two. Each lock was doubled so that boats could pass in both directions simultaneously, and lengthened so that two standard barges could fit inside simultaneously. He replaced the Rochester aqueduct with a wider one.

The original canal had been completed with amazing rapidity, given the difficulties the builders faced. The enlargement dragged on far longer than anyone could have imagined. First came the Panic of 1837, then economic depression and a clouded future. Workers, less docile than their predecessors, staged strikes. For several years, beginning in 1842, a reluctant faction of the New York Democratic Party known as the Locofocos halted the project entirely. Railroads, cheaper to build and far more versatile, soaked up investment.

Interest in canal-building flagged. The enlargement was not finished until 1862. Yet the Erie Canal continued to thrive, and revenues kept flowing into state coffers.

One of those urging on the work was Jesse Hawley. By 1840, he was a successful businessman in Lockport. "No single act," he declared, "has done so much to promote the public prosperity and produce a new era in the history of the country."

THUNDERER

During the summer of 1834, America experienced its first great student rebellion. The cause was the republic's original sin: the enslavement of human beings. The uprising found its perfect leader in Theodore Dwight Weld. Converted to Christianity by Charles Finney, Weld had been a star of the Rochester revival three years earlier. He embodied the Romantic age: an unkempt bohemian dressed in what he called "John the Baptist attire." He proudly asserted that "my bearish proportions have never been licked into City Shape." A female admirer noted that "his appearance is just what I anticipated." She recognized in him "a God like and expanded soul." He had *presence*.

After Rochester, Weld, with his typical energy, had toured the nation as agent of the Society for Promoting Manual Labor in Literary Institutions, which was bankrolled by New York's Tappan brothers. He traveled 4,500 miles and made more than two hundred public addresses in the cause.

Weld identified the Lane Seminary, a training academy for young evangelists in Cincinnati, as a likely western headquarters for the rapidly accelerating reform movement. He became a leader at the school and helped transfer the manual-labor system that had governed the Oneida Academy to this recently founded institution in the west. Many Oneida students, who idolized Weld and were eager to be on the forefront of evangelical reform, transferred to Lane.

Unable to attract Finney to head the school, Lane trustees hired Lyman Beecher. The renowned Boston minister had moved closer to his onetime nemesis, finally accepting Finney's revival "methods." He had vigorously promoted Christian reform, suggesting to followers that giving up booze could spur the millennium.

During his travels, Weld had become a thoroughgoing abolition-ist. "Abolition *immediate universal* is my desire and prayer to God," he wrote in an 1833 letter. "I hardly know how to contain myself." Obsessed with the issue, he embraced the slaves' cause as his own. "My heart aches with hope deferred," he said.

About the issue of slavery, Beecher was just as cautious as Finney. The topic was too controversial both inside and outside the churches. One had to consider "what was expedient" as well as what was right. Never one to rock the boat, Beecher favored the position of the American Colonization Society, a group that envisioned compensat-ing slave owners and sending freed slaves to Africa. It was an idea that at the time was embraced by the majority of antislavery advocates. Beginning in 1820, the Society settled several thousand freed blacks in the section of West Africa that was to become Liberia.

In February 1834, against his better judgment, Beecher al-lowed his students to hold a series of debates about two questions: Should slavery be immediately abolished? Should Christians support colonization?

Weld, an experienced and persuasive talker, took the lead. The abolitionists among the students had stacked the deck. They had spent months pushing their ideas on classmates. The debates were really a barrage of antislavery sentiment aimed at converting the un-decided to become full-fledged soldiers in the cause. The conclusion was foreordained: abolition, yes; colonization, no.

For eighteen days, regular classes were suspended while the stu-dents and guest speakers discussed the questions. James Bradley, a former slave who had worked five years to buy his freedom and was now a student at the Lane Seminary, testified to the humanity of black people. Southerners who had repented of their region's "pecu-liar institution" detailed its cruelties. The tactic worked. Almost to a man, the students converted to the radical, unpopular idea of imme-diate abolition of slavery without compensation to owners.

It was a dangerous opinion. Sabbath breakers or those who en-joyed an occasional glass of whiskey became only mildly incensed when holier-than-thou types derided their vices. To slave owners, abolition meant the loss of an enormous and essential investment. The effrontery of ignorant northern idealists out to wreck the south-ern economy and way of life infuriated them to the point of madness.

And it was not just southern plantation masters. Cotton, grown in the South by slaves, was processed in northern factories. It was a critical asset of the young republic. Businessmen north and south insisted that the end of slavery would bring the nation's commerce to its knees. Workers imagined freed slaves taking their jobs. White men's heads came alive with panicked visions of black men molesting their women. An apocalyptic race war was a vivid fear.

The Lane students, who now embraced the antislavery cause as their creed, dismissed all objections. They went into the community of free blacks in Cincinnati and started schools. They stayed in black homes, escorted black students to the seminary. "While I was at Lane Seminary," Weld remembered, "my intercourse was with the Colored people at Cincinnati, I think I may say *exclusively*. . . . If I ate in the City it was at *their* tables. If I slept in the City it was at their homes." The summer of 1834 would have an echo 130 years later, when blacks and whites united to defy Jim Crow in the Freedom Summer of 1964.

A Cincinnati newspaper labeled Weld "a proud, arrogant, self-conceited, disorganized man" who was "a compound of folly, madness, vanity, ambition, self-complacency, and total contempt of law and public sentiment."

Lyman Beecher admired Theodore Weld and feared him. "Great economic and political questions," the clergyman stated, "can't be solved so simply." Beecher believed that the students should leave the issue of slavery to clergymen, who viewed the matter from a broader perspective than mere individual conscience. Teaching blacks was fine. But visiting their homes, walking in the street with them—it was too provocative. America would never accept blacks socially. Colonization would leave everyone better off.

Weld and his fellow students would have none of it. Abolition was "the cause of God." Drunk with righteousness, the students saw themselves as the nation's only hope. "The pulpit is overawed," Weld declared, "the press panders to power, conscience surrenders to expediency."

One of their allies, a preacher in a nearby Ohio church who took up the cause, was attacked for "niggerism" and labeled a "traitor to Christ and his country." A Lane student who went to Nashville to sell Bibles was caught with abolitionist handbills in his possession. He was tried before two clergymen and seven Presbyterian elders.

Found guilty of inciting slaves, he was publicly beaten and thrown out of the city.

The students were criticized for defying public opinion—a majority of citizens across the country tolerated slavery. Weld scoffed at the notion. Should high moral issues be decided by "which side of the question is popular: which will be huzza'd and hosanna'd? Which will tickle the multitude?"

The Lane trustees became alarmed at the students' defiance. "Madness rules the hour," one commented. They asked Weld and his fellows to cease "mixing" with blacks. They fired a professor sympathetic to the cause, accused Weld of "monomania," limited campus societies, and ordered the students to give up their abolitionist activities.

In response, almost all the rebels walked out. A school, they insisted, should be concerned with Truth. If not, Weld said, "better the mob demolish every building." The millennium was coming. The cause was urgent. They wanted to be treated "as men." In fact, Weld was thirty-one, most of the others in their late twenties.

The Lane students enrolled in the newly organized Oberlin Collegiate Institute, two hundred miles to the north in Ohio. Oberlin, the first permanent coeducational college in the world, was also among the first to freely admit black students. The Tappan brothers shifted their financial support from Lane to Oberlin.

And who better to play a lead role in the new institution than Charles Finney? The great evangelist was at the height of his powers. He was preaching at the grand Broadway Tabernacle in New York and had just published his influential book *Lectures on Revivals of Religion*, which would serve as an instruction manual for generations of evangelists. But seeing a slow decline in enthusiasm for his revivals, he wanted to mobilize a new cadre of preachers trained in his methods. The west was where he had seen his great success. He agreed to leave New York and take over the Oberlin theology department. He would eventually become the college's president as well.

Theodore Weld was also offered a professorship at the college. He declined. The fight against slavery was "superior to every other cause." He would abandon academia to go out and convert the nation to abolitionism. During the next two years, Weld would change the moral debate in America. Before he was done, colonization would no longer be seriously talked about. Abolition would move from an idea on the radical fringe to a pressing concern across the northern states. He effected the change by leveraging the moral energy of those caught up in the excitement of the recent revivals.

Weld faced enormous resistance. Clergymen preached against abolition. Civil authorities actively thwarted him. Mobs threatened and attacked him. President Jackson, who had built his wealth on slavery, blocked the distribution of abolitionist literature through the mails.

To the majority of Americans, abolition was not just an erroneous policy, it was anathema, even lunatic. They could offer proof. In Virginia a few years earlier, a slave and visionary named Nat Turner had undergone a mystical experience that promised freedom. In 1831, he preached liberty to fellow slaves. They threw off their shackles and armed themselves with knives and axes. Before the rebellion was suppressed, they had killed sixty white men, women, and children. Retaliation took the lives of many innocent blacks. The Turner uprising stalked the dreams of the entire nation.

Weld became a leading member of the American Anti-Slavery Society. Abolitionist firebrand William Lloyd Garrison had written the organization's manifesto. Money from Arthur and Lewis Tappan paid the bills. The goal was the "immediate emancipation of the whole colored race." Members were further determined to free the colored man "from the oppression of public sentiment." During the next few years, an antislavery newspaperman would be shot dead in Illinois, abolitionists would be hounded from Missouri, and a reward of $20,000 was offered for the delivery of Arthur Tappan to the levee of New Orleans for lynching.

Known as the "thunderer of the West," Weld embarked on a furious series of antislavery lectures. He started in Ohio and worked his way eastward along the Erie Canal. He preached to western audiences with force and colloquial clarity. "A *stump* is my throne," he asserted, "my element the *everydayisms* of plain common life."

Borrowing from Finney, he ran his programs like revivals. He orated day after day—at times he gave two dozen speeches in one city. He drove home the logic, the pure rightness of his message. He played skillfully on listeners' emotions. "If it is not FELT in the very vital tissues of the spirit," he wrote, "all the reasoning in the world is a feather thrown against the wind." He met resistance at first, but gradually the crowds at each lecture stop would grow. Even adamant opponents would sometimes succumb to his impassioned arguments.

At Lockport, Weld was "almost shouted down by hostile demonstrators." Yet he spoke for four hours, convincing hundreds to sign a constitution for the Niagara County Anti-Slavery Society. The group would soon attract 21,000 members. In Rochester, he convinced eight hundred citizens to join the local Anti-Slavery Society branch. In Utica, nineteen hundred joined the Society or signed abolitionist petitions.

The success of his appeal drove his enemies wild. Outside his meeting places, they screamed, banged tin pans, blew bugles, and let loose barking dogs. They threw stones and eggs—at one point Weld was stunned by a brickbat to the head. He pointed to the virulence of the opposition as a sign of his success. He described himself as "the most mobbed man in America."

By the end of 1835, talk of abolition was buzzing across the northern states. The idea was daring, visionary, exciting. For a time, it seemed unstoppable. The number of abolitionist newspapers grew from three to thirty-five in a single year. Local antislavery societies proliferated—in a few months there were two hundred. Weld had helped make abolition the most celebrated cause in America.

THE BONES OF GOD

In December 1838, Joseph Smith, having barely escaped execution for treason, had languished in a filthy, freezing jail cell in Liberty, Missouri. A year later, he walked into the White House for a meeting with the president of the United States.

He had made the long trip to the nation's capital in order to plead with Martin Van Buren to redress the Mormons' many grievances over their treatment by Missouri's inhabitants and public officials. A Washington newspaper described the prophet as "a tall muscular man, with . . . much shrewdness of character." He had the appearance of "a plain yeoman, intended rather for the cultivation of the soil, than the expounding of prophecy." He was a great talker, resolute and determined. The writer estimated the number of Mormons in the country at 200,000 and "still on the increase. Persecution swells their ranks."

Van Buren, elected vice president as Andrew Jackson's running mate in 1832, was known as the Little Magician because of his short stature and the political canniness with which he had maneuvered into the presidency in 1837 as Jackson's successor. He met with Smith, but he gave the Mormons no satisfaction. The president was not about to alienate the state of Missouri. A newspaper account said that he listened a few moments to the Mormons' tale of injured innocence, then abruptly left the room. They waited, he did not return, and they had to leave "disappointed, and chagrined."

Feeling insulted, Smith was reported to have said that Van Buren was not as fit "as my dog, for the chair of state." The president had bigger worries than vigilantism on the frontier. The country was still reeling from the Panic of 1837, and he was being blamed. In the 1840 election, Whig Party candidate William Henry Harrison would drive him from office. Missouri would be one of only seven states Van Buren managed to carry.

Smith and his entourage returned to Nauvoo. His life there for the next four years was as hectic and varied as ever. On a typical day in 1842, he noted, "I read in the Book of Mormon, transacted a variety of business in the Store and City, and spent the evening in the Office with [two elders] interpreting dreams &c." As in Kirtland, he had started a dry goods shop in the center of Nauvoo, adding a merchant's duties to his many responsibilities with the Church and town government.

One day he was chopping wood. The next he would spend talking with Hyrum about the details of the priesthood. He and Emma gave huge dinner parties, hosting as many as a hundred Mormon neighbors, who ate in shifts. He purchased a surplus steamboat from the Army Corps of Engineers—the agent handling the deal was an officer named Robert E. Lee.

In 1840, Chicago was the largest city in Illinois, with a population of 4,500. The state capital at Springfield had 2,500 citizens. The population of Nauvoo was 3,000, and it would more than triple over the next five years. Converts came by the Erie Canal and lake steamers. Riverboats from New Orleans began to bring immigrants from England by the hundreds. Across the Atlantic, Brigham Young had used his formidable proselytizing skills to spread the word of the fabulous New World revelation to the teeming masses of desperate English factory workers.

Most new Church members were poor; some walked all the way from the East. But not all. William Law, an astute businessman, arrived from Canada with a comfortable financial cushion. Law would quickly climb the Mormon hierarchy to become a member of the First Presidency and a close counselor to Smith. Nauvoo received its city charter in 1840 with the support of an Illinois legislator named Abraham Lincoln. The document allowed Smith to add considerable temporal power to his religious authority.

Following a revelation, Joseph no longer required members to "consecrate" property to the Church. Instead, they were to "tithe" a tenth of their income. But local land still had to be plotted, apportioned, sold, traded, and taxed. Ordinances had to be drawn up about everything from unruly children to the prohibition of bordellos. Church officials, guided by Smith's revelations, planned another huge temple for ritual and worship. The cornerstones were laid on April 6, 1841, the eleventh anniversary of the founding of the Church. The edifice would be more than three years in the building.

Lawsuits and court cases were unremitting. Joseph was legally still a fugitive from various charges in Missouri. From time to time, he had to go into hiding to avoid a sheriff or a posse. He ducked both civil and criminal cases on technicalities.

More grave were the losses within his family. Joseph Smith Sr. died in September 1840. The next August, malaria claimed Don Carlos, the youngest of Joseph's four remaining brothers, at twenty-five. A short time later, illness also killed Joseph and Emma's young son, whom they had named Don Carlos after his uncle. Emma, now thirty-seven, soon lost another baby in childbirth, her fifth child to die in infancy.

Always drawn to translation, Joseph continued to revise the Bible and to apply himself to ancient Egyptian scrolls. He oversaw the production of a new edition of the *Book of Mormon*. He studied Hebrew. He tried to master German.

In a sense, Joseph Smith was a man who never grew up. Or rather, he was a man with a knack for drawing from the well of youth long into adulthood. He loved games, loved make-believe. He traveled to a nearby town in Illinois where he bested the strongest man in the village in "stick pulling," and threw the best wrestler. He played baseball and took up fencing. Whether meeting with the president of the United States or with Indian chiefs, he made of his life a fantastic adventure.

Through it all, he continued to push his wild new religion further and further from orthodox Christianity. "It may seem to some to be a very bold doctrine that we talk of," Joseph admitted. Not for him the careful modifications with which Charles Finney had deflected the evangelical mainstream. One by one, Smith was bursting all limits.

The Mormons had always believed in baptism by immersion. In 1840, Joseph declared that the dead could, indeed must, be baptized. The idea was connected with what Smith called "the powers of the Holy Priesthood." What you bind on earth shall be bound in heaven. A ritual on earth could affect the destiny of those who had passed their earthly existence. Mormon zealots baptized George and Martha Washington into the true Church. They did the same to Thomas Jefferson, in life a deist skeptic.

"In the beginning," the Bible began, "God created the heaven and the earth." No, Joseph insisted, God did not make the world "out of Nothing; for it is contrary to a Rashanall mind & Reason. that a something could be Brought from a Nothing." The "elements" were eternal; the Almighty had recycled planets to create the earth we know.

"There is no such thing as immaterial matter," Smith told a Methodist inquirer. "All spirit is matter." It was a singular statement. When our bodies are purified, he assured the faithful, "we shall see that it is all matter."

Angels, like men, had physical bodies. To tell if a messenger from God was genuine, the prophet advised, "request him to shake hands with you. If he be an angel he will do so, and you will feel his hand." If the figure was a devil, you would feel nothing.

God's substance was not essentially different from ours. "The Father has a body of flesh and bones as tangible as man's," Joseph revealed. The angels "do not reside on a planet like this earth. But they reside in the presence of God, on a globe like a sea of glass and fire." This sphere where God lived was "a great Urim and Thummim."

Like the magical spectacles that Moroni had given Joseph, the crystal globe allowed heavenly beings to see reality in all its glory.

This was all passing strange, but no article of dogma carried Smith further from the shore of received wisdom than his notion of plural marriage. The controversy that had arisen over Fanny Alger was just the beginning.

THE WHOLE OF AMERICA

In April 1841, Joseph Smith Jr. instructed Joseph Noble to marry him to Noble's sister-in-law Louisa Beaman, whom Smith had met seven years earlier when she was a teenager. Now twenty-six, Louisa attended the ceremony dressed in a man's hat and coat. Joseph made up the words on the spot. Afterward, he told Noble, "I have placed my life in your hands."

Joseph knew how explosive his doctrine was. Even his younger brother Don Carlos had stated, "Any man who will teach and practice the doctrine of spiritual wifery will go to hell, I don't care if it is my brother Joseph."

Smith was an expert at hairsplitting. Mormons did not practice polygamy, he said, "in the ordinary and Asiatic sense of the term." They opposed it, along with "spiritual wifery."

To avoid the Biblical injunction against adultery, Smith turned his sexual adventures into complex ritual practices. He understood that many of these "plural marriages" had all the appearance of philandering and so hid them from the public—and from his wife. Eliza Snow, a friend of Emma whom Joseph would make his twelfth wife in 1842, called the doctrine "a deep intricate puzzle, a tangle of strings."

A tangle. Joseph devised a system of code words to maintain secrecy. Insiders knew that references to the holy order, eternal marriage, or the endowment meant more than others might imagine.

Keeping such a radical dogma under wraps in a community where he was constantly in the public eye taxed Joseph's abundant ingenuity. He decided to extend the doctrine to his inner circle of male followers, insisting that they not only could but *must* take plural wives if they were to enter the highest level of celestial glory. He said an angel had threatened to kill him if he did not take additional wives himself.

Many of those to whom Joseph revealed the teaching were appalled and disgusted. "It was the first time in my life," Brigham Young wrote, "that I had desired the grave." Heber Kimball begged Smith "to remove the requirement." Many expressed "shock, horror, disbelief, and general emotional confusion." Some threatened to leave the Church.

Joseph said he was teaching them "the Ancient order of things for the first time in these last days." Secrecy was essential. "The Lord makes manifest to me many things," he said, "which it is not wisdom for me to make public."

Historians and detractors have often compiled lists of Joseph Smith's "wives." The secrecy surrounding the practice makes any enumeration guesswork, but his dangerous liaisons certainly totaled more than two dozen. He took women in their thirties, like Lucinda Morgan, and even in their fifties. He preferred youth. Two of those he debauched were fourteen. He married the wives and daughters of his followers. He seduced young women whom he and Emma had taken into their home as servants, including the sisters Emily and Eliza Partridge. These girls, nineteen and twenty-two, were the daughters of Edward Partridge, the first Mormon bishop, who had died in 1840.

No amount of prudishness could disguise the frankly sexual nature of Smith's affairs. When Heber Kimball suggested that Eliza Snow was Smith's wife in name only, she replied, "I thought you knew Joseph better than that."

The women to whom Smith proposed the unconventional relationship were astounded, mortified, confused, sometimes flattered. When Joseph approached seventeen-year-old Lucy Walker, she said, "My astonishment knew no bounds. This announcement was indeed a thunderbolt to me."

Spirituality was a tool of seduction for Smith. "It is a command of God to you," he told Walker. "If you reject this message the gate will be closed forever against you." He gave her a deadline of the next day. Lucy said, "This aroused every drop of scotch in my veins." But she thought about it, prayed about it, and submitted. "It was not a love matter," she later wrote, "but simply the giving up of myself as a sacrifice."

When Joseph came for Heber Kimball's daughter Helen, she thought that to accept a doctrine "so contrary to all of our former ideas" was "utterly repugnant." But the charismatic prophet told her, "It will ensure your eternal salvation & exaltation and that of . . . all of your kindred." Only fourteen, she consented. "I would never have been sealed to Joseph," Helen later wrote, "had I known it was anything more than a ceremony."

Smith set his sights on Sidney Rigdon's nineteen-year-old daughter Nancy. Warned of his intentions, she refused him. Smith wrote to her, "Happiness is the object and design of our existence. . . . That which is wrong under one circumstance, may be, and often is, right under another." When her father confronted the prophet, Joseph claimed he had only been testing her virtue.

Joseph's behavior gave rise to an anguished melodrama in the Smith household. Emma knew and did not know. She suspected, heard rumors, tried not to believe it was true. She spied on her husband, confronted him, erupted in anger. Some of her closest friends became his lovers and successfully hid the arrangement from her.

Emma was president of an important organization known as the Female Relief Society, which was charged with organizing aid for the many destitute converts to Mormonism who were continually arriving at Nauvoo. Members were also intended to watch over the community's morals. Hoping to tamp down rumors, Joseph attended a meeting of the group and told them to "hold your tongues about things of no moment." He was afraid that loose talk could "draw the indignation of a gentile world upon us."

Emma was not cowed. "All who walk disorderly must reform," she said. "I want none in this society who have violated the laws of virtue."

Friends described Emma as "a woman of commanding presence." She was intelligent, a brilliant conversationalist, high-spirited, witty. But Joseph's persuasion and her fear of his increasingly public philandering finally wore down her resistance. Perhaps easy access to the girls in their home would placate him. Whatever her motivation, she consented to his having the Partridge sisters. They became Joseph's wives in May 1843, and Emily "roomed" with him that night. Emma was ignorant of the fact that he had "married" the sisters several months earlier. Nor could she shake her qualms. Emily Partridge reported that after the marriage ceremony, Emma was "more bitter in her feelings than ever before," and berated her husband late into the night.

Around the same time, Joseph convinced Emma to accept his marriage to Sarah and Maria Lawrence. The sisters were teenage orphans who had inherited eight thousand dollars. The Smiths had taken them into their busy home and Joseph had arranged to be appointed their guardian. For much of the next year, the four young women lived in an awkward ménage with Smith and his wife.

Emily Partridge said Emma often made things unpleasant for the girls, "but I have nothing in my heart towards her but pity." It was the pity of a pretty young girl for a middle-aged woman. Emma regretted having agreed to the arrangement, but, as Emily knew, "it would have been the same with or without her consent." At one point, Emma suggested to Joseph that if he continued to "indulge himself, she would too."

Hyrum suggested to his brother that a revelation from God might be in order. Hyrum would take it to Emma and Joseph would "hereafter have peace." The revelation announced that if a man "have ten virgins given unto him by this law, he cannot commit adultery." Speaking in the voice of God, Joseph added, "I command mine handmaid, Emma Smith, to abide and cleave unto my servant Joseph, and to none else."

Emma, more than anyone alive, knew the game Joseph was playing. When Hyrum returned, Joseph asked, "How did you succeed?"

"I have never received a more severe talking to in my life," his brother said. "Emma is very bitter and full of resentment and anger."

"I told you you did not know Emma as well as I did." The revelation, issued in July 1843, remains a part of Mormon scripture.

In August of that year, Emma threatened to divorce Joseph if he would not "relinquish all for her sake." Once, when she found out about yet another "wife," she berated him so much that "he had to use harsh measures to put a stop to her abuse but finally succeeded."

Yet the dynamics between Joseph and Emma were deep and complex. Mormon convert Benjamin Johnson spent time in the Smith home when younger and more brilliant "wives" were present, "yet Emma the wife of his youth—to me apeared the Queen of his heart."

During the early 1840s, the suspicion and hostility that had plagued the Mormons in Missouri began to crop up in Illinois, whose citizens had at first welcomed the Saints. A local editor said his newspaper was "bound to oppose the concentration of political power in a religious body, or in the hands of a few individuals." He went on to ask "if there is not need of an Anti-Mormon Party in this country."

Illinois governor Thomas Ford was wary of Mormons. They were a powerful voting bloc whose numbers made them an effective pressure group. Any politician "too proud to court their influence" could see himself turned from office. "Let us vote as kissing goes," Brigham Young joked, "by favors."

An anti-Mormon conference in Carthage, fifteen miles southeast of Nauvoo, accused the Saints of following a "pretended Prophet" with "Heaven-daring assumption." Participants resolved to stop this "latter-day would be Mahomet," by force if necessary.

Joseph was not about to have his people driven from Illinois as they had been from Missouri. "Beware, oh earth!" he wrote, "how you fight against the Saints of God." In 1841, he formed the Nauvoo Legion. Although it was an official state militia unit under the orders of the governor, the force was also Smith's private army. The authorities allowed him to assume the exalted rank of lieutenant general. More than 2,500 Mormons signed up. Two years later, Smith prepared a message to President John Tyler. He wanted permission to enlist 100,000 men to protect Texas and the Pacific Northwest.

Increasingly, Smith, like many Americans, was looking westward. He sent scouts to explore New Mexico and Oregon, imagining a Mormon empire in the vast and largely empty territory. James Gordon Bennett, editor of the New York *Herald* and a Smith sympathizer, wrote that he "should not be surprised if Joe Smith were made Governor of a new religious territory in the west."

The Mormon leader declared himself in favor of *theodemocracy*, "where God and the people hold the power." Harking back to the days before the Constitution erected a wall between church and state, he imagined seizing the reins of power and bringing on a new age in which faith and government would again be one. Why should God not rule on earth through his servant Joseph?

In January 1844, he decided to run for president of the United States. He saw himself as a combination of priest and king, above the corruption of politics. The Twelve Apostles nominated him. With the Democrats dividing their support among President Tyler, former president Martin Van Buren, and dark horse candidate James Polk, success seemed possible. In any case, Smith's campaign would allow him to air Mormon grievances nationwide. He would use the Church's many missionaries to canvass for him. He could not have hit on any surer scheme to excite the fear or elicit the venom of his opponents.

"The whole of America is Zion," Smith declared in April 1844. He had two months to live.

O BLESSED YEAR

During the spring of 1843, a month of advertisements in local newspapers raised expectation in Rochester to the sky. On June 23, the much-ballyhooed Millerites came to town. The giant circus tent went up in the middle of the city. Hordes crowded under the sun-baked canvas to listen to Joshua Himes and Adventist luminaries explain the dire truth.

As the end grew nearer, Adventist leaders concentrated their attention on the spiritually fertile Erie Canal corridor. Audiences ranging from five hundred to thousands streamed into the big tent every day for two weeks. Many accepted the Adventist reasoning, many more were half-convinced or just curious. Prayer meetings and Bible study gave the event the feel of a revival.

Congregants were startled when a sudden rain storm and gust of wind blew one side of the enormous tent loose, threatening the crowd inside. Himes said the fact that all the participants escaped uninjured was a sign. When the Adventists returned to the city in November, Father Miller came along as the star attraction. Twice a day for an entire week, he preached to overflow crowds. Farmers and villagers packed the streets with carriages and wagons, eager for the spectacle.

That year, 1843, *the* year, had begun with a spasm of excitement. On January 1, Miller declared: "This year—O blessed year!—the trump of jubilee will be blown." He was sure that in a few short months a shout of victory would be heard from heaven and "time will be no more."

In February the brightest comet in seven hundred years stretched its luminous tail across the sky. During March, the Great Comet of 1843 blazed in full daylight. Himes said, "I could not but think of '*the Sign of the Son of Man in heaven.*'" Signs were everywhere.

So widespread was talk of the end time that crass merchants incorporated it into advertising. An Adventist angel in one newspaper notice bore a banner reading, *The Time Has Come!* The time had indeed come, the ad said, to try Wistar's Balsam of Wild Cherry, a consumption cure. Another headline read, *The End of the World!* It advertised a cigar to savor while you still had time.

Individual Adventists, in their enthusiasm, continually proposed dates when they expected the final trumpet to sound. The anniversary of the day when Napoleon occupied Rome in 1798. The Jewish feast of Passover, the Christian Pentecost, the autumn equinox. "Expectation with many was on tip-toe," an Adventist leader said.

The sheer strangeness of Millerism made many in the community anxious and angry. Mobs gave believers the same treatment they doled out to abolitionists. They broke up Millerite meetings by jeering, clapping, and stamping their feet. They threatened violence.

January 1, 1844, was initially a blow to the Advent movement. The year that Miller had first pointed to, the blessed year, had passed. He was not daunted. "Never has my faith been stronger than at this very moment," Miller affirmed. Interest in the looming apocalypse accelerated. Only thirteen weeks remained until March 21. "I feel confident that the Savior will come, and in the true Jewish year."

But March 21 came and March 21 went. Three days later, Miller wrote to Himes, "I am still looking for the dear Saviour, the Son of God, from heaven." Neither he nor Himes was discouraged. It was not safe to assume Christ's return was anything but imminent.

Yet the failure inevitably raised doubts. "We would not disguise the fact at all," Himes admitted, "that we were mistaken in the precise time of the termination of the prophetic periods."

In May, Miller frankly wrote: "I confess my error." He was shaken but not downhearted. How could anyone complain "if God should give a few days or even months more as probation time, for some to find salvation."

As was his habit, Miller turned back to his Bible. From Habakkuk and Matthew, he drew the idea that God had briefly delayed the end. Hebrews, chapter 10, advised, "For ye have need of patience." The world had entered the tarrying time. Mankind was on probation. God was giving the skeptical a last chance even as he tested the resolution of the faithful. Glorious hope was still alive and all plans now were contingent on the proviso, "if time continues."

For the leaders of the movement, the path was clear. Himes wrote that they had to continue with "lecturing, Conferences, Tent and Camp-Meetings, and the distribution of publications." He insisted on "more zeal, decision, and perseverance, than ever." He planned to travel to England to spread the word, should time continue long enough to allow it.

Miller was now more of a celebrity than ever. In June, thousands were turned away from his lectures in Boston. In July, Miller and other Adventist preachers headed down the Erie Canal toward points west, the scene of earlier successes. They drew enormous crowds to a two-week camp meeting in Scottsville, New York, a village south of Rochester.

When they returned to the East in August, everyone was talking about a new date for the end of the world.

AS IT IS

In May 1836, Theodore Weld brought his abolitionist message to Troy, New York. The opposition was ferocious. A mob gathered outside the church where he planned to give an oration, prevented access, and intimidated the elders. The churchmen canceled Weld's invitation to speak. Rioters surrounded his lodgings and continued their shouting long into the night.

Weld moved to another church. A proslavery mob broke in and stampeded down the aisles. They tried to drag him from the pulpit, while his supporters resisted. "Stones, pieces of bricks, eggs, cents, sticks, etc. were thrown at me while speaking," Weld later reported. Crowds harassed him in the street. City officials actively opposed him.

Weld vowed that he would continue to press his case until the authorities enforced his right to free speech or he was killed. The fanatic in him took flame. Every abolitionist must decide whether he was willing to "die a martyr."

Even the fiery William Lloyd Garrison urged Weld to relent. The mayor of Troy finally told the abolitionist to leave the city or be forcefully removed. Weld had no choice. He left without a victory.

Alarmed by Weld's uncompromising stand, Charles Finney appealed to him to make abolition secondary to saving souls, "as we made temperance an appendage of the revival in Rochester." An uncompromising push for abolition, Finney warned, could "roll a wave of blood over the land."

Finney admitted that race bias was "a silly and often a wicked prejudice." But a man may, "from constitutional taste," refuse to marry or allow his daughter to marry a black person. Opposition to "amalgamation," he said, was merely a prejudice. It deprived no man of his rights. Forcing the races to mix would hurt the antislavery cause. Converting citizens to Christianity would end slavery without conflict.

Weld and the Tappan brothers, Arthur and Lewis, treated black Americans as fellow human beings. Finney could not bring himself to take that step. Like many Americans, he was held back by ingrained attitudes. "Abolitionists are good men," he wrote to Weld, "but there are but few of them wise men. Some of them are reckless." He asked Weld if he did not fear the country was "going fast into a civil war?"

Barely more than a decade earlier, Charles Finney had been labeled "the madman of Oneida." Now the man who had condemned lukewarmness in religion was himself taking the moderate view.

Finney's warning about the potential consequence did not quench Weld's fever. Regrouping from his defeat in Utica, the abolitionist set off to find reinforcements. He was determined to recruit abolitionist orators, men of "the most obstinate constancy," who would carry on his lecture program. By November, he had selected fifty candidates and brought them to New York City for training. Weld poured everything into the effort.

He spoke for hours, conveying to his followers the glorious, redemptive message of abolishing slavery. Sessions lasted long into the night. He taught his pupils the methods he had learned from Finney:

how to argue like a lawyer, how to counter objections, how to speak in plain language. By the final day of the training, Weld "could not speak above a whisper." He had ruined his voice, just as years earlier he had ruined his eyes in a frenzy of studying.

No longer physically capable of fiery oratory, Weld published an influential book in 1837 titled *The Bible Against Slavery*. It was an attempt to convince his fellow evangelicals that Scripture left no room for the toleration of human bondage.

Weld continued his alliance with others who were fighting the abomination. The sisters Angelina and Sarah Grimké had been raised in Charleston, South Carolina, and had seen slavery in action. In addition to abolition, the Grimké sisters fiercely advocated for the rights of women. Their speeches were controversial even within the abolitionist community—most Americans of the time had never heard a woman speak in public. Angelina thought that female ministers would be a good idea. "We abolitionist women," she said, "are turning the world upside down." She joined activists like Lucretia Mott and Elizabeth Cady Stanton in demanding women's rights. Weld wrote to her, questioning her mixing of the woman issue with abolition. Her peremptory answer reflected his own uncompromising vehemence: "Abandon the law of expediency NOW!"

By February 1838, Weld was contacting the spirited young woman on a different subject. "For a long time," he wrote, "you have had my whole heart." He was delighted when Angelina replied, "I feel my Theodore that we are the two halves of one whole."

Both were unconventional. Weld regarded courtship as "artificial and facetious . . . a misshapen compound of sentimentality." But finding himself in love, he was hardly immune to poetic reverie—he could not decide whether a meeting with Angelina was "an actual reality or an Eden dream." In May 1838, they were married in Philadelphia before a group of friends, with no minister or magistrate present. Six former slaves attended the vows.

The day of their wedding, a large auditorium called Philadelphia Hall was dedicated as a center of abolitionist activity in that city. Two days later, a women's antislavery convention there drew a crowd of three thousand. A mob gathered outside and began to smash the building's windows. Angelina convinced the audience to remain for the speeches. On leaving, white women surrounded the few black attendees to protect them from a barrage of rocks. The next day, mobs burned the building to the ground.

Theodore Dwight Weld was among the small group of Americans who had forced the nation to look its most dire sin square in the face. But the 1837 panic and depression had bankrupted the Tappans and forced the wealthy philanthropists to reduce their support. The American Anti-Slavery Society lacked the funds to pay its agents. The wind went out of the movement. For a while, anyway.

Theodore and Angelina settled on a farm in New Jersey. Her sister Sarah, thirteen years older, lived with them. Angelina was briefly intrigued by the fashionable message of Millerism. Friends grew concerned about her "mental excitement" as she became fixated on the end of the world. She gradually regained her equilibrium and came to see Miller's predictions in only a spiritual light. Yet the idea of the millennium still excited her, as it did all who were swept up in revivals and reforms. "A great and mighty revolution is at hand," she wrote.

Aided by Angelina and her sister, Weld began a new antislavery project, bringing to it his typical obsessive thoroughness. The three were determined to disprove the persistent claim that southern plantation owners treated their slaves humanely. To do so, they scoured twenty thousand southern newspapers, clipping stories that referred to the mistreatment of slaves. They added the testimony of those southerners who knew slavery intimately, including former slave owners and the Grimké sisters themselves.

In 1839, the American Anti-Slavery Society published their resulting book, *American Slavery As It Is: Testimony of a Thousand Witnesses*. In the introduction, Weld stated, "Reader, you are empanelled as a juror to try a plain case and bring an honest verdict." It was pure Charles Finney, simultaneously convincing the mind and moving the heart. No reasonable person could resist. The book catalogued unconscionable horrors. It detailed the baroque tortures that masters inflicted on men and women in bondage. It cited numerous instances of slaves poorly fed, overworked, forced to live in cramped quarters, severely beaten, and routinely treated as animals. The authors meticulously documented every charge. Angelina remembered from her childhood the sickening sight of a poor slave girl "stripped naked and whipped."

The Anti-Slavery Society published 100,000 copies of this groundbreaking book. Its lurid accounts shocked Lyman Beecher's daughter Harriet Beecher Stowe. Thirteen years later, she published *Uncle Tom's Cabin*, which conveyed in fictional form the evidence laid out in *Slavery As It Is*. Stowe's novel, the best-selling book of the century, helped reignite the abolition debate in the run-up to the Civil War.

Theodore Weld had once told a fellow abolitionist, "I *feel* that I know the mind of God." Moral certainty never left him. He worked for a while in Washington, helping former president, now congressman, John Quincy Adams in his efforts to oppose slavery. But Weld soon settled into farming and raising a family. He and Angelina set up a progressive school at their home, where they taught the children of well-known abolitionists, including those of Henry and Elizabeth Cady Stanton. "There is a fighting era in everyone's life," Weld said. "While you feel it so, fight on." But when the time passed, a man had to move to "another and a higher view."

STRONG MEAT

Sometime in 1842, Mormon convert William Law put his arms on Joseph Smith's shoulders and, with tears in his eyes, pleaded with the prophet to give up the teaching of polygamy. Joseph said that he could not. The doctrine was a command from God, not a personal whim. Law was not sure at the time that Smith and his inner circle had put the doctrine into practice. But he was convinced that if the rumors of multiple wives were confirmed, it would ruin the Church.

Law and his wife Jane had converted to Mormonism in 1836 and came to Nauvoo three years later with a wagon caravan of new believers. William started a steam mill for grinding flour and sawing wood.

Joseph was impressed by the sophisticated, pious young couple. William was noted for a "great suavity of manners and amiability of character." William and his brother Wilson, who had accompanied him to Nauvoo, generously loaned money to the Church and to Joseph personally. In 1840, when Hyrum succeeded his late father as

Patriarch, Joseph selected Law to take his place, making him counselor to the First Presidency, Joseph's right-hand man.

After pleading with the prophet, Law tried to ignore what was becoming common knowledge. He relied on the *Book of Mormon*, which explicitly condemned polygamy. Late in 1843, Hyrum showed William Law the original copy of Joseph's revelation establishing plural marriages and admonishing his wife Emma. Law could no longer deny the rumors. He learned that the taking of additional wives was not just an option. No man could be sealed to his first wife for eternity who had not married others. The very idea of accepting the doctrine, Law wrote, "paralizes the nerves, chills the currents of the heart, and drives the brain almost to madness."

Distraught, Law again went to Joseph to point out that the revelation about polygamy directly contradicted other revelations. Joseph said the previous teaching "was given when the church was in its infancy, then it was all right to feed the people on milk, but now it is necessary to give them strong meat."

Joseph sensed correctly that Law could become an enemy. The first week in January 1844, he removed Law from his high Church position. Law did not bend. He and other dissenters in Nauvoo raised questions about Smith's alleged self-dealing in city real estate, as well as about polygamy. Jane Law admitted to her husband that Joseph Smith had tried to seduce her, "by preaching the spiritual wife system to her." Law and Smith traded accusations. In April 1844, William and Jane Law were excommunicated from the Church for "unchristianlike conduct."

That same month, Smith agreed to give a commemorative address in honor of an elder named King Follett. A stonemason, Follett had been killed while digging a well, work that Joseph knew from his youth. The sermon was a highlight of the spring Church conference. Ten thousand Mormons attended the outdoor event. They strained to hear as a stiff wind kept tearing Smith's words to shreds. Four scribes in the audience took notes for an official version of the sermon. Yelling into a mighty wind for more than two hours, Joseph unfolded for his people the supreme mystery of the universe.

"God himself," he said, "was once as we are now, and is an exalted man, and sits enthroned in yonder heavens! That is the great secret."

God was once a man? "God himself, the Father of us all, dwelt on an earth," he said. What was more, there were many gods. A council of "Gods came together & concocked the plan of making the world & the inhabitants."

To any orthodox Christian, this was rank blasphemy. The prophet was leaping far beyond the teachings of even the most eccentric religious visionaries of the time. Those who heard his words were stunned.

"You have got to learn how to be Gods yourselves," he declared, "the same as all Gods have done before you." Each believer had to move "from grace to grace, from exaltation to exaltation . . . until you arrive at the station of a God." Saints today, Gods tomorrow. It was too wonderful.

Finally he spoke of himself. "You don't know me," he told his listeners, "you never knew my heart." His spiritual journey had left him alone among men. "When I am called by the trump of the archangel," he concluded, "you will all know me then. I add no more. God bless you all. Amen."

The dissenters whom Joseph had excommunicated had not gone away. William Law and his brother still operated their milling business and exerted a contentious influence in Nauvoo. At the same time, the Illinois citizens who surrounded Nauvoo were growing more and more hostile. Rumors of mob action ignited memories of the violence that had taken lives and driven the Mormons from Missouri.

"The Lord has constituted me so curiously that I glory in persecution," Joseph boasted from the pulpit in May 1844. "I will come out on top at last."

William Law said that when he met Emma in the street "she used to complain especially because of the girls whom Joseph kept in the house, devoting his attention to them." Law decided to publicly accuse Joseph of adultery for living with Maria Lawrence, who was now twenty-one. He brought the charge not in Nauvoo, but in Carthage, the county seat. A grand jury indicted the prophet for perjury and polygamy.

The Law brothers bought a printing business in Nauvoo and planned to publish a newspaper. They advocated for a repeal of the Nauvoo city charter, which rested so much power in the hands of Joseph Smith. They railed against "gross moral imperfections wherever they may be found."

Their paper, the *Nauvoo Expositor*, would aim to restore the religion "originally taught by Joseph Smith," which the editors acclaimed as the truth. The Nauvoo dissenters, like those in Kirtland, wanted to return to the simpler message of the *Book of Mormon*. They were determined to oppose the pernicious doctrines "taught secretly and denied openly." They rejected Joseph's idea "that there are innumerable Gods."

On June 7, the Law brothers published a thousand copies of the first issue of the *Expositor*, more a broadside than a newspaper. A long "Preamble" laid out their case against the prophet. "We are earnestly seeking to explode the vicious principles of Joseph Smith," they wrote, "and those who practice the same abominations and whoredoms." They included a melodramatic depiction of how innocent girls were ensnared in the net of polygamy by "some individual feigning to be a God."

Joseph declared the publication to be "a greater nuisance than a dead carcass." He ordered city marshals to act. A posse of a hundred men broke into the offices on June 10 and "removed the press, type, and printed papers, and fixtures into the street, and fired them." Smith declared that, in spite of the action, he was for freedom of the press for any newspaper that would print the truth.

Although he enjoyed virtually limitless power in Nauvoo, Smith was still subject to state law. The mob action and the trampling on one of Americans' most revered rights struck a nerve in the larger community. The day after the suppression of the *Expositor*, attendees at a public meeting in Carthage vowed "to exterminate—UTTERLY EXTERMINATE, the wicked and abominable Mormon leaders."

Smoldering animosity burst into flames. On June 21, Illinois governor Thomas Ford, generally a reasonable man, declared that Smith's destruction of the dissidents' press "was a very gross outrage upon the laws and liberties of the people." Even if the *Expositor* had been full of libels, he told Smith, "this did not authorise you to destroy it." Joseph said he was willing to comply with Ford's orders and to appear "before any legal tribunal in the state." But he refused to submit to a court where witnesses would be intimidated by a "blood thirsty mob."

Ford guaranteed Smith's safety, but declared that if the prophet did not give himself up, he would have to call out the militia. "I have great fears that your city will be destroyed and your people many of them exterminated."

Joseph Smith was not about to buckle. "I have got all the truth which the Christian world possessed and an independent revelation in the bargain," he declared, "and God will bear me off triumphant."

AWFUL FOREBODINGS

While William Miller and his colleagues were touring the Middle West during the summer of 1844, eastern Adventists were journeying to a huge camp meeting in Exeter, New Hampshire, by way of the new Boston and Maine Railroad. Preachers unrolled their charts. They began their explanations of the calculations that proved the imminent end. But the audience was bored. They had heard it before.

Mrs. John Couch stood up in the middle of a sermon, interrupted the preacher, and voiced the feelings of the crowd: "It is too late to spend our time upon these truths, with which we are familiar." She said there was one speaker there, whom few had heard, who had a new, fresh message for the believers.

The man was thirty-eight-year-old Samuel S. Snow. Raised in the orthodox Congregational Church, Snow had lost his faith and for a time edited the Boston *Investigator*, a skeptical newspaper. He had proclaimed the Bible to be "nothing but gross absurdities." In 1839, he purchased one of Miller's books from a peddler, expecting it to be "moonshine." But it inspired him to search the Scriptures. After three months of study, he converted to Christianity and accepted "the soon-coming Saviour."

Snow was, like Miller, a self-taught Bible scholar. He dove into the great prophetic morass, trying to discern the hidden meanings. When he emerged, he too had determined the date of the end. He did not qualify it with words like "if" or "about." He insisted that "God is an exact time keeper." And Snow knew the exact time. The end would come on the Hebrew day of atonement, the tenth day of the seventh month of the Jewish calendar. That day fell on October 22, 1844.

Snow's message was a lighted match tossed into dry grass. It "worked like leaven throughout the whole camp," a Millerite said. In one tent, prayer continued all night, "attended with great excitement." The believers shouted until their voices gave out and clapped until their hands were raw with blisters. The participants went home, intent on conveying their enthusiasm to the world. Snow started his own periodical, *The True Midnight Cry*. The day he had named was only eight weeks away.

Joshua Himes and other leaders were wary of setting yet another date. They knew that disappointment could discourage believers. But George Storrs, an associate of Miller and editor of the magazine *The Bible Examiner*, latched on to the prediction and began to preach it with gusto. Miller's message had been "but the *alarm*," he said. Now the true cry was sounding.

"We are then within a *few days* of the event," Storrs said on September 24. It was an awful moment for those who were unprepared, a glorious one for those who were ready. On September 30, Himes noted that "this thing has gone over the country like lightning." It must come from God, he thought, so strongly had it encouraged believers, so thoroughly had it reduced them to a sober state of mind. "I dare not oppose it."

Adventists all over the country waited to see what Miller would say. On October 6, a bit more than two weeks before the day, he finally sent a letter to Himes. "I see a glory in the seventh month which I never saw before," he wrote.

The fact was that the Adventist devotees, although many still called them Millerites, had sprinted past Father Miller. The movement he had led was now leading him. He dropped all doubts and all fears and proclaimed, "God's word is true." He became as close to ebullient as his modesty allowed. "Oh, how I wish I could shout," he wrote. An old-school Calvinist at heart, he did not believe in any such outward displays of excitement. When the King of Kings came, then he would shout.

Miller was sure the Lord would not tarry a second time. He was delighted to see among his followers "a forsaking of the world, an unconcern for the wants of life." When he next wrote to Himes, he concluded, "I do not expect to see you again in life."

It was October 12. Ten days left.

Adventist editors worked four presses pumping out publicity. Hundreds of thousands of copies of the final issue of *The Midnight Cry* were thrust into the hands of believers and skeptics alike. A reporter for the Philadelphia *Public Ledger* wrote that a Millerite had shuttered his store and hung out a sign: "This shop is closed in honor of the King of kings, who will appear about the 20th of Oct. Get ready, friends, to crown him Lord of all."

A prosperous hatter in Rochester threw open his doors, a newspaper reported, and invited the crowd to "help themselves to hats, umbrellas, etc., which they naturally did." Many Adventists pulled their children out of school. Why prepare for a future that would not come? The Cleveland *Herald* reported that "many have suspended their usual avocations, and now devote their whole time and substance to the work of proselytizing."

That was October 19. Three days to go.

Scoffers reported bizarre activities among Miller's followers. Most of the stories were fabricated, but they made for juicy gossip. Insane asylums, it was said, were crammed with deluded Adventists. The Millerites were providing themselves with "ascension robes," white garments appropriate for strolling the sidewalks of heaven. Mills were operating overtime to produce the fabric. Zealots planned to gather in cemeteries to welcome the dead who would be rising. They would climb atop barns or haystacks to make their heavenward journey shorter.

In rare cases, believers did go to extremes. But most spent their last days in continual prayer meetings that involved "deep searching." In Rochester, on the eve of the end, believers gathered at Cobb's Hill, a traditional site of Easter morning services.

Mobs of scoffers had been harassing Millerites in recent weeks, smashing windows of their meeting halls, setting off Roman candles to panic the nervous believers. In some cities, the police had barred formal Adventist gatherings. A New York newspaper reported that Millerites "formed themselves into small parties at their several houses, to comfort and bear each other company in their anticipated trip."

They faced a tomorrow that even the wildest imagination could barely comprehend. William Miller, back home in Low Hampton, reported, "We held meetings all day and our place of worship was crowded to overflowing with anxious souls."

Many who had accepted the Adventist message were people unhinged by the modern world, by the acceleration of time, the shortening of distance, the sudden changes in daily life. They could not take it, did not want it, were ready to say good-bye to the earth.

Now, on this last night, they waited for the "Son of man, clothed with a garment down to the foot." They waited with a unique sensation of terror and hope, trepidation and relief. "Some were exceedingly frightened with awful forebodings." None entertained a doubt that the pending cataclysm was real. Gerrit Smith, a prominent upstate New York abolitionist and Millerite, wrote that "we have just had family worship—perhaps for the last time."

As the sun went down for the final time and darkness seeped into the sky, Adventists everywhere waited, gripped by a penetrating idea of the marvelous, and by faith in the imminent, miraculous appearance of Jesus Christ.

O LORD, MY GOD

On Tuesday, June 18, 1844, eight days after the destruction of the *Expositor* press, Joseph Smith donned a fancy gold-braid uniform that "would have become a Bonaparte or a Washington." The man who hoped to be elected president of the United States buckled on his sword and stood atop the framework of a house under construction. The Nauvoo Legion assembled before him, several thousand strong. With mobs in nearby Warsaw, Illinois, calling for the Mormons' extermination, Joseph was placing the city under martial law. He told his soldiers to mount pickets around the city. They should secure their gunpowder and ammunition. Mormons on outlying farms should prepare to come into the city for refuge.

Governor Thomas Ford arrived in Carthage, the inland county seat that formed a triangle with Nauvoo and Warsaw along the river.

The militia of three counties accompanied him. Joseph wrote him another letter proclaiming his innocence. Three tense days passed.

Joseph's impulse was to flee. That Saturday, June 22, he and Hyrum crossed the Mississippi to Iowa. One plan was to make their way to Washington for yet another appeal to federal authorities. Maybe Joseph could persuade President John Tyler to give the beleaguered Mormons justice. Alternatively, the brothers could light out for Oregon or Texas or the Rocky Mountains.

He sent a message to Emma. "Do not despair," he told her. "If god ever opens a door that is possible for me I will see you again." He also wrote to his "wives," Sarah and Maria Lawrence, telling them to get out of Nauvoo. "I want for you to tarry in Cincinnati until you hear from me."

After he left the city, terror spread through the Nauvoo citizenry. The people feared that a posse or state militia force would tear up the town searching for Joseph. Heber Kimball's wife Vilate wrote that people were "tryed almost to death to think Joseph should leve them in the hour of danger."

"Let us go back and give ourselves up," Hyrum suggested, "and see the thing out." Joseph listened to his older brother. The next day they climbed into boats and rowed back across the Mississippi.

On Monday, June 24, Joseph and Hyrum, along with the sixteen others who had been named in the *Expositor* plot, headed for Carthage. They encountered a state militia company led by Captain James Dunn. He rode with the Mormons back to Nauvoo. The Legion members handed their muskets, which were state property, over to Dunn and his men. It was part of Ford's plan to defuse the powder keg. The accused Mormons, accompanied by the militiamen, reached Carthage just before midnight.

The town was swarming with loud, rough rustics, who hooted at the arrival of the prophet. What prophet? He was an ordinary looking man. Joseph swung down from his horse. He still walked with a slight limp, a reminder of the illness and awful surgical ordeal of his boyhood. The Mormons checked into the Hamilton House hotel. The night was mild, thick with summer.

The next day, the defendants appeared before a judge. With two lawyers at his side, Smith felt he had a good case. Nauvoo's city charter gave him the same right to close down a lying newspaper as it did to remove the carcass of a dead horse. The judge, perhaps eyeing the crowds peering through the courtroom windows, decided to release the defendants charged with rioting on bail of five hundred dollars each. But Joseph and Hyrum were accused of treason for declaring martial law and for calling out the Legion against the state militia. Treason was not a bailable offense. They were arrested and led to the county lockup a few blocks away.

The two-story Carthage jail had been constructed from thick blocks of ochre-colored limestone. The Smiths occupied a ground-floor cell the first night, but were allowed to stay in an upstairs bedroom the second. Eight members of the state militia unit known as the Carthage Greys stood guard. They were there as much to bar the rabble, who milled in the jail's yard, as to keep the prisoners from escaping. Other members of their unit were camped in the town square, several blocks from the jail.

Two of the Twelve Apostles stayed in the jail with their leader. John Taylor was editor of two Mormon newspapers in Nauvoo; Willard Richards, a physician, was the prophet's personal secretary.

On Wednesday, June 26, the case was delayed until Saturday. In jail, the men received a stream of visitors, including lawyers, Joseph's uncle John Smith, and Mormon officials. One of them, Cyrus Wheelock, slipped Joseph a pepperbox pistol, an early form of revolver. Another man armed Hyrum with a single-shot handgun.

On the morning of Thursday, June 27, the guards stopped allowing the aides who left the jail to return. The broiling day grew tense. Joseph sent a clerk with a message to his lawyers about potential witnesses. The man rode away quickly to avoid the rough characters surrounding the jail. Suspicious, they fired on him. He escaped and a rumor spread through town that he was riding to summon the Nauvoo Legion.

Joseph wrote a letter to Emma that "there is no danger of any exterminating order." He wanted to reassure the Saints in Nauvoo. If they kept quiet, they could avoid violence. "I am very much resigned to my lot," he wrote to his wife. "Give my love to the children."

The close midsummer day became stifling. Local people milled around town, repeating rumors they had heard and nervously discussing what to do. Guns were being loaded all over the county.

Governor Ford rode to Nauvoo with Captain Dunn's company of militia. He had ordered all other militia units to disband. Only the Greys should remain to keep order in Carthage. Those nervous militiamen were certain that an attack was imminent.

They were wrong. The armed men approaching Carthage were members of the Warsaw Regulators. These militiamen had set out to join the governor, but a messenger had met them on the prairie with the order to disband. Some did turn around. Some, disappointed that their "Nauvoo picnic" had been canceled, headed for Carthage instead.

Governor Ford arrived in Nauvoo and found the city peaceful, the people apprehensive. He took time to shave before climbing atop the same building frame from which Joseph Smith had addressed his soldiers. He advised citizens to put down their arms and to respect the property of the dissenters. If not, thousands would assemble for the total destruction of their city. He could not protect them from the mobs. Would they keep the peace? Although suspicious of gentile promises, they all raised their hands.

In Carthage, the four Mormons who occupied the unlocked upstairs bedroom were sweating in the oppressive afternoon heat. They removed their coats and opened the window to catch a breeze. They felt "unusually dull and languid." Hyrum read from a history of the Jews. The ever-talkative Joseph chatted with the guards. John Taylor sang a Mormon hymn. The pudgy, forty-year-old Willard Richards told Joseph that, if he could, he would allow himself to be hanged in place of the prophet. The jailer's son brought water from the well just below their window.

Four o'clock came. Cicadas droned, then suddenly fell silent. The sun pressed its sweaty palm onto the flat prairie, which stretched out to the limits of the sky. Members of the Warsaw Regulators arrived at the outskirts of town, dismounted, and began to cut through the jimsonweed and horse nettle. Well fortified by whiskey, they stopped to mix damp clay with gunpowder. They blackened their faces. A housewife in the village caught sight of them. Assuming them to be Mormons, she raised the alarm. Someone cried: "The Danites are coming for the Smiths!" Panic began to sprint through the streets.

At the jail, Richards gave the jailer's son a dollar to buy wine. The prisoners drank to revive their spirits. They passed the bottle to a guard to share with his men. Everyone was suffering from the heat.

Shouts echoed from downstairs, a commotion. Taylor looked out the window and saw a hundred armed men jostling each other in the yard. More shouts. A heavy tread of feet up the stairs. Joseph and Hyrum drew the guns from their coats. The men braced themselves against the closed door.

Suddenly, an enormous blast shattered the quiet. The keyhole splintered. Another shot sent a ball through the door panel. This one struck Hyrum in the face. He spun. Another bullet tore into his back. He fell dead to the floor.

For the remaining men, events took on a visionary, slow-motion, adrenaline-fueled lucidity. "I remember feeling," Taylor later wrote, "as though my time had come." Joseph opened the door a few inches, reached through and pulled the trigger of his pistol again and again. Bullets struck three men on the landing.

"Streams of fire as thick as my arm passed by me," Taylor said. The attackers thrust muskets and bayonets through the opening. Taylor batted at them with a heavy walking stick. Then he rushed across to the window, hoping to jump out and alert friends in the town. A bullet stabbed through his thigh. He stumbled against the window frame. Outside, he saw only the devilish, blackened faces of the militiamen. He teetered on the edge and fell backward into the room. Three more shots hit him as he crawled under a bed, wounded but alive.

Joseph shared Taylor's instinct to rush to the window. He too made it as far as the sill. Two shots from the door hit him in the back. He paused. He called out: "O Lord, my God." One of the militiamen below shot him in the chest.

Joseph fell heavily to the ground outside. A stranger dragged his body to the curb of the well. Four men raised their muskets and fired bullets into his body. The Mormon prophet, six months shy of his thirty-ninth birthday, was dead.

EPILOGUE

TODAY

"Still in the cold world!" a Millerite lecturer sighed after what was called the Great Disappointment. An Adventist leader acknowledged that "our fondest hopes and expectations were blasted." As midnight came and went on October 22, 1844, he said, "We wept and wept till the day dawned." In the morning, "all were silent except to inquire, 'Where are we?' and 'What next?'"

The Millerites would not bounce back as they had after the failure of previous prophecies. Some plunged into a crisis of faith. "If this had proved a failure," one asked, "what was the rest of my Christian experience worth?"

William Miller was shaken but undaunted. "My hope in the coming of Christ is as strong as ever," he said. Joshua Himes organized relief efforts to provide sustenance for those who had given up everything in expectation of the end of time.

Many skeptics and scoffers had secretly dreaded that Miller might be correct. Now they turned on the fanatical, self-righteous Millerites with a vengeance. "It seemed as though all the demons from the bottomless pit were let loose on us," an Adventist remembered. In Scottsville, in Rochester, in the small towns along the canal where the millennial fire had burned so bright, mobs wrecked and burned Adventist meeting places. Men in blackface attacked Millerites with clubs and knives and with tar and feathers.

The truest believers continued their obsession with the end. Christ would surely come in April 1845. In July. On Passover or Pentecost. Maybe in 1846. At each date, the glory eluded them. But no matter. Tomorrow, surely. It was all "visionary nonsense," Joshua Himes declared. He was done with setting dates.

Himes, Miller, and some other Adventist leaders held the enfeebled movement together for a few more years. But without a date to sustain their enthusiasm, most Millerites dispersed, some returning to the churches from which they had "come out."

In Maine, Ellen G. Harmon, a seventeen-year-old convert to Miller's doctrine, was dismayed by the Disappointment but held tight to her belief. Two months later, in December 1844, she saw herself "rising higher and higher, far above the dark world." She returned from the clouds believing that the October date had been momentous in heaven, if not on earth. She married an itinerant Millerite preacher named James White. They saw that the seventh day of the week, the true Sabbath, held mystical significance for the interpretation of prophecy.

Ellen White became one of America's most influential prophets in her own right. Her visions and revelations, which focused on Christ's coming and the millennium that would follow, guided the Sabbatarian Adventist movement. She published pamphlets, documents, and books to spread her message. Her ideas were especially well received in western New York; she and her husband lived for a time in Oswego and Rochester. The Sabbatarians adopted strict vegetarianism, rejecting alcohol and coffee. One of their later converts, John Harvey Kellogg, invented corn flakes. His brother Will turned breakfast food into an industry.

In 1863, the Sabbatarians formed the Seventh-day Adventist Church. Although William Miller would not have approved of the members' "fanaticism," these believers represented the last major remnant of his own movement.

Before Joshua Himes died in 1895, at the age of ninety, he asked to be buried in a particular cemetery near his home in Sioux Falls, South Dakota, because "he wanted to be on the top of a hill when Gabriel blows his trumpet."

William Miller lived for five years after his predicted apocalypse. "I have fixed my mind upon another time," he declared, "and here I mean to stand until God gives me more light." With the wisdom of disappointment, he came to see the real time of Christ's returning. "And that is Today, TODAY, and TODAY, until He comes."

EVERYTHING

Emma Smith loved to sing. Her beautiful voice and her book of hymns had added music to the Mormon vision. In Nauvoo at summer dusk, she sometimes heard the four plaintive notes of a Chuck-will's-widow, an elusive, twilight-loving bird.

Before the dawn sun skimmed the earth on June 28, 1844, her anxious ears caught the hollow staccato of horses' hooves. A hard-riding messenger was hurrying toward Nauvoo. Emma's heart rose to her throat. Across town a rooster crowed.

The dreaded word arrived. Joseph was dead. A friend tried to comfort Emma. Her sorrow would be the crown of her life, he told her. "My husband," she replied, "was my crown."

How could this have happened? She could not help thinking of a handsome stranger walking into her father's house in Harmony in 1825, or of that Palmyra evening when she and Joseph rode into the darkness to fetch the golden treasure. Her seventeen years with him had passed in a blink.

Later that same day, Emma's sensitive ears picked up the distant sound of brass horns from the prairie. The town band was playing a dirge. Two sorrowful wagons were drawing relentlessly closer.

At first, Emma, who was pregnant with Joseph's last child, was not allowed to see her husband's remains. Nor was Hyrum's wife Mary allowed to see his. Not until the corpses had been washed and dressed in fine clothes.

Emma entered the room but could not look on her husband. Could not face the sight of Joseph, who had radiated such an abundance of life, now lying still. She fainted away twice. Elders helped her from the room. Mary went next. She "trembled at every step," but reached the bier. Her two children, a son six and a daughter three, clung to her "shrieking in the wildness of their wordless grief."

Two men assisted Emma back into the room. One held his hat to shield her from the sight of her husband's corpse. She gathered herself. "Now I can see him," she said. "I am strong now." She looked. She bent and took his face in her hands. She sank onto his body. "Joseph," she moaned. "Joseph."

Finally it was Lucy's turn. At sixty-nine, she was a veteran of heartbreak. She had lost her eldest and favorite, Alvin. She had lost her youngest, Don Carlos. She had lost two farms. She had lost her dear husband. Now two more of her sons, beautiful grown men, lay dead before her. Her soul "filled with horror past imagination." She sat down between them and put a hand on the cold flesh of each.

"Now Joseph is gon," Brigham Young later wrote, "it seamd as though menny wanted to draw off a party and be leders." Hyrum would have been the natural heir. Samuel, one of two surviving Smith brothers and a high Church official, seemed to many a likely successor. But the fevers still common in Nauvoo claimed his life only a month after Joseph's murder. The last brother, William, was an unstable character and never a serious contender for Church leadership.

The erratic Sidney Rigdon had clashed with Joseph but later regained his favor. He had established a branch of the Church in western Pennsylvania. At the time of the assassination, he had been campaigning as Joseph's vice-presidential candidate. He returned to Nauvoo and tried to take over.

He was not the only one. James Strang was a lawyer and recent convert to Mormonism. Only thirty-one, he produced a letter, allegedly signed by Joseph, naming him successor. Strang established a Mormon outpost he called Voree in southern Wisconsin. He emulated Joseph in receiving revelations, and he even produced some ancient metal plates to support his role as a translator. Some of the Ohio apostates, including the Whitmer brothers and Joseph's old financial backer Martin Harris, eventually joined Strang's sect. The group would remain a minor offshoot of Mormonism.

On August 6, 1844, Brigham Young returned to Nauvoo from Boston—he and the other Apostles had been traveling to proselytize and to promote Joseph's candidacy for president. He quickly pushed aside Rigdon, who had unwisely criticized Joseph for his most unorthodox teachings, especially polygamy. Young based his own claim of Church leadership on his role as one of the Apostles. He told the Saints that the Twelve possessed an "organization that you have not seen." They held "the keys of the Kingdom."

Young was not the visionary that Smith had been. Nor did he have Rigdon's powers of oratory. What he had was confidence and a personal sense of authority. When he spoke, a witness said, "it seemed in the eyes of the people as though it was the very person of Joseph which stood before them." Young later said, "I never pretended to be Joseph Smith." He could not be the man who had produced the *Book of Mormon.* But the barrel-chested, forty-three-year-old Young was an excellent and practical organizer. Like Joseph, even more than Joseph, he knew how to build a church.

Emma would never follow Brigham Young. She knew too well that he had enabled Joseph's polygamy practices—Young would eventually marry fifty-five women himself. Nor, in spite of his strict and respectful adherence to Joseph's principles, did Young win over Lucy or the other members of the Smith family.

The Mormons' relations with non-Mormons in Illinois festered for two more years. In 1846, the conflict again broke into open warfare. The Mormons abandoned Nauvoo, settling briefly in Iowa. The next April, Brigham Young led the bulk of the Saints westward on their famous trek to the valley of the Great Salt Lake in Utah.

Emma returned to her home in Nauvoo. The once thriving city had become nearly a ghost town. She married a non-Mormon and operated a store there. Lucy stayed with her and died ten years later at the age of eighty. Emma's son, Joseph Smith III, went on to head the Reorganized Church of Jesus Christ of Latter Day Saints. The members of this sect, staunchly opposed to polygamy, never reconciled with the much larger body of Utah Saints. At the age of seventy-four, Emma said of her husband Joseph, "I believe he was everything he professed to be."

HIGHWAY

During the first decades of the nineteenth century, the finger of God touched down with remarkable frequency in the region of western New York through which men had slashed the great ditch. "There is no country in the world," Tocqueville wrote in the 1830s, "where the Christian religion retains a greater influence over the souls of men than in America."

Visionaries along the canal's path played a critical role in the formation of Americans' God-hungry character. The canal was itself the product of inspiration, its construction an act of faith.

DeWitt Clinton correctly predicted that the waterway would serve to bind the United States together. It would form a link between the Atlantic Seaboard and the vast interior. But even as the canal was fostering commerce and connection, a new split was opening.

One of the consequences of the canal was to populate the upper Middle West—Ohio, Indiana, Michigan, Illinois, and beyond—with settlers from the North, many of them New England Yankees. Their influx drew a sharp line between the slave states and the free—the word *southern* as a political term came into use two years after the canal's completion. Influenced by the wave of revival and reform that spread during the 1830s, northerners were less inclined to tolerate the great sin that was staining the nation's soul. The abolitionist cry would assault American ears for another quarter century, harbinger of the cataclysm of the 1860s.

The Erie Canal was a psychic highway, the scene of visions and religious upheavals. Charged with the preaching of men like Charles Finney and Theodore Weld, it was also a moral highway. It was in Buffalo that the first National Convention of Colored Men was held in 1843. Four years later, Frederick Douglass, the escaped slave from Maryland who did so much to affirm the dignity of his people, settled in Rochester, where he published his abolitionist paper *The North Star*. The towns along the canal served as some of the final links for the Underground Railroad, which helped escaped slaves reach safety in Canada. In 1848, Elizabeth Cady Stanton, who had marveled at Finney's preaching in Rochester, helped organize a convention to advance the struggle for women's rights. She and her colleagues gathered in Seneca Falls, the same town where the idea of a canal across the state had set fire to Jesse Hawley's imagination in 1805.

MARTYR

William Morgan, whose abduction had touched off the earliest of the excitements to scorch the Erie Canal region, was not soon forgotten. It is a testament to the vehemence and durability of the Anti-Masonic furor that fifty-six years after Morgan's disappearance, two thousand people from around the United States and Canada pledged money to erect a monument to his memory.

The organizer of the tribute was Jonathan Blanchard. As a young man in the 1830s, Blanchard had been one of those recruited as a lecturer by Theodore Weld to carry the banner of abolition. After the Civil War, Blanchard had revived the moribund Anti-Masonic Party, dedicating his efforts to fighting secret societies and to promoting temperance and Christianity.

In September 1882, a towering granite pillar, thirty-seven feet high, was erected in the corner of the Batavia Cemetery. Its inscription said that it commemorated "a respectable citizen of Batavia, and a martyr to the freedom of writing." Looking over the city from its pinnacle was a statue of William Morgan.

Among the letters read aloud at the monument's dedication was one from eighty-five-year-old Thurlow Weed, who was suffering from the illness that would kill him two months later. The revival of Morgan's memory was a touching reminder of the Anti-Masonic movement that had helped Weed become one of the great political fixers in American history. He had guided the party away from its fanatical roots and broadened its focus. He had overseen the transition of Anti-Masonry into a powerful faction of the Whig Party, which for twenty years opposed Andrew Jackson and his Democrats. When the Whigs crashed onto the rocks of the slavery controversy in the 1850s, Weed had served as one of the midwives at the birth of a new political faction, the Republican Party.

OLD MULE

With the arrival of the twentieth century, New Yorkers debated whether to rebuild the Erie Canal, which had not seen a major upgrade in forty years. Some said the proposed $100 million cost, more than the value of all the public schools in the state, was a waste. Voters in the cities the canal had built, especially Buffalo and New York, envisioned a waterway that would allow much larger vessels to continue the flow of grain, iron ore, limestone, lumber, and other bulky products to and from the interior. The legislature gave its approval.

This was to be no mere enlargement. The availability of steam-powered excavation equipment and plentiful concrete meant that the canal could be entirely remade. Builders deepened the channel to twelve feet and installed high-lift locks, their doors operated by electric motors. The earlier canal was abandoned from Albany to Rome. The Mohawk River itself, canalized and fed by giant reservoirs, became the eastern canal. The river's rapids were erased by a series of dams, with locks to allow boats to climb to each new height. At Lockport, two massive locks replaced the flight of five.

The new canal, finished in 1918, was christened with the workaday name, "Barge Canal." Tugboats and powered barges had already invaded the canal, and now all the vessels on the waterway would be motorized. The soft clop-clop of hooves, which had always accompanied boats gliding along the ditch during the nineteenth century, would be heard no more. The familiar song with the line, "I've got an old mule and her name is Sal," written in 1905 and sung by generations of American schoolchildren, commemorated this change.

The cry "Low bridge, everybody down!" faded into history. The minimum headroom under the three hundred bridges that crossed the new canal was fifteen feet. The Barge Canal sacrificed charm for efficiency, but it did not disappoint its proponents. Its vessels carried enormous amounts of cargo over the next half century and kept state commerce humming.

During the 1950s, rail and truck transport sucked the life out of the canal as a commercial venture. The St. Lawrence Seaway, a system of locks and canals that gave oceangoing ships access to the Great Lakes, opened in 1959 and provided a finishing blow. Tonnage on the canal declined, then dwindled to almost nothing. Now, with the name Erie Canal restored, the waterway is almost entirely the abode of pleasure craft.

"And you'll always know your neighbor, And you'll always know your pal . . ." Today, a trip along the Erie Canal's route is an occasion for wistful nostalgia. Just as the canal lost its reason for being in the latter half of the twentieth century, so did the cities along its path. Rochester had long ago ceased to be the Flour City; Buffalo no longer handled the bulk of the nation's grain; Syracuse's salt industry had evaporated. For decades, the canal cities prospered as industrial towns. But the decline of American manufacturing brought them to their knees. As factories rusted, Buffalo lost half its population; Rochester fell victim to crime and decay; Syracuse was blighted with abandoned buildings; Lockport, Rome, Utica, Schenectady, all struggled to maintain their vitality.

But the ribbon of water across the state remains. It still brings to mind the exuberance of the nineteenth century, the energy of the immigrants who worked on the colossal building project and the hopes of the settlers who populated its banks.

PAGEANT

In the 1920s, Mormons began to hold a yearly conference back in Palmyra, New York. During the event, they enjoyed acting out scenes from the *Book of Mormon*. They expanded the production in 1937 into a full-scale pageant, which they enacted on the side of Hill Cumorah. Every year since, except during World War II, Mormons from around the world have gathered near the original Smith homestead to mount an elaborate spectacle. More than seven hundred amateur actors, including many children, portray the journey of the ancient Israelites and their adventures in America.

Non-Mormon guests are welcome. In the balmy darkness, under a pepper of stars, figures dressed in costumes half Biblical and half Aztec leap around the terraced stage. Lush music and recorded dialogue pour from loudspeakers as the Saints act out their miracle play. The Nephites and Lamanites cross the Atlantic in a wave-sprayed boat, fight clanking battles, dance wildly, heed and ignore prophets, and stand in awe to watch Jesus Christ descend on the New World in a pillar of light.

When it's over, the gorgeous palaces and solemn temples, the whole insubstantial pageant, fades to darkness. The prophets were ordinary men, the battles bloodless, the gold mere glitter. All was make-believe. Surely Joseph Smith, the cheerful prophet whose dreams knew no bounds, would smile and approve.

SOURCE NOTES

PROLOGUE

2. *"ruminating over it"*: Koeppel, 37.
3. *"All my private prospects"*: Ibid., 7.
3. *"I will presume"*: Ibid., 40.
3. *"hitherto I have"*: Ibid., 48.
4. *"a burlesque"*: Ibid., 54.
4. *"in a century"*: Ibid., 52.
4. *"lies in the province"*: Ibid., 41.
4. *"the effusions of"*: Ibid., 51.
4. *"little short of"*: Ibid., 64.

CHAPTER 1

7. *"embarrassment of debt"*: Bushman, *Joseph Smith: Rough Stone Rolling*, 19.
7. *"There is nothing"*: Ibid., 20.
8. *"of the most eligible"*: Koeppel, 55.
8. *"Chaquagy [Chicago] and then"*: Bernstein, 151.
8. *"When the United States"*: Ibid., 117.
8. *"produced such expressions"*: Koeppel, 55.
10. *"some of them are"*: Thwaites, 148.
11. *"My parents were neither"*: Hambrick-Stowe, 4.
11. *"the idol of his pupils"*: Hardman, 31.
13. *"ashamed to have a human"*: Finney, *Memoirs*, 16.
13. *"to give my heart"*: Hardman, 41.
14. *"Deacon Barney"*: Ibid., 43.
15. *"hauteur of manner"*: Koeppel, 68.
15. *"irreligious and profane"*: Ibid., 79.
16. *"As yet, my friend"*: Shaw, 22.
16. *"the swarms of flies"*: Cornog, 111.
16. *"a violent rupture"*: Campbell, 43.
17. *"Our ears were invaded"*: Cornog, 111.
17. *"In one place"*: Campbell, 106.
17. *"wood-ducks, gulls"*: Cornog, 110.
18. *"from the evils"*: Campbell, 189.
18. *"Mr. Geddes proposes"*: Koeppel, 82.
18. *"the second wonder"*: Wisbey, 132.

18. *"she Conceived the Idea"*: Ibid., 10.
18. *"I was sincerely"*: Ibid., 30.
19. *"Do you have faith?"*: John H. Martin.
19. *"She veils herself"*: Campbell, 175.
19. *"Too great a national"*: Cornog, 112.
20. *"Outbreaks occur"*: Tocqueville, 142.
21. *"hair-hung and breeze-shaken"*: Hardman, 6.
21. *"Must a man draw"*: Hatch, 55.
22. *"the people appeared"*: Ibid., 173.
23. *"While I was a Deist"*: Rowe, 39.
23. *"with an intensity"*: Ibid., 20.
23. *"many contradictions"*: Ibid., 41.
23. *"What a scene!"*: Numbers, *The Disappointed*, 18.
24. *"moross and ill natured"*: Rowe, 51.
24. *"To go out like"*: Ibid., 56.
24. *"cling to that hope"*: Ibid.
24. *"God by his Holy"*: Ibid., 67.
25. *"To believe in"*: Ibid., 73.
25. *"There never was a book"*: Cross, 291.
25. *"I wondered why"*: Rowe, 72.
26. *"one of the most frightful"*: Stommel, 7.
26. *"Our teeth chattered"*: Ibid., 30.
26. *"so desolate it would"*: Bernstein, 361.
27. *"the visionary rather than"*: Cross, 139.
27. *"without parallel"*: Koeppel, 117.
28. *"determined to seize"*: Ibid., 121.
28. *"had a delicate and difficult"*: Ibid., 129.
30. *"woods of hemlock"*: Ibid., 142.
30. *"swamp and swale"*: Ibid.
31. *"The mystery of the level"*: Ibid., 223.
32. *"The mind is lost in wonder"*: Ibid., 144.
32. *"Let us conquer space"*: Ibid., 158.
32. *"suddenly become wonderfully"*: Ibid., 161.
33. *"big ditch would be buried"*: Bernstein, 182.
33. *"too great for the state"*: Koeppel. 180.
33. *"The man who will enter"*: Ibid., 185.
33. *"Who is this James Geddes"*: Bernstein, 259.
36. *"under no less Penalty"*: Bullock, 17.
37. *"create a stir"*: Brown, 15.
38. *"No subject has ever"*: Goodman, 3.

CHAPTER 2

41. *"Geddes will be found"*: Koeppel, 204.
41. *"one of the grandest"*: Ibid., 193.
41. *"each vieing with"*: Sheriff, 9.
42. *"snug log house"*: Bushman, *Joseph Smith: Rough Stone Rolling*, 33.
42. *"trees of all ages"*: Kaledin, 179.
43. *"destitute of friends"*: Bushman, *Joseph Smith: Rough Stone Rolling*, 33.
43. *"I am the wealthiest"*: Bushman, *Joseph Smith and the Beginnings of Mormonism*, 203.
44. *"the soberest of men"*: Ibid., 60.
44. *"with as much ease"*: Persuitte, 17.

44. *"All their good feelings"*: Bushman, *Joseph Smith: Rough Stone Rolling*, 37.
44. *"to get Religion too"*: Ibid.
44. *"Never did any passage"*: Ibid., 38.
44. *"my toung seemed"*: Ibid., 40.
44. *"A pillar of light"*: Ibid., 39.
44. *"The Lord opened"*: Ibid.
45. *"all their Creeds"*: Smith, *The Joseph Smith Papers, Extract.*
45. *"they did in reality"*: Bushman, *Joseph Smith and the Beginnings of Mormonism*, 230.
45. *"thin and weather-beaten"*: Sellers, 91.
45. *"taken up by a whirlwind"*: Dow, 4.
46. *"In a religious point of view"*: Morone, 124.
46. *"One hath thousands"*: Hatch, 132.
47. *"His manners have been"*: Ibid., 255.
48. *"The object of our measures"*: Ibid., 199.
49. *"practical nature is every thing"*: Koeppel, 127.
49. *"native farmers, mechanics"*: Way, *Common Labour*, 62.
50. *"a spectacle that must awaken"*: Bernstein, 211.
50. *"from which the muck"*: Koeppel, 254.
52. *"resembled the Welch lime"*: Ibid., 240.
52. *"Baffled at first"*: Ibid., 241.
53. *"The zeal of all"*: Taylor, 24.
53. *"variegated sampler of all"*: Hatch, 164.
53. *"diminutive stature"*: The Wayne Sentinel 3, no. 35 (May 26, 1826).
53. *"red-bearded giant"*: The American Baptist Magazine 1, no. 9 (May 1818).
54. *"beginning to be gathered in"*: Barrus.
54. *"Oh-a, Ho-a"*: Ham, 296.
54. *"Our readers will recollect"*: The Vermont Chronicle 6, no. 26 (June 24, 1831).
55. *"pretend to marry"*: Barrus.
55. *"the marriage of the flesh"*: Neal, 23.
55. *"It is not I that speak"*: Ibid., 24.
55. *"They run about"*: Morse, 7.
55. *"In admonition she was quick"*: Burns, 32.
56. *"They have everything"*: Ibid., 40.
56. *"The joys of the celibate"*: Nordhoff, 160.
56. *"accompanied by a gentle"*: Church of England Magazine 15, no. 414 (July 14, 1843).
56. *"with a sort of galvanized hop"*: Morse, 156.
57. *"All appeared happy"*: Ibid., 154.
57. *"in school houses"*: Hambrick-Stowe, 35.
58. *"have gone down to hell"*: Finney, *Lectures*, 2.
58. *"You have taken your stand"*: Hambrick-Stowe, 36.
58. *"You admit that what"*: Finney, *Memoirs*, 62.
58. *"The Spirit of God"*: Hambrick-Stowe, 37.
59. *"A sinner under"*: Ibid., 38.
60. *"Gospel salvation seemed"*: Finney, *Memoirs*, 14.
60. *"like cannonballs"*: William C. Martin, 40.
60. *"Oh, God, smite"*: McLoughlin, 125.
61. *"feast of reason"*: Rowe, 81.
61. *"The Bible is a system"*: Ibid., 74.
62. *"the end of all things"*: Ibid., 83.
62. *"I believe"*: Ibid., 82.
62. *"a great favorite"*: Brodie, 29.
63. *"glorious beyond description"*: Bushman, *Joseph Smith and the Beginnings of Mormonism*, 61.

63. *"written upon gold plates"*: Persuitte, 30.
64. *"The whole family were"*: Bushman, *Joseph Smith and the Beginnings of Mormonism*, 76.
64. *"they would try to take"*: Bushman, *Joseph Smith: Rough Stone Rolling*, 46.

CHAPTER 3

66. *"a swindler and a dangerous"*: Weed, 216.
66. *"never saw men"*: Stoler, 35.
68. *"There was danger"*: Finney, *Memoirs*, 161.
69. *"men of the strongest"*: Ibid., 163.
69. *"Ministers came in"*: Ibid., 164.
69. *"Religion . . . was the principal"*: Hardman, 73.
69. *"It is fanaticism"*: Finney, *Memoirs*, 165.
69. *"That man is mad"*: Ibid., 167.
69. *"I was obliged to preach"*: Ibid., 168.
69. *"Go where you would"*: Ibid., 171.
70. *"My meetings soon"*: Ibid., 289.
70. *"I said 'you'"*: Ibid., 83.
70. *"is not plain-telling"*: Hambrick-Stowe, 56.
70. *"descriptions of hell"*: Sweet, 136.
71. *"levelling of all distinctions"*: Sellers, 229.
71. *"that my flesh literally"*: Finney, *Memoirs*, 193.
71. *"The next morning"*: Ibid., 180.
71. *"I heard of several cases"*: Ibid., 177.
71. *"sunk down, and burst"*: Ibid., 183.
72. *"Good evening, we've"*: Hardman, 89.
73. *"My father was a real"*: Abzug, 47.
73. *"those great staring"*: Ibid., 39.
73. *"I was so ashamed"*: Ibid., 48.
73. *"his heart all broken"*: Finney, *Memoirs*, 187.
74. *"put an end to my studying"*: Hardman, 88.
74. *"It seemed to me like"*: Koeppel, 320.
75. *"where large timber"*: Ibid., 321.
75. *"plan to prevent their"*: Ibid., 255.
76. *"No person without experience"*: Way, *Common Labour*, 139.
76. *"Although great exertions"*: Koeppel, 255.
77. *"wages on the canal"*: Sheriff, 43.
77. *"I don't know"*: Mayo County Library.
77. *"several plates of brass"*: *Western Farmer* 1, no. 27 (September 19, 1821).
77. *"fed with a Vain"*: Taylor, 15.
77. *"who do in the simplicity"*: Brodie, 18.
78. *"poor but credulous people"*: Taylor, 22.
78. *"the MANIA of"*: Bushman, *Joseph Smith and the Beginnings of Mormonism*, 212.
79. *"It proved not to"*: Vogel, 458.
79. *"by which he could discern"*: Bushman, *Joseph Smith: Rough Stone Rolling*, 48.
79. *"The heat of the sun"*: Brooke, 31.
79. *"by some clever spirit"*: Taylor, 11.
79. *"on account of enchantment"*: Ibid., 13.
80. *"deluded beings would"*: Ibid., 9.
80. *"become insolent and"*: Ibid., 15.
80. *"Joseph can see any"*: Ibid., 14.
81. *"a valuable mine"*: Joseph Smith, "The Joseph Smith Papers, Appendix I."
82. *"At the center of all"*: Morison, 6.

83. *"would one day pass"*: Shaw, 34.
83. *"Economy induced us"*: Koeppel, 323.
83. *"I take the average"*: Barnes, 8.
84. *"appears to be correct"*: Koeppel, 324.
86. *"did not want to go"*: Bernard, Appendix 1, 1.
87. *"most of whom were"*: Ontario Repository 24, no. 28 (October 11, 1826).
87. *"are of a very strong"*: Ontario Repository 24, no. 30 (October 25, 1826).
88. *"outrages and oppressions"*: Geneva Gazette 17, no. 20 (October 18, 1826).
88. *"the said Morgan"*: Ontario Repository 24, no. 38 (December 20, 1826).
88. *"several persons have been"*: Ontario Repository 24. no. 40 (January 3, 1826).
88. *"unparalleled outrages upon"*: Ontario Repository 24, no. 38 (December 20, 1826).
89. *"that if living"*: Ibid.
89. *"We have bought the place"*: Vogel, 315.
89. *"Oh, no matter"*: Bushman, *Joseph Smith and the Beginnings of Mormonism*, 67.
89. *"The anxiety of mind"*: Vogel, 321.
90. *"I did not feel so keenly"*: Ibid.
90. *"fine looking, smart"*: Newell, 18.
90. *"would be my choice"*: Bushman, *Joseph Smith: Rough Stone Rolling*, 53.
91. *"a certain stone"*: Persuitte, 41.
91. *"discovered that time"*: Brooke, 152.
91. *"I had no intention of marrying"*: Newell, 1.
91. *"Joseph's wife was"*: Brodie, 42.
92. *"They want me to look"*: Bushman, *Joseph Smith: Rough Stone Rolling*, 54.
93. *"I have got a key"*: Ibid., 59.
93. *"The money-diggers"*: Brooke, 156.
94. *"my family will be placed"*: Brodie, 416.
94. *"I do not wish to make myself a fool"*: Bushman, *Joseph Smith: Rough Stone Rolling*, 62.
95. *"a man of very pleasant"*: Koeppel, 250.
97. *"an ingenious and enterprising"*: Ibid., 327.
97. *"Who can contemplate"*: Shaw, 129.
97. *"prodigious violence"*: Koeppel, 328.
97. *"see that no bad material"*: Ibid.
98. *"In conversation"*: Wyld, *40 x 8 x 4*, 27.
98. *"the most stupendous"*: Shaw, 130.
98. *"the grandest single"*: Koeppel, 329.
99. *"so conducive to health"*: Lender, 47.
100. *"was provided bountifully"*: Koeppel, 350.
100. *"Along the line"*: McGreevy, 78.
100. *"You wouldn't expect"*: Way, "Evil Humors," 1414.
100. *"Fever, and death"*: Ibid.
100. *"quarrel in their drink"*: Muelder, 14.
101. *"cold-water, pale-faced"*: Johnson, *Shopkeeper's*, 60.
102. *"The importance of"*: Abzug, 46.
102. *"throw us back in civilization"*: Hardman, 126.
102. *"a softness and delicacy"*: Ibid., 127.
102. *"Illiterate men"*: Hatch, 18.
102. *"his shocking blasphemies"*: Hardman, 109.
103. *"Our spiritual dignity"*: Finney, *Memoirs*, 213.
104. *"talking to God"*: Hardman, 84.
104. *"lukewarmness in religion"*: Hardman, 143.
104. *"meet you at the State"*: Ibid., 144.
104. *"We crossed the mountains"*: Ibid.
106. *"an art which"*: Johnson, *Sam Patch*, 53.

107. *"He may now challenge"*: Ibid., 124.
107. *"gentlemen who feel"*: Ibid., 134.
107. *"like an army drawn"*: Ibid., 153.
108. *"between a horse race"*: Ibid., 158.

CHAPTER 4

115. *"I frequently wrote"*: Waterman, 89.
116. *"should be forthcoming"*: Morris.
116. *"would apper in Brite"*: Bushman, *Joseph Smith: Rough Stone Rolling*, 72.
116. *"You must study"*: Ibid., 73.
117. *"We experienced great"*: Ibid., 75.
117. *"These days were never"*: Ibid., 73.
117. *"Day after day"*: Waterman, 89.
118. *"one of the most serious"*: McGreevy, 32.
119. *"without consulting any one"*: Koeppel, 332.
120. *"more like dog-kennels"*: Way, *Common Labour*, 144.
122. *"respect there is paid"*: McGreevy, 178.
123. *"at the peril of his life"*: Weed, 213.
124. *"must have been over-zealous"*: Ibid.
124. *"the vultures of Masonry"*: Haigh, 14.
124. *"the horrors of suspense"*: Formisano, 118.
125. *"for the purpose of giving"*: Haigh, 4.
127. *"entirely alone"*: Bushman, *Joseph Smith: Rough Stone Rolling*, 79.
128. *"I command you"*: Bushman, *Joseph Smith and the Beginnings of Mormonism*, 106.
128. *"I beheld with my eyes"*: Bushman, *Joseph Smith: Rough Stone Rolling*, 78.
128. *"'Tis enough"*: Ibid., 78.
128. *"relieved of a burden"*: Ibid., 79.
129. *"stout, round, smooth-faced"*: Weed, 358.
130. *"spindle shanked ignoramus"*: Bushman, *Joseph Smith and the Beginnings of Mormonism*, 120.
130. *"the greatest fraud"*: Bushman, *Joseph Smith: Rough Stone Rolling*, 82.
130. *"it partakes largely"*: Ibid., 112.
132. *"more difficult to remove"*: McGreevy, 52.
132. *"The explosions (cannonading)"*: Ibid., 55.
133. *"One stone weighing"*: Ibid., 80.
133. *"on some days the list"*: Ibid., 81.
133. *"the rough perpendicular"*: Riley, 52.
134. *"retain all the advantages"*: Morone, 200.
134. *"freeborn Yankees"*: Sheriff, 40.
134. *"extraordinary kind of artillery"*: Koeppel, 362.
135. *"a work of the first magnitude"*: Ibid., 334.
135. *"strikes the traveler"*: McGreevy, 134.
135. *"The last barrier is past"*: Ibid., 112.
135. *"I was more astonished"*: Sheriff, 31.
135. *"September 24th"*: *The Orleans Whig* 1, no. 15 (October 10, 1827).
136. *"No feature of it was"*: Weed, 315.
136. *"no doubt but"*: Ibid.
136. *"People left their busy"*: *Rochester Daily Advertiser* 2, no. 305 (October 19, 1827).
137. *"the contradiction"*: Weed, 318.
137. *"That is a good enough"*: Van Deusen, 41.
138. *"There is no blood"*: Ibid., 48.
138. *"Public opinion is"*: Bernard, 487.
139. *"This Institution"*: Ibid., 430.

139. *"dark, unfruitful"*: Ibid., x.
140. *"strong feeling"*: Ibid., xvii.
140. *"What great moral"*: Ibid., 476.
143. *"chloroform in print"*: Bushman, *Joseph Smith: Rough Stone Rolling*, 84.
143. *"He could never tell"*: Brodie, 26.
143. *"infant baptism, ordination"*: Bushman, *Joseph Smith: Rough Stone Rolling*, 89.
144. *"every error"*: Ibid., 90.
144. *"It was a young city"*: Finney, *Memoirs*, 297.
144. *"one of the wonders"*: Bernstein, 273.
145. *"dignity and majesty"*: Hambrick-Stowe, 109.
146. *"When the bubbling"*: Weed, 357.
146. *"encouraged that soul"*: McKelvey, 40.
146. *"Rochester was the place"*: Finney, *Memoirs*, 286.
146. *"the duty to publish"*: Numbers, *The Disappointed*, 21.
147. *"texts would occur"*: Rowe, 83.
147. *"I told the Lord"*: Ibid., 84.
147. *"any practice"*: Ibid., 94.
147. *"a few Evidences"*: Ibid., 96
148. *"began to speak"*: Bliss, 83.
148. *"We are a visionary house"*: Bushman, *Joseph Smith: Rough Stone Rolling*, 113.
148. *"I have lived to see"*: Ibid., 110.
149. *"Criticism, . . . even by"*: Ibid., 296.
149. *"a seer, a translator"*: Ibid., 130.
150. *"setting the country"*: Ibid., 117.
150. *"Let thy soul delight"*: Newell, 33.
151. *"alter or erase"*: Bushman, *Joseph Smith: Rough Stone Rolling*, 120.
151. *" his countenance change"*: Newell, 32.
151. *"Brother Joseph"*: Bushman, *Joseph Smith: Rough Stone Rolling*, 121.
153. *"into the burning depths"*: Sernett, 17.
153. *"some measure that"*: Finney, *Memoirs*, 288.
154. *"All Rochester was moved"*: Hardman, 210.
154. *"The revival took"*: Finney, *Memoirs*, 293.
155. *"lady of high standing"*: Ibid., 287.

CHAPTER 5

158. *"by the use of accurate"*: Koeppel, 367.
159. *"by laborious industry"*: Ibid., 366.
159. *"coarse epithets"*: Ibid., 372.
160. *"this great work"*: Monticello.
160. *"marks a new era"*: Koeppel, 373.
160. *"in a manner suited"*: Ibid., 378.
160. *"smile most propitiously"*: Ibid., 378–79.
161. *"I always loved"*: Givens, 15.
161. *"the serene and penetrating"*: Ibid., 88.
162. *"the people stood"*: Bushman, *Joseph Smith: Rough Stone Rolling*, 124.
162. *"We began to talk"*: Hatch, 188.
163. *"treated a laborer"*: Ibid., 121.
163. *"Hear my voice"*: Bushman, *Joseph Smith: Rough Stone Rolling*, 125.
163. *"Simultaneously hundreds"*: Hardman, 209.
164. *"the divided self"*: James, 185.
164. *"All sin consists"*: McLoughlin, 128.
164. *"was the greatest work"*: Hamrick-Stowe, 113.
164. *"nation after nation"*: Morone, 128.

165. *"Why do we call"*: Johnson, *Sam Patch*, 179.

166. *"Whether in exercise"*: Abzug, 61.

166. *"universal insecurity"*: Ibid., 58.

167. *"If the church will"*: Hardman, 152.

167. *"There is an increasing"*: Rowe, 103.

168. *"I sometimes feel"*: Ibid., 100.

169. *"See, . . . see, the angel"*: Ibid., 109.

169. *"It will start"*: Ibid.

170. *"No time should be lost"*: Numbers, *The Disappointed*, 39.

170. *"What can an old farmer"*: Ibid., 27.

171. *"Newel K. Whitney"*: Newell, 38.

171. *"native cheery Temperament"*: Bushman, *Joseph Smith: Rough Stone Rolling*, 141.

171. *"spirit of lightness"*: Ibid., 170.

172. *"I have never seen"*: Newell, 217.

174. *"an account of his marvilous"*: Bushman, *Joseph Smith: Rough Stone Rolling*, 234.

174. *"rallying signals"*: Adams, 288.

174. *"Antimasonry is bottomed"*: Goodman, 54.

175. *"darkest and deepest"*: Ibid., 57.

175. *"Why are six hundred"*: Bernard, 495.

175. *"Damn him"*: Adams, 186.

176. *"Morgan's abductors"*: Stoler, 37.

176. *"bound, hoodwinked"*: Brown, 43.

179. *"The waters of salvation"*: Hambrick-Stowe, 213.

180. *"the whole orthodox"*: Johnson, *Shopkeeper's*, 110.

180. *"is either gathering"*: Hardman, 281.

180. *"the ecstasy of sanctimony"*: Roth, 2.

180. *"triflers and blasphemers"*: Sellers, 230.

181. *"I don't give"*: Johnson, *Shopkeeper's*, 121.

181. *"Once get that region"*: Hambrick-Stowe, 116.

182. *"to renounce themselves"*: Finney, *Memoirs*, 215.

182. *"Measures adopted here"*: Hambrick-Stowe, 129.

183. *"The City is in great"*: Ibid., 138.

183. *"divert the attention"*: Ibid., 142.

183. *"most dangerous"*: Ibid., 143.

184. *"truly great and wonderful"*: Bushman, *Joseph Smith: Rough Stone Rolling*, 189.

185. *"the time had not yet"*: Newell, 65.

185. *"I was the first"*: Ibid.

185. *"tampering with our slaves"*: Ibid., 49.

186. *"break down the walls"*: Abanes, 118.

187. *"The religious tenets"*: Bushman, *Joseph Smith: Rough Stone Rolling*, 328.

187. *"Are you not ashamed"*: Ibid., 171.

187. *"His language and manner"*: Ibid., 231.

187. *"he was a quear man"*: Newell, 57.

187. *"On shaking hands"*: Bushman, *Joseph Smith: Rough Stone Rolling*, 231.

188. *"a varry nice & Comly"*: Newell, 66.

188. *"by no means a paternal"*: Compton, 34.

189. *"a dirty, nasty, filthy"*: Newell, 66.

189. *"of the old-fashioned"*: Larkin, 40.

191. *"race of non-producers"*: Schlesinger, 152.

191. *"There is a union"*: Johnson, *Shopkeeper's*, 134.

191. *"We are all becoming"*: Stahr, 24.

192. *"at war with"*: Masur, 94.

194. *"in his sanctum"*: Turner, 31.

194. *"with whiskey, perfumed"*: Bushman, *Joseph Smith: Rough Stone Rolling*, 311.

194. *"the angels are coming"*: Turner, 46.
194. *"the Lord standing"*: Ibid.
196. *"If I was to harbor"*: Ibid., 51.
197. *"We were immediately"*: Compton, 49.
197. *"To my utter astonishment"*: Thompson.
197. *"They are Eastern men"*: Bushman, *Joseph Smith: Rough Stone Rolling*, 327.
198. *"selling his lands"*: Ibid., 348.
198. *"oppose his own"*: Ibid., 353.
199. *"From this day and hour"*: Ibid., 355.

CHAPTER 6

202. *"brigandish guise"*: Sheriff, 145.
202. *"Commending my soul"*: Shaw, 197.
203. *"We often passed"*: Trollope, 244.
203. *"to hop down"*: Shaw, 206.
203. *"every quarter"*: Ibid., 209.
205. *"Iced-water (without sugar)"*: Trollope, 231.
205. *"an interminable"*: Koeppel, 391.
205. *"the air was so foul"*: Shaw, 207.
205. *"whither dreams betake"*: Koeppel, 392.
206. *"You are actually sailing"*: McGreevy, 133.
206. *"so low that"*: Shaw, 214.
207. *"full, strong, and"*: Reiss, 42.
207. *"some of those cunning"*: Ibid., 115.
209. *"the white circle of tents"*: Whittier, 426.
209. *"a radical and an enthusiast"*: Rowe, 160.
210. *"distinct in his utterance"*: Ibid., 173.
210. *"You can have"*: Ibid., 172.
210. *"disposed to make"*: Ibid., 180.
210. *"convince him that"*: Ibid., 138.
211. *"If you intend"*: Barkun, 40.
211. *"an event scarcely"*: Ibid., 98.
211. *"done us so much"*: Knight, 146.
211. *"I am confirmed"*: Numbers, *The Disappointed*, 46.
212. *"undefiled works"*: McGreevy, 212.
212. *"It is written in the"*: Abzug, 67.
212. *"such scenery is too"*: Sheriff, 61.
212. *"beautiful from end"*: Bourne, 132.
212. *"vulgar and worldly"*: Koeppel, 392.
212. *"in time, the wondrous"*: Ibid., 391.
212. *"Nature is fairly"*: Bernstein, 282.
212. *"as Niagara Falls are"*: Sheriff, 58.
212. *"every man moved"*: Bourne, 133.
212. *"Pork and Flour coming"*: Sheriff, 63.
212. *"The bowels of the nation"*: Bourne, 161.
213. *"I think for us young"*: Sheriff, 118.
214. *"loafing about the city"*: Ibid., 147.
214. *"the Boys who Drive"*: Ibid., 142.
214. *"they are only specimens"*: Ibid., 150.
214. *"one continual stream"*: Bernstein, 337.
214. *"than the negroes"*: Bushman, *Joseph Smith: Rough Stone Rolling*, 357.
215. *"Lawlessness prevailed"*: Ibid., 363.
216. *"the Mormons must"*: Givens, 138.

217. *"about as badly scared"*: Bushman, *Joseph Smith: Rough Stone Rolling*, 367.
217. *"I carried him into"*: Newell, 75.
218. *"Dear Emma"*: Bushman, *Joseph Smith: Rough Stone Rolling*, 381.
218. *"fanciful and flowe[r]y"*: Ibid., 379.
219. *"was frank open & familiar"*: Ibid., 382.
219. *"Build up a city"*: Ibid.
219. *"so unhealthy"*: Ibid., 384.
220. *"in the size of our canal"*: Koeppel, 389.
220. *"the country's first"*: Ibid., 390.
221. *"No single act"*: Ibid.
221. *"John the Baptist"*: Abzug, 124.
221. *"my bearish proportions"*: Ibid., 146.
221. *"his appearance"*: Ibid., 151.
222. *"Abolition immediate"*: Young, 179.
222. *"My heart aches"*: Abzug, 85.
223. *"While I was at Lane"*: Ibid., 95.
223. *"a proud, arrogant"*: Ibid., 98.
223. *"Great economic and political"*: Ibid., 112.
223. *"The pulpit is overawed"*: Ibid., 121.
223. *"traitor to Christ"*: Ibid., 116.
224. *"which side of the question"*: Ibid., 107.
224. *"Madness rules the hour"*: Ibid., 119.
224. *"better the mob"*: Ibid., 121.
224. *"superior to every"*: Ibid., 123.
225. *"immediate emancipation"*: Muelder, 163.
225. *"thunderer of the West"*: Abzug, 151.
225. *"A stump is my throne"*: Ibid., 146.
225. *"If it is not FELT"*: Ibid., 129.
226. *"almost shouted down"*: McGreevy, 191.
226. *"the most mobbed man"*: Sernett, 43.
226. *"a tall muscular man"*: Barney.
227. *"disappointed, and chagrined"*: Ibid.
227. *"as my dog"*: Ibid.
227. *"I read in the Book"*: Joseph Smith, "The Joseph Smith Papers, *History*."
229. *"It may seem to some"*: Marquardt, 319.
229. *"out of Nothing"*: Bushman, *Joseph Smith: Rough Stone Rolling*, 421.
229. *"There is no such thing"*: Ibid., 419.
229. *"request him to shake"*: Doctrines and Covenants, Section 129.
229. *"The Father has a body"*: Doctrines and Covenants, Section 130.

CHAPTER 7

232. *"I have placed my life"*: Bushman, *Joseph Smith: Rough Stone Rolling*, 438.
232. *"Any man who will"*: Newell, 96.
232. *"in the ordinary"*: Ibid., 113.
232. *"a deep intricate"*: Ibid., 120.
233. *"It was the first time"*: Ibid., 98.
233. *"the Ancient order"*: Bushman, *Joseph Smith: Rough Stone Rolling*, 452.
233. *"The Lord makes"*: Newell, 114.
233. *"I thought you knew"*: Ibid., 136.
233. *"my astonishment"*: Brodie, 477.
233. *"It is a command"*: Ibid., 478.
234. *"so contrary to all"*: Compton, 499.
234. *"Happiness is the object"*: Newell, 111.

234. *"hold your tongues"*: Ibid., 115.
234. *"All who walk"*: Ibid.
234. *"a woman of commanding"*: Ibid., 150.
235. *"more bitter in her"*: Ibid., 143.
235. *"but I have nothing"*: Ibid., 145.
235. *"hereafter have peace"*: Ibid., 151.
235. *"have ten virgins"*: Ibid., 153.
235. *"How did you succeed"*: Ibid., 152.
235. *"relinquish all"*: Ibid., 158.
235. *"he had to use harsh"*: Bushman, *Joseph Smith: Rough Stone Rolling*, 496.
235. *"yet Emma the wife"*: Newell, 166.
236. *"bound to oppose"*: Bushman, *Joseph Smith: Rough Stone Rolling*, 428.
236. *"too proud to court"*: Ibid., 509.
236. *"Let us vote as kissing"*: Turner, 82.
236. *"pretended Prophet"*: Bushman, *Joseph Smith: Rough Stone Rolling*, 510.
236. *"Beware, oh earth"*: Remini, 161.
236. *"should not be surprised"*: Bushman, *Joseph Smith: Rough Stone Rolling*, 518.
236. *"where God and the"*: Turner, 105.
237. *"The whole of America"*: Bushman, *Joseph Smith: Rough Stone Rolling*, 519.
237. *"This year—O blessed"*: Bliss, 174.
238. *"I could not but think"*: Knight, 131.
238. *"Expectation with many"*: Ibid., 130.
238. *"Never has my faith"*: Rowe, 184.
238. *"I am still looking"*: Bliss, 254.
238. *"We would not disguise"*: Knight, 164.
238. *"I confess my"*: Bliss, 256.
239. *"lecturing, Conferences"*: Knight, 168.
239. *"Stones, pieces of bricks"*: Abzug, 148.
240. *"as we made temperance"*: Davis, 431.
240. *"a silly and often"*: Hardman, 318–19.
240. *"Abolitionists are good"*: Gospel Truth.
241. *"could not speak"*: Abzug, 152.
241. *"We abolitionist women"*: Muelder, 18.
241. *"For a long time"*: Abzug, 188.
241. *"artificial and facetious"*: Ibid., 166.
241. *"an actual reality"*: Ibid., 196.
242. *"A great and mighty"*: Ibid., 239.
243. *"There is a fighting"*: Ibid., 202.
243. *"great suavity"*: Bushman, *Joseph Smith: Rough Stone Rolling*, 528.
244. *"paralizes the nerves"*: Ibid., 528.
244. *"was given when"*: Beam, 98.
244. *"by preaching the spiritual"*: Bushman, *Joseph Smith: Rough Stone Rolling*, 580.
245. *"God himself"*: Joseph Smith, "King Follett Sermon, Part 1."
245. *"You don't know me"*: Joseph Smith, "King Follett Sermon, Part 2."
245. *"The Lord has constituted"*: Brodie, 374.
245. *"she used to complain"*: Newell, 161.
246. *"gross moral"*: Newell, 181.
246. *"originally taught"*: Bushman, *Joseph Smith: Rough Stone Rolling*, 539.
246. *"We are earnestly seeking"*: Krakauer, 129.
246. *"a greater nuisance"*: Beam, 9.
246. *"removed the press"*: Bushman, *Joseph Smith: Rough Stone Rolling*, 540.
246. *"to exterminate"*: Newell, 181.
246. *"was a very gross"*: Bushman, *Joseph Smith: Rough Stone Rolling*, 545.
247. *"I have great fears"*: Ibid., 546.

247. *"I have got all"*: Beam, 127.
247. *"It is too late"*: Knight, 187.
247. *"nothing but gross"*: Ibid., 192.
248. *"God is an exact"*: Ibid., 188.
248. *"worked like leaven"*: Ibid., 189.
248. *"We are then within"*: Ibid., 192.
248. *"this thing has gone"*: Ibid., 202.
248. *"I see a glory"*: Ibid., 203.
248. *"Oh, how I wish"*: Ibid., 204.
249. *"a forsaking of the world"*: Ibid.
249. *"This shop is closed"*: Cross, 307.
249. *"help themselves"*: Knight, 206.
249. *"many have suspended"*: Ibid., 208.
249. *"formed themselves"*: Nichol, 244.
250. *"We held meetings"*: Rowe, 191.
250. *"we have just had"*: Kobler, 106.
250. *"would have become"*: Bushman, *Joseph Smith: Rough Stone Rolling*, 423.
251. *"Do not despair"*: Newell, 186.
251. *"I want for you"*: Ibid., 187.
251. *"tryed almost to death"*: Ibid., 188.
251. *"Let us go back"*: Beam, 153.
252. *"there is no danger"*: Bushman, *Joseph Smith: Rough Stone Rolling*, 548.
253. *"The Danites"*: Newell, 194.
254. *"I remember feeling"*: Presidents of the Church.
254. *"Streams of fire"*: Ibid.
254. *"O Lord, my God"*: Bushman, *Joseph Smith: Rough Stone Rolling*, 550.

EPILOGUE

256. *"Still in the cold"*: Nichol, 248.
256. *"We wept and"*: Ibid., 247.
256. *"If this had proved"*: Ibid., 248.
256. *"My hope in"*: Ibid., 266.
256. *"It seemed as"*: Rowe, 193.
257. *"rising higher"*: Numbers, *Prophetess*, 56.
257. *"he wanted to be"*: Numbers, *The Disappointed*, 56.
257. *"I have fixed my mind"*: Ibid., 33.
258. *"My husband"*: Newell, 196.
258. *"trembled at every"*: Ibid., 197.
258. *"Now I can see him"*: Ibid., 197.
258. *"filled with horror"*: Lucy Smith, 298.
259. *"Now Joseph is gon"*: Turner, 111.
259. *"organization that you"*: Ibid., 112.
259. *"it seemed in the eyes"*: Ibid., 113.
260. *"I believe he was"*: Newell, 25.
260. *"There is no country"*: Kyle, 23.
263. *"I've got an old"*: by Thomas S. Allen.

SOURCES CITED

Abanes, Richard. *One Nation under Gods: A History of the Mormon Church*. New York: Four Walls Eight Windows, 2002.

Abzug, Robert H. *Passionate Liberator: Theodore Dwight Weld and the Dilemma of Reform*. New York: Oxford University Press, 1980.

Adams, John Quincy. *Letters Addressed to William L. Stone, Esq. of New-York, and to Benjamin Cowell, Esq. of Rhode-Island, Upon the Subject of Masonry and Antimasonry*. Providence, R.I.: Edward and J. W. Cory, 1833.

Barkun, Michael. *Crucible of the Millennium: The Burned-over District of New York in the 1840s*. Syracuse, N.Y.: Syracuse University Press, 1986.

Barnes, Joseph W. "Bridging the Lower Falls." *Rochester History*, Vol. 36, No. 1 (January 1974).

Barney, Ronald O. "Joseph Smith Goes to Washington, 1839–40." rsc.byu.edu, https://rsc.byu.edu/archived/joseph-smith-prophet-and-seer/joseph-smith-goes-washington-1839-40 (accessed October 27, 2015).

Barrus, Clair. "Isaac Bullard, Bizarre 19th Century Prophet." Examiner.com. http://www.examiner.com/article/isaac-bullard-bizarre-19th-century-prophet (accessed September 21, 2015).

Beam, Alex. *American Crucifixion: The Murder of Joseph Smith and the Fate of the Mormon Church*. New York: Public Affairs, 2014.

Bernard, David. *Light on Masonry: A Collection of All the Most Important Documents*. Utica, N.Y.: W. Williams, 1829.

Bernstein, Peter L. *Wedding of the Waters: The Erie Canal and the Making of a Great Nation*. New York: W. W. Norton, 2005.

Bliss, Sylvester. *Memoirs of William Miller, Generally Known as a Lecturer on the Prophecies, and the Second Coming of Christ*. Boston: J. V. Himes, 1853.

Bourne, Russell. *Floating West: The Erie and Other American Canals*. New York: Norton, 1992.

Brodie, Fawn. *No Man Knows My History*. New York: Alfred A. Knopf, 1945.

Brooke, John L. *The Refiner's Fire: The Making of Mormon Cosmology, 1644–1844*. Cambridge, U.K.: Cambridge University Press, 1994.

Brown, Henry. *A Narrative of the Anti-masonick Excitement, in the Western Part of the State*. Batavia, N.Y.: Adams & McCleary, 1829.

Bullock, Steven C. *Revolutionary Brotherhood: Freemasonry and the Transformation of the American Social Order, 1730–1840*. Chapel Hill: University of North Carolina Press, 1996.

Burns, Amy Stechler. *The Shakers: Hands to Work, Hearts to God*. New York: Aperture Foundation, 1987.

Bushman, Richard L. *Joseph Smith and the Beginnings of Mormonism*. Urbana: University of Illinois Press, 1984.

———. *Joseph Smith: Rough Stone Rolling*. New York: Alfred A. Knopf, 2005.

Campbell, William W. *The Life and Writings of De Witt Clinton*. New York: Baker and Scribner, 1849.

Compton, Todd. *In Sacred Loneliness: The Plural Wives of Joseph Smith*. Salt Lake City, Utah: Signature Books, 1997.

Condon, George E. *Stars in the Water: The Story of the Erie Canal*. Garden City, N.Y.: Doubleday, 1974.

Conkin, Paul Keith. *American Originals: Homemade Varieties of Christianity*. Chapel Hill: University of North Carolina Press, 1997.

Cornog, Evan. *The Birth of Empire: Dewitt Clinton and the American Experience, 1769–1828*. New York: Oxford University Press, 1998.

Cross, Whitney R. *The Burned-over District: The Social and Intellectual History of Enthusiastic Religion in Western New York, 1800–1850*. Ithaca, N.Y.: Cornell University Press, 1950.

Davis, David B., editor. *Antebellum American Culture: An Interpretive Anthology*. University Park: Pennsylvania State University Press, 1997.

Doctrines and Covenants. "Section 129," lds.org, https://www.lds.org/scriptures/dc-testament/dc/129 (accessed September 24, 2015).

———. "Section 130," lds.org. https://www.lds.org/scriptures/dc-testament/dc/130.22 (accessed September 24, 2015).

Dow, Lorenzo. *History of Cosmopolite*. Cincinnati: Applegate, 1854.

Finney, Charles G. *Lectures on Revivals of Religion*. New York: Leavitt, Lord & Co., 1835.

———. *Memoirs of Rev. Charles G. Finney*. New York: A. S. Barnes & Company, 1876.

Formisano, Ronald P. *For the People: American Populist Movements from the Revolution to the 1850s*. Chapel Hill: University of North Carolina Press, 2008.

Givens, Terryl L., and Matthew J. Grow. *Parley P. Pratt: The Apostle Paul of Mormonism*. New York: Oxford University Press, 2011.

Goodman, Paul. *Towards a Christian Republic: Antimasonry and the Great Transition in New England, 1826–1836*. New York: Oxford University Press, 1988.

Gospel Truth. "Letter of Charles Finney to Theodore Dwight Weld, 21 July 1836." gospeltruth.net, http://www.gospeltruth.net/Finneyletters/finlets/finlet%201830-1839%20done/finlet1836-07_21.htm (accessed September 24, 2015).

Haigh, Elizabeth B. *New York Antimasons, 1826–1833*. Unpublished Ph.D. thesis, University of Rochester, 1980.

Ham, F. Gerald. "The Prophet and The Mummyjums: Isaac Bullard and the Vermont Pilgrims of 1817." *Wisconsin Magazine of History*, Vol. 56, No. 4 (Summer, 1973).

Hambrick-Stowe, Charles E. *Charles G. Finney and the Spirit of American Evangelicalism*. Grand Rapids, Mich.: W. B. Eerdmans, 1996.

Hardman, Keith. *Charles Grandison Finney, 1792–1875: Revivalist and Reformer*. Syracuse, N.Y.: Syracuse University Press, 1987.

Hatch, Nathan O. *The Democratization of American Christianity*. New Haven, Conn.: Yale University Press, 1989.

Howe, Daniel Walker. *What Hath God Wrought: The Transformation of America, 1815–1848*. New York: Oxford University Press, 2007.

James, William. *The Varieties of Religious Experience: A Study in Human Nature*. New York, Modern Library, 1936.

Johnson, Paul E. *Sam Patch, the Famous Jumper*. New York: Hill and Wang, 2003.

———. *A Shopkeeper's Millennium: Society and Revivals in Rochester, New York, 1815–1837*. New York: Hill and Wang, 1978.

Kaledin, Arthur. *Tocqueville and His America: A Darker Horizon*. New Haven, Conn.: Yale University Press, 2011.

Knight, George R. *Millennial Fever and the End of the World: A Study of Millerite Advent-ism*. Boise, Idaho: Pacific Press, 1993.

Kobler, John. *Ardent Spirits: The Rise and Fall of Prohibition*. New York: G. P. Putnam's Sons, 1973.

Koeppel, Gerard T. *Bond of Union: Building the Erie Canal and the American Empire*. Cambridge, Mass.: Da Capo Press, 2009.

Krakauer, Jon. *Under the Banner of Heaven: A Story of Violent Faith*. New York: Anchor Books, 2004.

Kyle, Richard G. *Evangelicalism: An Americanized Christianity*. New Brunswick, N.J.: Transaction Publishers, 2006.

Larkin, F. Daniel. *Pioneer American Railroads: The Mohawk and Hudson & the Saratoga and Schenectady*. Fleischmanns, N.Y.: Purple Mountain Press, 1995.

Lender, Mark E. *Drinking in America: A History*. New York: Free Press, 1987.

Marquardt, H. Michael. *The Joseph Smith Revelations: Texts & Commentary*. Salt Lake City, Utah: Signature Books, 1999.

Martin, John H. "Saints, Sinners and Reformers: The Burned-Over District Re-Visited." *The Crooked Lake Review*, Fall 2005. http://www.crookedlakereview.com/books /saints_sinners/martin5.html (accessed October 28, 2015).

Martin, William C. *A Prophet with Honor: The Billy Graham Story*. New York: William Morrow, 1991.

Masur, Louis P. *1831: Year of Eclipse*. New York: Hill and Wang, 2001.

Mayo County Library. "Work in America." Mayolibrary.ie. http://www.mayolibrary.ie /en/LocalStudies/Emigration/WorkinAmerica/ (accessed September 22, 2015).

McGreevy, Patrick. *Stairway to Empire: Lockport, the Erie Canal, and the Shaping of America*. Albany, N.Y.: State University of New York Press, 2015.

McKelvey, Blake. *Rochester on the Genesee: The Growth of a City*. Syracuse, N.Y.: Syracuse University Press, 1993.

McLoughlin, William G. *Revivals, Awakenings, and Reform: An Essay on Religion and Social Change in America, 1607–1977*. Chicago: University of Chicago Press, 1978.

Monticello. "Erie Canal." Monticello.org. http://www.monticello.org/site/research-and-collections/erie-canal (accessed September 23, 2015).

Morison, Elting. *From Know-How to Nowhere: The Development of American Technology*. New York: Basic Books, 1974.

Morone, James A. *Hellfire Nation: The Politics of Sin in American History*. New Haven, Conn.: Yale University Press, 2003.

Morris, Larry. "The Conversion of Oliver Cowdery." BYU Religious Education. https:// rsc.byu.edu/archived/days-never-be-forgotten-oliver-cowdery/2-conversion-oliver -cowdery (accessed October 28, 2015).

Morse, Flo. *The Shakers and the World's People*. New York: Dodd, Mead, 1980.

Muelder, Owen W. *Theodore Dwight Weld and the American Anti-slavery Society*. Jefferson, N.C.: McFarland, 2011.

Neal, Julia. *The Shaker Image*. Boston: New York Graphic Society, 1974.

Newell, Linda King. *Mormon Enigma: Emma Hale Smith*. Urbana: University of Illinois Press, 1994.

Nichol, Francis David. *The Midnight Cry: A Defense of the Character and Conduct of William Miller and the Millerites*. Takoma Park, Washington, D.C.: Review and Herald Publishing Association, 1944.

Nordhoff, Charles. *The Communistic Societies of the United States*. New York: Harper & Brothers, 1970.

Numbers, Ronald L., editor. *The Disappointed: Millerism and Millenarianism in the Nineteenth Century*. Knoxville: University of Tennessee Press, 1993.

———. *Prophetess of Health: Ellen G. White and the Origins of Seventh-day Adventist Health Reform*. Knoxville: University of Tennessee Press, 1992.

Persuitte, David. *Joseph Smith and the Origins of the Book of Mormon.* Jefferson, N.C.: McFarland, 2000.

Presidents of the Church. "John Taylor—Third President of the Church." Lds.org. https://www.lds.org/manual/presidents-of-the-church-teacher-manual-religion -345/john-taylor-third-president-of-the-church?lang=eng (accessed October 30, 2015).

Reiss, Benjamin. *The Showman and the Slave: Race, Death, and Memory in Barnum's America.* Cambridge, Mass.: Harvard University Press, 2001.

Remini, Robert V. *Joseph Smith.* New York: Viking, 2002.

Riley, Kathleen L. *Lockport: Historic Jewel of the Erie Canal.* Charleston, S.C.: Arcadia, 2005.

Rorabaugh, W. J. *The Alcoholic Republic, an American Tradition.* New York: Oxford University Press, 1979.

Roth, Philip. *The Human Stain.* Boston: Houghton Mifflin, 2000.

Rowe, David L. *God's Strange Work: William Miller and the End of the World.* Grand Rapids, Mich.: William B. Eerdmans, 2008.

Schlesinger, Arthur M., Jr. *The Age of Jackson.* Boston: Little, Brown, 1945.

Sellers, Charles C. *Lorenzo Dow: The Bearer of the Word.* New York: Minton, Balch & Company, 1928.

Sernett, Milton C. *North Star Country: Upstate New York and the Crusade for African American Freedom.* Syracuse, N.Y.: Syracuse University Press, 2002.

Shaw, Ronald E. *Erie Water West: A History of the Erie Canal, 1792–1854.* Lexington: University Press of Kentucky, 1966.

Sheriff, Carol. *The Artificial River: The Erie Canal and the Paradox of Progress, 1817–1862.* New York: Hill and Wang, 1996.

Smith, Joseph. *The Joseph Smith Papers*, "Appendix I," josephsmithpapers.org. http://josephsmithpapers.org/paperSummary/appendix-1-agreement-of-josiah-stowell -and-others-1-november-1825 (accessed October 30, 2015).

———. *The Joseph Smith Papers*, "Extracts from the History of Joseph Smith, the Prophet Chapter 1," josephsmithpapers.org. https://www.lds.org/scriptures/pgp /js-h/1.19?lang=eng (accessed [date]).

———. *The Joseph Smith Papers*, "History, 1838–1856, volume C-1 [2 November 1838–31 July 1842]," josephsmithpapers.org. http://josephsmithpapers.org/paperSummary /history-1838-1856-volume-c-1-2-november-1838-31-july-1842?p=445#!/paper Summary/history-1838-1856-volume-c-1-2-november-1838-31-july-1842&p=444 (accessed September 24, 2015).

———. "The King Follett Sermon, Part 1." Lds.org. https://www.lds.org/ensign/1971/04 /the-king-follett-sermon?lang=eng (accessed September 24, 2015).

———. "The King Follett Sermon, Part 2." Lds.org. https://www.lds.org/ensign/1971/05 /the-king-follett-sermon?lang=eng (accessed September 24, 2015).

Smith, Lucy. *Biographical Sketches of Joseph Smith the Prophet and His Progenitors for Many Generations.* Lamoni, Iowa: Reorganized Church of Jesus Christ of Latter-day Saints, 1912.

Stahr, Walter. *Seward: Lincoln's Indispensable Man.* New York: Simon & Schuster, 2012.

Stoler, Margaret. "The Disappearance of William Morgan." *Rochester History*, Vol. 53, No. 4 (Fall 1991).

Stommel, Henry M. *Volcano Weather: The Story of 1816, the Year Without a Summer.* Newport, R.I.: Seven Seas Press, 1983.

Sweet, Leonard I., editor. *The Evangelical Tradition in America.* Macon, Ga.: Mercer University Press, 1997.

Taylor, Alan. "The Early Republic's Supernatural Economy: Treasure Seeking in the American Northeast, 1780–1830." *American Quarterly*, Vol. 38, No.1 (Spring 1986).

Thompson, John E. "The Mormon Baptism of William Morgan." lds-mormon.com. http://www.lds-mormon.com/morgan2.shtml (accessed September 23, 2015).

Thwaites, Reuben G. *Early Western Travels, 1748–1846, Volume 8.* Cleveland: A. H. Clark Company, 1904–7.

Tocqueville, Alexis de. *Democracy in America, Volume II.* New York: E. Walker, 1850.

Trollope, Frances Milton. *Domestic Manners of the Americans.* New York: Alfred A. Knopf, 1949.

Turner, John G. *Brigham Young: Pioneer Prophet.* Cambridge, Mass.: Harvard University Press, 2012.

Van Deusen, Glyndon G. *Thurlow Weed, Wizard of the Lobby.* Boston: Little, Brown, 1947.

Vaughn, William Preston. *The Antimasonic Party in the United States, 1826–1843.* Lexington: University Press of Kentucky, 1983.

Vogel, Dan, editor. *Early Mormon Documents.* Salt Lake City, Utah: Signature Books, 1996.

Waterman, Bryan, editor. *The Prophet Puzzle: Interpretive Essays on Joseph Smith.* Salt Lake City, Utah: Signature Books, 1999.

Way, Peter. *Common Labour: Workers and the Digging of North American Canals, 1780–1860.* Cambridge, U.K.: Cambridge University Press, 1993.

———. "Evil Humors and Ardent Spirits: The Rough Culture of Canal Construction Laborers." *The Journal of American History*, Vol. 79, No. 4 (March 1993).

Weed, Thurlow. *Life of Thurlow Weed Including His Autobiography and a Memoir.* Boston: Houghton Mifflin, 1883.

Whittier, John Greenleaf. *Prose Works of John Greenleaf Whittier.* Boston: Ticknor and Fields, 1866.

Wisbey, Herbert A. *Pioneer Prophetess: Jemima Wilkinson, the Publick Universal Friend.* Ithaca, N.Y.: Cornell University Press, 1964.

Wyld, Lionel D. *Low Bridge! Folklore and the Erie Canal.* Syracuse, N.Y.: Syracuse University Press, 1962.

———, editor. *40 x 28 x 4, the Erie Canal, 150 Years.* Rome, N.Y.: Oneida County Erie Canal Commemoration Commission, 1967.

Young, Michael P. *Bearing Witness Against Sin: The Evangelical Birth of the American Social Movement.* Chicago: University of Chicago Press, 2006.

INDEX

Abiff, Hiram, 32–4, 38, 93
abolitionist movement, 170, 182–3,
    222–6, 238–43, 250, 261
Adams, John Quincy, 122–3, 138–9,
    192, 243
Adventism (Millerism)
    camp meetings, 208–11, 239, 247
    and "come-outers," 211
    and Great Disappointment, 256–7
    and predicted return of Christ, 18,
        18, 62, 168–9, 211, 237–9, 242,
        247–50
    Sabbatarian Adventists, 182, 257
    Second Adventist Association, 208
    See also Himes, Joshua; Miller,
        William
alcohol, 79, 99–101, 165–7, 181–2,
    285, 204, 222, 257
Alger, Fanny, 188–9, 198, 230
American Anti-Slavery Society, 225,
    242
    American Slavery As It Is: Testimony
        of a Thousand Witnesses, 242–3
    See also abolitionist movement
American Revolution, 6, 15, 17, 40,
    77–8, 134, 178, 191
Anthon, Charles, 114
Anti-Masonry
    and Book of Mormon, 143
    influence on Adventism, 208–9
    and Morgan affair, 107, 124–6,
        136–7, 147, 174–5, 190–1, 261–2
    and politics, 125–6, 129, 136–40,
        175, 192–3, 261–2

See also Freemasonry; Weed,
    Thurlow
apocalypse, 53, 60–2, 184, 209,
    238, 257. See also Adventism
    (Millerism)

Bank of the United States. See
    Second Bank of the United
    States
Barnum, Phineas Taylor, 206–11
Bartow, Andrew, 52
Bates, David Stanhope, 81–5, 95–9
Beecher, Catherine, 102
Beecher, Lyman, 101–4, 164, 181–2,
    221–3, 243
Bennett, James Gordon, 191, 236
Birdsall, John, 135
Blanchard, Jonathan, 261–2
Boggs, Lilburn, 215–16, 219
Book of Mormon, 150–1, 161–3, 167,
    187–8, 227–8
    and Hill Cumorah Pageant, 264
    and polygamy, 188, 244
    publication of, 129–30, 198, 228
    Smith's translating of, 113–17
    stories and themes, 140–4, 163,
        188
    See also Church of Jesus Christ of
        Latter-day Saints
Brainard, Jeremiah, 50
Brant, John, 178
Brittin, William, 97–8
Brownson, Orestes, 134
Bruce, Eli, 126, 138, 140, 175–6

Bullard, Isaac (the Prophet), 53–5, 57
Bullardites (Pilgrims), 53–5
Burr, Aaron, 15

Calhoun, John C., 32
Calvinism, 12, 43–4, 46–7, 101, 105, 167, 248
camp meetings, 21, 47, 168, 208–11, 239, 247
canal technology and materials, 49–50, 131–5
  aqueducts, 96–9, 206, 220
  cement, 48, 50–2
  limestone, 50–2, 96, 118, 131, 252, 262
  stump puller, 50
  See also Erie Canal
Champollion, Jean-François, 113–14
Chase, Willard, 93–4
Chesebro, Nicholas G., 67–8, 140
cholera, 167, 183, 186, 214
Church of Jesus Christ of Latter-day Saints
  anti-bank, 195
  baptism, 117, 130, 148–50, 229
  dissenters, 196–9, 244–6, 253
  endowments, 194, 232
  Hill Cumorah, 92, 95, 127, 129, 141, 173–4, 187, 264
  Hill Cumorah Pageant, 264
  and Illinois, 217–19
  Kirtland Temple, 173, 194–6
  lay church officials, 172–3
  Melchizedek priesthood, 173
  Missouri mob violence and expulsion of Mormons (1838), 214–17
  move to Salt Lake City, 260
  naming of, 131
  and Nauvoo Expositor, 246, 250–1
  polygamy (plural marriages), 185, 188–9, 230, 232–5, 243–6, 259–60
  priesthood, 173
  and Sons of Dan (Danites), 198–9, 215, 253
  Urim and Thummim, 93, 116, 229
  and Zion, 143, 171–3, 185–6, 197, 219, 237
  Zion's Camp, 186, 194
  See also Book of Mormon; Smith, Joseph Jr.
Clay, Henry, 66, 191–2
Clinton, DeWitt, 14–18, 260
  death of, 189
  elected governor of New York, 33
  and Erie Canal Commission and planning, 15–18, 27–8, 31–3, 40, 82
  and Erie Canal opening, 158, 160
  and Freemasonry, 66, 88, 95, 125
  and Morgan affair, 88, 125
  political background, 15
  removal of Sheriff Bruce, 138, 140
Clinton, George, 15
Clinton, James, 17
Cole, Abner, 130
Cole, Thomas, 144, 212
conversion, religious, 13–14, 46, 60–1, 69–72, 153–5, 164–7
Cowdery, Oliver, 162, 171, 173
  and "Article on Marriage," 188–9
  baptisms by, 149–50, 161
  disagreements with Smith, 151, 189
  excommunication of, 198
  and organization of Church of Christ, 131, 149
  as second elder, 149
  and translation of the Book of Mormon, 115–17, 126–30
Currier, Nathaniel, 210

Darwin, Charles, 118
Deep Cut, 131–5, 159, 206
Deism, 23–5, 229
Dibble, Orange H., 132
Dickinson, Emily, 57
Doniphan, Alexander W., 217
Douglass, Frederick, 261
Dow, Lorenzo, 45–8, 53, 102, 193, 208
du Pont, Éleuthère Irénée, 131
Durand, Asher, 161
Durfee, Lemuel, 89

Dyer, Russell, 123, 136

Eddy, Thomas, 18–19, 27, 75
Edwards, Jonathan, 164
Erie Canal
   *Act respecting Navigable
     Communications, An*, 33
   aqueducts, 30, 96–9
   Barge Canal rebuilding, 262–3
   Bonus Bill (1817), 32
   canal boys (hoggees), 213–14
   canal workers, 48–9, 75–7, 98–101,
     120–2, 133–4, 204
   and commerce, 212–13
   Commission, 14–20, 28
   construction of, 48–52, 74–7, 95–8,
     117–22, 131–5
   cost and funding, 32–3, 52, 214
   and crime, 214
   and daredevil jumping of Sam
     Patch, 104–9, 133, 144, 146, 165
   Deep Cut, 131–5, 159, 206
   and employment, 213
   enlargement of, 220–1
   feeder canals, 96, 220
   groundbreaking, 40–1
   Hawley's inspiration and
     "Hercules" essays, 3–4, 8, 15, 33,
     98–9, 158–9
   Irondequoit Embankment, 95–6,
     122–3, 206
   legacy of, 260–1
   and Lockport, 120–2, 132–5,
     159–60, 204, 206, 212–13, 221,
     226, 263
   locks, 10–11, 30, 32, 48, 50, 82, 95,
     117–22, 131, 134–5, 159, 204,
     220, 262–3
   Memoir of Durand sketches, 161
   and money-digging, 77–9
   and Niagara Falls, 2, 9–10, 18,
     21–2, 118, 134, 202, 212
   opening of, 158–6
   and Rochester, 81–3, 85, 96–9, 118,
     122, 144–6, 261, 263
   route, 3–4, 8–10, 18–19, 26–32
   and St. Lawrence Seaway, 263
   survey led by Geddes, 8–11

   typical journey on, 202–6
   See also canal technology and
     materials
Erie Canal Commission, 14–20,
   27–33, 40–1, 48–52, 75–6, 83,
   118, 131–2
evangelism, 13, 20, 145–9, 163–6, 173,
   180–3, 186–7, 221, 224, 229

Far West, Missouri, 186, 194, 196–8,
   215–17
Female Relief Society, 234
Finger Lakes (New York), 3, 25, 97,
   193, 220
Finney, Charles Grandison, 222, 224,
   225, 229, 240, 242, 261
   background and education, 11–12
   in Boston, 182
   conversion of, 13–14, 24, 46
   and evangelical millennium, 165–7,
     179–84
   Lectures on Revivals of Religion, 224
   marriage of, 59
   meeting with Miller, 210–11
   in New York City, 182–4
   as preacher, 57–60, 68–74
   religious influences, 12–13
   revival methods of, 48, 70–1, 101–4,
     164, 166, 208, 221, 224, 240
   in Rochester, 144–6, 151–5, 163–4,
     179–81
   and role of women, 186
   Utica revival, 69–72
Follett, King, 244
Ford, Thomas, 236, 246–7, 250–1,
   253
Fort Niagara, 22, 126, 174–8
Fox, Corydon, 176
Franklin, Benjamin, 36, 46, 77
Freemasonry
   Batavia Masonic Lodge, 87
   Canandaigua Masonic Lodge, 67
   and Hiram Abiff, 32–4, 38, 93
   members, 23, 66, 95, 139, 192
   and Morgan affair, 36–8, 85–8,
     123–5, 147, 174–9, 190–1
   and Morgan's *Illustrations of
     Masonry*, 38, 66, 88, 126, 129

origins of, 34–6
and politics, 66, 126, 137–9, 190–2
"The Temple's Completed"
  (hymn), 98
See also Anti-Masonry
Fulton, Robert, 4, 8

Gale, George, 12, 60, 166
Garrison, William Lloyd, 211, 225,
  240
Geddes, James, 8–11, 14–15, 18, 28,
  33, 40–1, 82–3, 118–19, 158
Genesee River, 11, 17–18, 35, 42,
  82–3, 88, 98, 104, 107, 175
Gibbs, Horace, 85
Giddins, Edward, 176
Gilbert, John, 130
Gillet, Moses, 68
Gilman, Caroline, 135
Grand Western Canal, 158. *See also*
  Erie Canal
Grandin, Egbert B., 129–30
Great Awakening, 20–2, 164. *See also*
  Second Great Awakening
Great Lakes, 2–4, 9, 78, 135, 159–60,
  263. *See also* Lake Erie; Lake
  Ontario
Greene, Samuel, 66–7
Grimké, Angelina, 241–2
Grimké, Sarah, 241–2

Hale, Emma. *See* Smith, Emma Hale
  (wife of Joseph Jr.)
Hale, Isaac, 90–2, 113–14
Harmon, Ellen G., 257
Harmony, Pennsylvania, 81, 90–1,
  94, 113–16, 126, 130, 149, 151,
  258
Harris, George W., 87, 179, 197–8
Harris, Martin, 80–1, 93–4, 113–14,
  127–30, 149, 259
Harrison, William Henry, 227
Harwood, Webb, 74–6
Haun, Jacob, 216
Hawkins, John Isaac, 51
Hawley, Jesse, 10, 40, 118, 220–1, 261
  and aqueduct celebration, 98
  and canal inspiration, 2–4
  and Erie Canal's opening, 158–9

"Hercules" essays by, 3–4, 8, 15,
  32, 98–9, 158–9
Heth, Joice, 206–7
Hill, R. H., 138
Himes, Joshua, 170–1, 208–11, 237–9,
  248–9, 256–8
Hooker, Isabella Beecher, 102
Hovey, Alfred, 97–8
Hudson River, 3–4, 10, 14, 78, 95–6,
  122, 160

Independence, Missouri, 173, 185,
  197, 217
Irondequoit Creek (New York), 18,
  81–3, 94–5, 122, 193, 206
Iroquois Confederacy, 9, 17–18, 78,
  159

Jackson, Andrew, 34, 66, 123, 125–6,
  138–9, 166, 173, 192, 195, 204,
  225, 227, 262
Jefferson, Thomas, 4, 14, 23, 46, 160,
  229
Jervis, John, 30–1, 95, 190, 220
Jewett, Ezekiel, 176

Kellogg, John Harvey, 257
Kimball, Heber, 193, 195–6, 233–4,
  251
Knight, Joseph, 90, 92–4, 115–16,
  149–50

Lafayette, Marquis de, 134–5
Lake Erie, 3, 8, 10, 14–15, 26–8, 79,
  118–20, 131, 134, 158, 160, 171,
  194, 206
Lake Ontario, 3, 9–11, 16, 56, 83, 98,
  118, 126, 135–6, 159, 174, 178
Lane Seminary (Cincinnati), 221–4
Latter-day Saints. *See* Church of
  Latter-day Saints
Law, William, 228, 243–6
Lawrence, Maria, 235, 251
Lawrence, Sarah, 235, 251
Lawson, Loton, 67–8, 140, 175
Lee, Ann (Mother Ann), 55, 219
Lee, Robert E., 227
Locofoco Party, 220
Lucas, Samuel D., 216–17

Lyell, Charles: *Principles of Geology*, 117–18

Madison, Dolley, 22
Madison, James, 27, 32
malaria, 76, 219, 228
Marsh, Joseph, 209
Masons. *See* Freemasonry
Meacham, Joseph, 55–6
Melville, Herman, 202, 214
Methodism, 12, 17, 20–1, 34, 44–6, 90, 149, 164, 167, 193, 229
Middlesex Canal (Massachusetts), 3
Miller, David, 37–8, 67, 87–8, 129, 136, 140, 177
Miller, William, 26, 53, 177, 184, 208–11, 247, 256
    apocalyptic beliefs, 61–2, 146–8, 165–71, 208–11, 237–9, 246, 248–50
    background and education, 22–3
    conversion of, 24–5
    Currier portrait of, 210
    Evidences from Scripture and History of the Second Coming of Christ, 169
    illness of, 210
    and War of 1812, 23–4, 61
    See also Adventism (Millerism)
Mohawk River, 2, 9, 14, 16, 29, 119, 203, 262–3
money-digging. *See* treasure-hunting and money-digging
Monroe, James, 32, 192
Morgan, Lucinda (later Lucinda Pendleton Morgan Harris), 33–8, 67, 85–8, 124, 126, 136, 174, 179, 197, 233
Morgan, William, 34–8, 107, 129
    background, 34–5
    disappearance of, 35–8, 68, 85–9, 107, 129, 123–6, 147, 190–2, 204
    and finding of a corpse on shores of Lake Ontario, 135–40
    and Freemasons, 34–5
    Illustrations of Masonry, 38, 66–7, 88, 126
    jailing of, 67–8
    monument in tribute to, 261–2

theories of his disappearance, 174–9
Morison, Elting, 82
Mormon (prophet), 127–8
Mormonism. *See* Church of Jesus Christ of Latter-day Saints
Morris, Gouverneur, 15–16, 20
Mott, Lucretia, 241
Mound Builders, 78
Mount Tambora, 26
Munro, Timothy, 137–8

Nauvoo, Illinois, 219, 227–8, 234, 236, 243–6, 250–3, 257–60
New Israelites, 52–3
New York City, 14–16, 27, 32, 114, 120, 122, 125, 158, 182–4, 187, 202, 209
New York City Anti-Slavery Society, 183
Newton, Isaac, 33, 82
Niagara Falls, 2, 9–10, 18, 21–2, 106–7, 118, 134, 146, 202, 212
Niagara River, 126, 131, 134, 136–7, 178
Noble, Joseph, 232

Oberlin Collegiate Institute, 224
Oneida Lake, 9, 14, 18, 41, 52, 82

Page, Hiram, 128, 151
Paine, Thomas: *The Age of Reason*, 23
Panic of 1819, 75
Panic of 1837, 220, 227
Partridge, Edward, 162
Partridge, Emily, 233–5
Partridge, Emma, 233–5
Patch, Sam (True Sam Patch), 104–9, 133, 144, 146, 165
Peck, Edward, 122, 185, 233
Platt, Ezra, 175
Polk, James, 237
polygamy (plural marriages), 53, 185, 188–9, 230, 232–3, 243–6, 259–60
Pratt, Orson, 179, 197
Pratt, Parley, 161–3, 179, 196, 216–17
Pratt, Sarah, 197

Presbyterianism, 21, 43, 57–60, 71, 94, 101, 122, 146, 223

Prichard, Ruth, 18–9

Puritanism, 12, 46–7, 102, 105, 119, 164, 173

Reorganized Church of Jesus Christ of Latter Day Saints, 260

Revelation, Book of, 61, 169

revivalism. *See* Finney, Charles Grandison

Revolutionary War. *See* American Revolution

Richardson, John, 41

Rigdon, Sidney, 161–2, 171–2, 179, 184, 196, 198–9, 215–18, 234, 259

Roberts, Nathan, 119–20, 131–2, 135

Rochester, Nathaniel, 96, 98

Rochester, New York
  and Charles Finney, 144–6, 151–5, 163–4, 179–81
  and Erie Canal, 81–3, 85, 96–9, 118, 122, 144–6, 261, 263

Rosetta Stone, 112–13

St. Lawrence River, 9

Second Adventist Association, 208. *See also* Adventism (Millerism)

Second Bank of the United States, 32, 195

second coming of Christ, 60–2, 167–71. *See also* apocalypse

Second Great Awakening, 20. *See also* Great Awakening

Seneca Falls Convention, 261

Seneca River, 14

Seventh-day Adventist Church, 257. *See also* Adventism (Millerism)

Seward William, 191

Shakers, 54–7, 149, 219

Six Nations, 17

Slater, Samuel, 105

slavery, 15, 46, 121, 134, 180, 182–5, 202, 207–8, 221–6, 239–43, 261–2. *See also* abolitionist movement

Smeaton, John, 51

Smith, Alvin (brother of Joseph Jr.), 42–4, 63, 78, 81, 89, 115, 258

Smith, Alvin (son of Joseph Jr.), 114, 172

Smith, Don Carlos (brother of Joseph Jr.), 27, 228, 232, 258

Smith, Emma Hale (wife of Joseph Jr.), 113–15, 125, 130, 149, 163, 171, 184–5, 217–9, 227
  baptism of, 150
  and death of Joseph Jr., 257–60
  and deaths of children, 114, 172, 228
  and Joseph Jr.'s multiple marriages, 188–9, 234–5, 245
  marriage to Joseph Jr., 90–2
  as president of Female Relief Society, 234

Smith, Hyrum (brother of Joseph Jr.), 42, 89, 93, 115, 128, 161, 186, 227, 235, 258
  arrested for treason, 251–4
  baptism of, 43
  and Church organization, 130–1, 148, 188, 259
  imprisonment of and escape, 217, 219
  and Joseph Jr.'s death, 254
  as Patriarch, 188, 243–4

Smith, Joseph Jr., 19, 23
  birth and childhood illness, 7–8
  and Brigham Young, 194–6
  conversion of, 44–5
  court-martial and imprisonment of (1838), 217–19, 228
  death and final days, 250–4, 258–260
  decision to run for president, 237
  discovery of golden plates on Hill Cumorah, 63–4, 79–81
  discovery of keys (Urim and Thummim), 92–3
  Doctrines and Covenants, 187
  early Church organization, 149–51, 161–3
  formation of Nauvoo Legion, 236–7
  indicted and jailed for perjury and polygamy (1844), 245–7, 250–4
  and Joseph Sr.'s baptism, 148–9
  marriage to Emma, 90–2

meeting with Van Buren, 226–7
and money-digging, 80–1
move to Harmony, Pennsylvania,
    94
move to Kirtland, Ohio, 171
in New York City, 184
personality and physical
    appearance, 44, 62, 171, 228–9
and plural marriages, 185, 188–9,
    197–8, 232–5, 243–6
publication of *The Book of Mormon*,
    129–30, 198, 228
religious influences, 44, 57
retrieval of and hiding of golden
    plates, 92–4
and revelations, 62–4, 114–16,
    141–3, 150–1, 163, 172, 185–8,
    228–30, 235, 244
translating of the golden plates,
    113–17, 126–7
trial for disorderly conduct (1826),
    91
trials in 1830, 150
visitation by Moroni, 62–4, 78, 80,
    90, 230
and witnesses to golden plates,
    128–9
See also Book of Mormon; Church of
    Jesus Christ of Latter-day
    Saints
Smith, Joseph Sr.
    baptism of, 148–9
    death of, 228
    early years with Lucy in Vermont,
        6–8
    farming and clearing land in
        Palmyra, 42–3
    ginseng farming, 6–7
    and Joseph Jr.'s discovery of golden
        plates, 62–4, 78–9
    loss of farm, 89–90
    move from Vermont to Palmyra,
        26–7
Smith, Joseph III, 184, 196
Smith, Lucy Mack (wife of Joseph
    Sr.), 52, 92
    attends revival meeting, 43
    and Brigham Young, 260
    and death of Joseph Jr., 258–9

early years with Joseph in
    Vermont, 6–8
on Emma (Joseph Jr.'s wife), 172
loss of farm, 89–90
move from Vermont to Palmyra,
    26–7
Smith, Samuel (brother of Joseph Jr.),
    43, 115–16, 130, 193, 259
Smith, Sophronia (sister of Joseph
    Jr.), 27, 43, 115
Snow, Eliza, 232–3
Snow, Samuel S., 247–8
Spalding, Lyman, 213
spiritual wifery, 232
Stanton, Elizabeth Cady, 153, 241,
    243, 261
Stoddard, Calvin, 89
Stone, Barton W., 21–2
stone-walling, 139
Stowe, Harriet Beecher, 102
    Uncle Tom's Cabin, 243
Stowell, Josiah, 81, 89–92, 94, 149–50
Strang, James, 259
Strong, Ezra, 136

Tappan, Arthur, 182–3, 221, 224–5,
    240, 242
Tappan, Lewis, 182–3, 221, 224–5,
    240, 242
textile industry, 71, 105–8
theodemocracy, 236–7
Throop, Enos T., 140
Tocqueville, Alexis de, 20, 42, 205–6,
    260
treasure hunting and money-digging,
    77–80, 90–4, 129
Trollope, Frances, 101, 203, 205, 212
Turner, Nat, 225
Twain, Mark, 143
Tyler, John, 236–7, 251

Unitarianism, 69, 74, 139
U.S. Constitution, 32, 59, 236
    Constitutional Convention, 15

Valance, Henry L., 125, 178
Van Buren, Martin, 125–6, 226–7,
    237
Van Rensselaer, Stephen, 15–16

volcanic eruption of 1815, 26

War of 1812, 20, 22–4, 33, 122, 134, 177
Washington, George, 22, 36, 229
Washington, Martha, 229
Weed, Thurlow, 78, 107, 122–6, 129, 136–40, 146, 178–9, 191–2, 208, 262
Weld, Theodore Dwight, 72–4, 165–7, 180–1, 212, 221–6, 239–43, 261
whiskey. *See* alcohol
White, Ansel, 119
White, Canvass, 51, 95, 119
White, Ellen (Harmon), 257
White, James, 257
Whitmer, David, 116, 127–8, 131, 149–50, 161–2, 171, 198, 259

Whitney, John, 178–9
Whitney, Newel, 171, 184–5
Whittier, John Greenleaf, 208–9
Whittlesey, Frederick, 107, 123–4, 138
Wilkinson, Jemima, 18, 44, 55, 130, 219
Wirt, William, 192
Wood, Nathaniel, 52
Wright, Benjamin, 28–33, 40–1, 51–2, 56, 82, 84, 96–9, 119, 158, 220
Wright, Lucy, 56

Young, Brigham, 193–6, 227–8, 233, 236, 259–60
Young, Samuel, 41
Young, Thomas, 113–14